THE THAMES IRONWORKS

THAMES IRON WORKS
SHIP-BUILDING ENGINEERING & DRY DOCK COMPANY LIMITED

THE THAMES IRONWORKS

A HISTORY OF EAST LONDON INDUSTRIAL AND SPORTING HERITAGE

BRIAN BELTON

The
History
Press

Half title verso: Thames Ironworks.

Above: HMS *Himalaya*.

First published 2015

The History Press
The Mill, Brimscombe Port
Stroud, Gloucestershire, GL5 2QG
www.thehistorypress.co.uk

© Brian Belton, 2015

The right of Brian Belton to be identified as the Author
of this work has been asserted in accordance with the
Copyright, Designs and Patents Act 1988.

British Library Cataloguing in Publication Data.
A catalogue record for this book is available from the British Library.

ISBN 978 0 7509 5834 9

Typesetting and origination by The History Press
Printed in Great Britain

CONTENTS

FOREWORD

As we prepare for the move to the Olympic Stadium, I guess all West Ham fans are becoming more and more aware of the history of the club. I have to say I have often wondered what the club's founder, Arnold Hills would have made of the move. I suspect he would approve, as he was the architect of the move from the Memorial Grounds to Upton Park.

As we all know, West Ham United was officially formed in 1900, but the club's forerunner was the Thames Ironworks, founded in June 1895 from the remnants of the Old Castle Swifts club, as announced in the *Thames Iron Works Gazette*. The founders were one of the shipbuilding company's foremen, David Taylor, who was a local football referee, and the owner of the company, Arnold Hills. Hills had a particularly enlightened attitude to employment and was well known for coming up with ideas to improve the lives of his employees. Initially playing as amateurs, the team featured several works employees including Walter Parks (clerk), Thomas Freeman (ships fireman), Tom Mundy, Walter Tranter and James Lindsay (all boilermakers), William Chapman, George Sage, William Chamberlain and apprentice riveter Charlie Dove.

Thames Ironworks' first game took place on 7 September 1895 against the Woolwich-based Royal Ordnance Reserves. It was played on the ground of the by then defunct Castle Swifts at Hermit Road, Canning Town. The game ended in a 1–1 draw.

In June 1897 the club moved to a new stadium at the Memorial Grounds in Straford, financed, of course, by Arnold Hills. It cost £20,000 to build. Season tickets for the 1897/98 campaign were priced at 5s, with admission for individual matches costing fourpence.

At the start of the 1897/98 season, the club's owner Arnold Hills wrote the following message to the team's players:

> To the players:– As an old footballer myself, I would say, get into good condition at the beginning of the season, keep on the ball, play an unselfish game, pay heed to your captain, and whatever the fortunes of the first half of the game, never despair of winning, and never give up doing your very best to the last minute of the match. That is the way to play football, and better still, that is the way to make yourselves men.
>
> (Quoted in *Iron in the Blood*)

The first sign that all was not well with the ownership of Thames Ironworks came on 7 March 1900 when it was reported in the *West Ham Guardian* that:

It is announced that the committee of Thames Ironworks FC are to consider some sort of reorganisation. A proposal is evidently on the table. For one who has it on authority says it will 'if adopted, undoubtedly be to the club's advantage.' This is good news. Supporters are tired of seeing the club so low down as fourth from the bottom.

The club's owner, Arnold Hills, was having cash flow problems, having agreed to buy John Penn & Sons, and needed to raise funds. He knew he couldn't pump further money into a football club. Shortly before the season's end the *West Ham Guardian* reported that local people would be asked to buy 500 shares at £1 each, with Arnold Hills matching the sum. A few weeks later the West Ham Football Club Company Limited was formed. However, some shares remained unsold for several years. Thames Ironworks resigned from the Southern League and were wound up in June 1900. On 5 July, West Ham United Football Club was formally registered and elected to the Southern League in Thames Ironworks' place. It may not have been the ending Arnold Hills had wished for, but there is little doubt that Mr Hills remains the great grandfather of the club we know today.

West Ham United started their illustrious history in the Southern League, a league they remained in for the next nineteen years until their election to League Division Two. Their first season started with a bang, with a 7–0 victory over Gravesend with new signing Billy Grassam scoring four goals. He finished as top scorer with fifteen goals and the club ended up in a creditable sixth place. Off the field the club's finances remained precarious with season ticket sales amounting to fewer than 200 and disappointing crowds.

By the end of the 1903/4 season, the club was verging on bankruptcy and only had the funds to pay one professional, Tommy Allison, over the summer. The club's main benefactor, Arnold Hills, had also hit on hard times and was in no position to reduce the rent on the Memorial Grounds Stadium. Luckily, a local brewery stepped in and put up £20,000 to finance the building of a new stadium on the site of the Boleyn Castle playing fields off Green Street in East Ham. However, a further hitch occurred when the Home Office objected to a football club using the land, which was under the ownership of the Catholic Ecclesiastical Authorities. The new manager, Syd King, took it upon himself to see local Conservative MP Ernest Gray. Gray smoothed the path and the 1905/06 season opened at the Boleyn Ground with an emphatic 3–0 win against Millwall.

And there we have remained for more than a century. We all have our individual memories of both the good times and bad times – of seeing fantastic players grace our pitch, and of course quite a few ordinary ones. But rarely do we remember those who started it all more than a hundred years ago.

This brilliant book by Brian Belton not only pays tribute to the club's founders and forefathers, it serves as a reminder to those who currently run the club that they are merely the club's custodians. Let's hope that in the year 2115 people will look back at the current owners and nod their heads in appreciation for the decision to move to the Olympic Stadium. Without that, West Ham would never have won the Champions League twenty times, they will say. Maybe.

Iain Dale, author of *West Ham: When Football Was Football* and editor of www.westhamtillidie.com

INTRODUCTION

Looking at the 1901 census, 15-year-old Samuel Poyser is detailed as a 'carrier for a rivotter'. Sam was, at that time, working at the Thames Ironworks. John, Sam's brother, was three years older and 'a painter of ships' during the same period. A third brother, 20-year-old Henry, was a 'holder up for a boiler rivotter'. You can, without too much effort, find many other men listed in the census who lived in the Canning Town/West Ham area, who looked to the Ironworks and to shipbuilding in general as the means to obtain their and their families' daily bread. Even at this point, the eastern reaches of London's great river had a long history of nautical industry. It was a place that was defined by, and grew out of water and perhaps the principal means by which its influence touched and changed global society.

This book looks at the life and times of Thames Ironworks. It is a story of ships, industrial history and the people that made both. It has to be said, however, that it is hard to write such a chronicle without including a biography of the football club that was part of the Ironworks, the former reflecting the latter, its development and soul. For many years history forgot the Ironworks. Renewed interest at the start of the twenty-first century arose largely because of the company's connection with the modern football industry.

The football team that represented Thames Ironworks and carried its name was the precursor of West Ham United, a club that was to become one of the most enigmatic of top professional sides in the English game. In fact, it would not be too far-fetched to say that West Ham carries, as part of its culture, echoes of the Ironworks it grew out of. If you like, the contemporary business could be thought of as being, in part, constituted on an archaeological ethos that is grounded in the great shipbuilding company that, for a time, dominated the district of West Ham as an enterprise, while shaping British and world maritime history.

A great deal of ink has been used on trying to describe the nature of West Ham as a football club. It is said to have a 'way', which brings to mind a sort of Zen-like persona. West Ham has been called a 'family club' and a 'community club', but quite what such expressions mean has never been clearly articulated. Perhaps these titles express something of a sense of belonging or a clear identity that is imbued through the club's location in the East End of London. This area has long been associated with the cloudy concept of 'community' and the ethereal 'loveable cockney character': at once a scoundrel and a threat, an idiot or clown but simultaneously an intelligently crafty archetype. In short, a vicissitudinous contradiction in terms: a conundrum of personality resonant of the 'cock's egg' from which the moniker is derived.

However, the deeper, more concrete roots of the sporting institution probably gives us stronger clues about its foundational nature, both its qualities and shortcomings. This pedigree was set in the complexities of Victorian class politics, industrial commercialism, philanthropy, paternalistic entrepreneurialism and the religious and humanitarian conscience of a society premised on the exploitation of the poor by the rich. To understand West Ham United as an organisation, its relationship to football as a phenomenon and a social institution, one needs to know something about its origins so firmly founded on iron; you need to understand the ships and something of the men who conceived, designed, built and sailed them.

More than a decade ago I wrote *Founded on Iron* that detailed the history of Thames Ironworks Football Club. When I was asked to build on this by developing a readable history of the Ironworks itself I spent not a little time thinking about how this might differ from that original work. A full and comprehensive history of Thames Ironworks would be a tome of much greater proportions than the information and narrative encapsulated in the pages that follow. It would be a hugely protracted enterprise, which would probably demand of the reader a considerable level of technical and specialist knowledge, but certainly personal commitment, to fully appreciate or understand. However, the purpose of the book I have written is more diffuse than a project of the latter magnitude. What I offer is something of a general prospect of the character of an organisation as it shifted within the confines of national and world history, while providing a perspective on how the sporting phenomenon that was to be its lasting legacy, was shaped and projected into the future. As such, my project was to capture something of the genesis and enduring spirit of a seminal facet of East London life and culture that touched, was part of and influenced the history and shape of the modern world.

This being the case, what follows is an introduction to the Ironworks, built on three pillars. Fundamentally there is the industrial, social, commercial foundation, the development and eventual demise of the company. Just as I found when writing *Founded on Iron*, when I started to write this book I quickly came to the conclusion that this would unavoidably mean interweaving into the text the birth and embryonic growth of the football club that sustains and gives contemporary meaning and resonance to the Ironworks, and has been a lasting monument to the shipbuilding company. Although in this case the (literal) thread of the story would need to be reversed; it would need to be led and concluded by a focus on the Ironworks rather than the football club.

The final element of this history is the ships built by Thames. These continue to carry a cargo of historical and social insight. They were a creation of the world in which they were constructed, and as such they embody in their biographies important and often hidden aspects of the time and place whose influence, in many cases, helped mould today's world.

Many of the craft built by Thames are listed as coming out of Blackwall, but most were, in fact, products of the Canning Town yard. Much of the documentation connected with the shipbuilding activity of Thames Ironworks was kept at the company's Blackwall offices and it is this location that is often given credit for the firm's contribution to the history of shipbuilding. This mainly administrative centre was moved to Canning Town in

1903, overlooking a dry dock. There was a small yard at the Blackwall site but the major shipbuilding projects of the Thames Ironworks were undertaken at Canning Town.

The company, in its time, was midwife to hundreds of craft of almost every type. It would be unrealistic to provide details of them all or even a majority in a publication of this size and scope. A full inventory would be a gargantuan project, covering every ship, vessel, construction and fabrication produced by Thames so choices had to be made. Considering this, I have looked to present components of the chronicle of industrial and sporting development, in unison. I have tried to portray something of the typical, the esoteric and the remarkable. I could have just gone for the latter of course, but that would present a skewed picture. I have tried to include at least a little bit of everything, but as in all such samples, there will always be more of one thing than another; this is no doubt a consequence of both conscious and unconscious forces – objectivity is confusingly a construct of subjective judgement.

So what we have is a representative selection of the ships built by Thames Ironworks, as well as touching on other constructions and innovations. However, I have looked to introduce ships and other craft that individually and collectively depict and, to some extent, personify and enact the impact and influence of the Ironworks in national and world history. The aficionado will undoubtedly protest at arguably vital omissions. I have not, for instance, included an exhaustive history of the *Warrior*, probably the most significant and lasting monument to Thames Ironworks. As much as I love that magnificent vessel (and I really do adore it, as an industrial and now also as an archaeological achievement, as well as in many other ways), robust and extensive electronic and hard histories are easily available. To merely replicate these would seem to be a waste of both the author's and the reader's time and energy. I have not provided a comprehensive biography of the *Thunderer* or the *Albion*, instead concentrating more on their impact on the history of the Ironworks.

For all this, ships are the underpinning element on which all that Thames Ironworks was or remains; West Ham United was 'Founded on Iron' and it is that heritage on which no mean legacy stands. West Ham United Football Club carries the mantle of the Ironworks and is its throbbing, vibrating, incandescent descendant. West Ham was incorporated on 5 July 1900 and, as the club minutes testified five days later, it was, like the ships, Thames-built, a product of the Ironworks.

BRIDGING THE GAP

In 1895 the owner of the Thames Ironworks and Shipbuilding Company, Arnold Hills, began to use a game to bridge the gaps between himself and his workforce. He founded and sponsored the Thames Ironworks Football Club. Football was chosen as a common language to meld management and worker into one efficient unit, but this opened up many more channels than Hills might have planned.

In its infancy football, as an organised affair, was in the hands of those who controlled society, the top of the social hierarchy who had been educated and trained to rule at public school and university. When a committee of workers took over Thames Ironworks

Football Club shortly after it came into being, this was part of a nationwide incursion of working people into the development and organisation of the sport. It had been going on before 1895 and was to continue over the next twenty years.

Thames Ironworks Committee included its chair, Mr F. Payne; treasurer, Mr G. Johnson and secretary, Mr A.T. Harsent. The committee was: C. Hill, A. Dance, Cameron Firth, Selby, W. Proctor, G. Patterson, T. Dearl, T. Robinson, D. Large, D. Taylor, E. Smith, E. Bickford and J. Cearns. F. Payne, G. Johnson, A.T. Harsent, C. Hill, E. Smith were selected to form an emergency committee.

The symbolic nature of this cannot be denied. One of the tools of the elite, ruling groups to forward its interests and values, which were synonymous, was hijacked and, in a relatively short time, turned into a means of making money. This was the very type of usurpation that those who had monopolised the organised football for the best part of a century feared in a more general way. The take-over of football represented something of their worst fears for society overall.

Association football, in its professional incarnation, destroyed the Athenian spirit that had guided its development as a sport and led to its demise in the public schools and universities, to be replaced by Rugby Union. One of the final nails in the coffin of football's elite age was banged home by West Ham United. After the 'Hammers' defeated the Corinthians, the most archetypal of the 'Old Boy' clubs, in the FA Cup of 1933, the former public schoolboys lost their exemption from the early rounds of the Cup, and eventually withdrew from the competition in protest. This can be seen to mark the last act of the start of the end of upper-class domination of the game.

However, the moneyed classes were quick to regroup. To paraphrase Gracie Fields in the 1930s, they were dead but wouldn't lie down and they stayed in control of the administration of football. Although many of the new professional clubs, arising out of working-class associations, church groups, workers clubs and the like, were owned by the rising middle classes and businessmen, the old aristocracy of the game remained involved at club level. This involvement was mainly through share ownership and ongoing monopolisation of football's umbrella organisations, such as the Football Association and Football League, which included control of the national teams of England, Scotland, Wales and, for the initial decades of organised game, Ireland.

Today it is a matter of some debate who actually 'owns' clubs. It depends on what one means by 'ownership'. What is not in doubt is that money dictates the direction of the upper echelon of football, so apart from the 'player revolts' of the 1950s and '60s, led at West Ham by Malcolm Allison and nationally by Jimmy Hill, the 'football revolution' of the late nineteenth and early twentieth centuries, seemed to have made very little difference in terms of where and with whom the organised power of the football presided.

This said, Arnold Hills wanted his footballing 'Irons', like his Ironworks, to be an extension of his personality, values and ambitions. While such intentions were never fulfilled, his shipbuilding company, as an organisation, existed for more than just the profit motive and more even than moving wonderfully innovative engineering ideas into reality. However, it must be said that some of these visions retrospectively look like something more akin to eccentric dreams than prospectively realisable innovation.

Thus the football team and the shipbuilders intertwine; one tells you about the other and to that extent they are historically symbiotic. However, as the industrial enterprise moved into the last phases of its existence, West Ham United was born as a quite different entrepreneurial incarnation.

So, what follows is neither a story of ships nor football. It is a tale of the synergy that existed between both, at a time and in a place which makes for a remarkable study of facets of the Victorian age that we have today inherited and continue to shape.

Ironclad *Vasco Da Gama* (as she was soon after her launch). A central battery ironclad, she was launched in 1876 and entered service with the Portuguese Navy later in the year. She served as the flagship of the Portuguese fleet for the majority of her long and peaceful career. She was rebuilt and heavily modernised between 1901 and 1903. Long-since obsolete by the 1930s, *Vasco da Gama* was finally sold for scrapping in 1935.

DITCHBURN, MARE AND ROLT

In a corner of today's Canning Town underground station there is a memorial, reputedly fashioned using original iron from a nineteenth-century warship, clad in numerous concrete panels. These are inscribed with a eulogy that commemorates the Thames Ironworks and Shipbuilding Company which was located in close proximity to where the memorial now stands.

Along with the Thames Ironworks, there were a number of other shipbuilding companies along the course of the River Thames. None of them survived to the modern era. In fact, Thames was the last major shipbuilding company based on the rambling old waterway to fade into history. However, this great industrial phenomenon did not appear out of the blue; it was no sudden incursion of the industrial age. The development and growth of the Ironworks represented much of the character of the Victorian age, the force that brought the company into the world, to be part of what would sustain that world.

In 1837 Queen Victoria succeeded her uncle, William IV, to the throne of England. She was the same age as 'painter of ships' John Poyser would be sixty-four years later, although 'Vicky' was not born east of the Thames and, even in 1819, she would not be subjected to the fact that infant mortality accounted for 25 per cent of all deaths at the time that John and his brothers came into the world over half a century later.

Three years prior to Victoria coming to the throne of the British Empire, the shipwright Thomas Ditchburn, who had been involved in shipbuilding at Rotherhithe, and naval architect Charles J. Mare joined forces to found the first iron shipbuilding yard on the Thames. Unsurprisingly, they called it 'Ditchburn and Mare'. The modest location was laid out on the south side of the River Thames at Deptford. After a fire gutted the yard they transferred to the northern bank of the Thames, taking over a 5-acre, disused shipbuilding premises along Orchard Place, between the East India Dock Basin and the mouth of the River Lea. This area is often referred to as Bow Creek and it is where the Thames cuts a majestic curve away from the Isle of Dogs at Blackwall.

There had been shipbuilding at Blackwall since 1587, but the confined nature of the spit meant that only ships of less than 1,000 tons could be built there. At that time there was no convenient rail links and this made the cost of bringing in iron plate from the north prohibitive. This also caused delays in the delivery of raw materials. Mare saw that these difficulties could be alleviated by smelting wrought iron plate and building rolling mills on site. However, if this ambition were to be made a reality the company would need to relocate to allow an appreciable expansion of plant.

Charles Mare identified a site with the potential to facilitate what he saw as the necessary growth of the company. It was an area of open land, just across Bow Creek on the eastern bank of the River Lea where it melds with the River Thames in (what was then) the borough of West Ham, Essex. However, Mare's partner, Thomas Ditchburn, didn't feel secure about this location as it would be subjected to flooding from spring high tides. In those days, the River Lea at Silvertown Way was 50ft wide at low water, but over 200ft wide at high tide. For all this, Mare was so keen to undertake this new venture that he changed the nature of his partnership with Ditchburn and purchased around 10 acres of marshland for a new, larger yard on the northern, Canning Town bank of the Lea.

Mare staked out the site personally, aided by a young apprentice, Clement Mackrow, who was to become Naval Architect to Thames Ironworks. By 1843 two new slipways, capable of taking four ships each, were staked out for the purpose of building small iron steamers for the Citizen Ship Company. However, the first site of the Thames Ironworks, that was also to continue to be known as Ditchburn and Mare for much of the rest of the century, was also to produce several innovative iron racing yachts, including the most famous of these, the *Mosquito*, which was built in 1846. She was an impressive 70 footer with a 15ft 2in beam. She is included in the *Guinness Book of Yachting Facts*.

The second half of the nineteenth century saw a revolution in communications. In 1840 Samuel Morse patented his invention of the code that bears his name. The telegraph spread rapidly in the next ten years. It was also a time of colonial expansion and struggle. The Battle of Blood River in Natal, South Africa took place in 1838 which resulted in the defeat of the Zulus by the Boers. The British occupied Aden in 1839 and the Opium War between Britain and China began, which was to last until 1842. Britain was also involved in protracted and bloody hostilities in Afghanistan (a conflict that, as we know, never really ended). Turkey invaded Syria and was heavily defeated in the Battle of Nesib (part of the Turks' lack of enthusiasm to openly intervene in more contemporary conflicts in and with Syria). There were rebellions in Upper and Lower Canada, whilst New Zealand was in the process of becoming a British Crown Colony. The latter was ratified in 1840 under the Treaty of Waitagi. At around the same time the Treaty of London was signed whereby Britain, Russia, Prussia and Austria agreed to limit Egyptian expansion. The British Navy bombarded Beirut and the Penny Post was introduced in Britain.

The Metropolitan Building Act of 1844 was a defining event in the history of East London as it introduced a raft of legislation that included the banning of toxic and noxious industry within the boundary of London. The County Borough of West Ham, wherein the new ironworks was situated, was located just outside the metropolitan area. Thus the eastern bank of the River Lea was encompassed in the immediate positive impact on manufacturing businesses (if not for the throats and lungs of local inhabitants) drawing development and relocation of industry to the area as a result. Mare's move from the Blackwall side of the Lea to Canning Town was part of this.

The situation caused a huge increase in the local population which made for cheaper labour. In 1841 the borough had fewer than 13,000 residents; by 1901 the area had a population of 267,000. This made West Ham the ninth most populous town in England.

This influx put a massive strain on what facilities there were and on those that could be created over a few decades. Housing and concomitant sewage systems were by no means even close to adequate at any stage during this period of time. Indeed, much of the housing that was huddled within the vicinity of the Ironworks from the 1850s on would have been blatantly unfit for human habitation by even the most primitive standards.

Nevertheless, the situation made for a good time for the shipbuilding industry on and around the banks of West Ham's patch of the Thames and throughout the 1850s and into the 1860s, East London firms in Limehouse, Millwall and Blackwall flourished as they were the first to have adjusted to the demand for large, iron vessels.

ARGO

By the mid-1800s Thames Ironworks had moved into crafting large scale ships like *Argo*. This was the first steamship to intentionally circumnavigate the world, as the *New York Times* of 19 November 1853 reported:

'A Short Voyage Around the Globe'

The iron screw steamer *Argo*, recently arrived at Southampton, Eng., has been round the globe in 128 days. She was 64 days on her passage from Southampton to Melbourne, via the Cape of Good Hope. She is completely shipped rigged, and has an auxiliary steam power of 300 horse, to be used in adverse winds and calms. She has used 2.105 tons coal, about 17 tons a day, and has averaged 230 miles a day, about 9½ miles an hour during the entire voyage. In fair winds under canvas, the *Argo* made 13 and 14 knots an hour for successive days; and 11 and 12 knots, close hauled, with the screw feathered ... Our Yankee clippers must look to their honors, if John Bull has got to building such vessels as the *Argo*. (*Boston Traveller*)

Argo was launched on 24 December 1852, constructed for the General Screw Steam Shipping Company, a British concern established in 1848 by James Laming which has an interesting history of its own. In the late 1849 it inaugurated a service between Liverpool, Gibraltar, Malta and Constantinople, deploying the new 500-ton *Bosphorus*, also an iron screw steamer. A few years later GSSSC were operating a mail service between the UK and Australia and, like many others, their ships were chartered as troop transports during the Crimean War.

Argo was an early incarnation of a screw-propelled vessel but she had a sail rig. Her screw could be feathered so she was able, if necessary, to become a totally wind-powered ship. In testing she achieved up to 10 knots under sail only, which was about the same speed she could make under steam. The transition from stopping the engines to sail could, remarkably, be effected in under seven minutes. Innovatively, and probably usefully, the screw could be raised for inspection while at sea.

With her four decks weighing in at 1,815 tons, *Argo* was nearly 245ft long, with a beam of 39ft and cost £75,000 by the time she went to sea. *Argo* had a complement of 120 and was made to accommodate 210 passengers.

Argo, being ahead of her times, adventurous and, in the worst case scenario, continuing to look to those who put faith in her, reflected the future character of the Ironworks and West Ham United. Her biography can be understood as an archaeological footprint in the history of the organisation and the football club that the following pages chronicle. That said, as you will read later, her crew were not always the best behaved.

On 8 May 1853 *Argo* set sail for Australia from Southampton, under Captain George Hyde. With 55 passengers and a full cargo of 375 tons, including jewellery to the value £11,500, there was just one stop planned to take on coal at Cape St Vincent. This was in response to steamships making the Australian run having a problematic reputation. As such, the single stop was part of an effort to provide a speedy passage.

After her sixty-four days at sea, on 14 July 1853 *Argo* arrived at Sydney, Australia only to be detained at her mooring in the harbour for a week due to the mutinous conduct of her crew. On arrival at, what was then, a British colony, they had immediately attempted to leave the ship. Acting on instructions given to him prior to leaving Britain, the ship's skipper, Captain Hyde, had the crew taken into custody and detained on board a convict hulk until the ship departed for its return to Britain.

Argo left Australia on 27 August 1853 carrying 100 passengers and 103,766 ounces of gold, the value of which at that time was £567,777 (£7.5m nowadays). She had been scheduled to sail two days previously but Captain Hyde had to find new crew members, as he wanted to leave some of the men who had mutinied to serve out their sentences. They had physically assaulted him, even though the police had been present when he was attacked. However, it seems that the offenders found the food in custody relatively good and preferred their comparative idleness to the prospect of rounding the Horn under the command of their victim; this was completely rational and, as such, understandable.

Argo arrived back in Britain in October 1853 to substantial acclamation, having become the first steamship to deliberately circumnavigate the globe. One passenger had died en-route, which was not bad going for the period. She had made the return voyage, rounding Cape Horn, in one day less than the outward journey.

Later, a month after transporting from Australia to England a huge amount of cargo for the Paris Exhibition, *Argo* was requisitioned by the government as a transport vessel and was fitted for cavalry in April 1855. In the same month *Argo* set course for the Crimea, transporting 190 horses, a troop of the Royal Horse Artillery and a battery of artillery that consisted of four brass 9lb guns, two 24lb howitzers, one 12lb rocket tube and ammunition.

On 7 March 1856 *Argo* left Southampton with C battery of Royal Artillery and horses, plus 210 tons of freight, which included guns and gun-carriages. She was heading once again for the Crimea.

Following hostilities, under Captain H.B. Benson, *Argo* was occupied shipping cargo and passengers across the Atlantic. However, in December 1857 she sailed from Spithead for India with detachments of troops, an event to warrant recording at the time:

The European and American Steam Navigation Company's splendid ship *Argo*, under Captain Benson, will receive her troops this day alongside Portsmouth Dockyard jetty. Captain Benson had barely eight clear working days to metamorphose the

Argo from a first-class Transatlantic passenger packet into a Government troop-transport, rendering necessary an entire revolution in the whole interior of the ship except the state saloon. This has been done in an able and masterly manner. The *Argo* is an iron ship, of 2,249 tons burden, 300-horse (screw) power, and the height between decks is 7ft 2in. She prepared for berthing 850 troops and about 50 officers. Her ventilation is unequalled. She has 68 port holes or scuttles on the troop deck, which is a clean sweep of space fore and aft, uninterruptedly presenting a line of benches and hammocks like a vista of stalls. She has also 11 ventilating shafts and a number of rotary ventilators in various parts of her, rendering the below berths as cool as the saloon deck. She is a good sailer, having Cunningham's patent self-reefing topsails and every other modern improvement; she steams on an average nine knots, and only consumes about 35 tons of coal per day. It is estimated with such advantages, and most experienced officers, she must make at least as good a passage out to India as the Company's other steamer, the *Golden Fleece*.

On New Year's Day 1858 *Argo* arrived at St Vincent. An extract from a letter from the ship told how:

Every one on board is in excellent health and tiptop spirits, and I think I may say that there is not a discontented man in the ship out of nearly 900. Yesterday (the 2nd inst) we astonished the natives by having a cricket match, which went off very successfully – tents pitched and band playing. The *Australasian*, with the head-quarters of the 68th, and the *Medway*, which takes home this mail, arrived here yesterday afternoon, and we are consequently quite a party in this desolate island. Coaling is very slow here, labour being extremely scarce, and Captain Benson thinks the 6th about the time we shall get away.

However, the journey back from India was a different story. On 12 May 1858 Lieutenant R.G. Bell, of the 37th Regiment (who had left England in December 1857 in the *Argo*) died on board. He had been invalided home with consumption immediately on arrival at Calcutta, and re-embarked on her leaving in April. It was on 6 June that Lieutenant D. Hay, who took a prominent part in the defence of Lucknow[1], died. He had also been sent back to Britain with consumption, said to have been caused by 'fatigue and privation'. Later that month, arriving at St Vincent, four men had died among the invalid troops on the passage from the Cape, the ship had embarked from there at the end of May. By the time *Argo* reached Plymouth in early July the majority of the troops had contracted diseases from those who had embarked carrying disease. Three days later she arrived

---

1. Lucknow was the capital of the former state of Awadh, India. The Residency (the local office of colonial administration) within the city was laid siege to during the Indian Rebellion of 1857. Following two successive relief attempts the defenders and civilians were evacuated, and the Residency abandoned. The protracted defence by the British was to be one of the key events of the uprising (there were over 2,500 casualties, mostly Indians; overall about 8,000 British troops faced 30,000 rebels).

in the Thames with the invalid troops from India. They were landed at Gravesend and forwarded to Fort Pitt Hospital, Chatham.

From mid-1858 *Argo* returned to her transatlantic duties, having been chartered to the Galway Line. On her first homeward voyage for the Galway Line, sailing from Newfoundland on 28 June 1859, she ran onto a reef in thick fog, which thankfully involved no loss of life. The *New York Times* of Monday, 13 July 1859 reported:

'Loss or the Steamer *Argo* – Personal Narrative of one of her Passengers.'
The Atlantic Royal Mail Steamship Navigation Company's steamer *Argo*, Capt. Halpin left New York on Thursday, June 23rd, with two hundred passengers; her officers and crew amounting to about one hundred and twenty men. The voyage up to the time of the loss of the ship was as favorable as could be desired; the weather was fine, and the comfortable accommodations of the ship together with the attentive and gentlemanly deportment of the Captain and officers, elicited universal approbation. On Tuesday, morning, at about 3½ o'clock, Cape Pine was made, being about twelve mile distant. The ship's course was altered, so as to clear Cape Race twenty miles. At about 4 o'clock a dense fog set in, the weather having been previously perfectly clear. A few minutes before six a fishing schooner was hailed, and we were informed that we were on the eastern side of Trepassey Bay, a mile and a half or two miles from land. The helm was put hard to port, and the course of the ship altered.

In five minutes the breakers were seen and the engines stopped and reversed, but too late. The ship struck a rock on Freshwater Point, on the eastern side of Trepassey Bay, and about seven miles from Cape Race. She struck so lightly that some of the passengers who were asleep in their berths were not awakened. She was fast aground, however, and soon began to thump violently and fill in the forward compartments. Minute guns were fired, and the boats got ready and supplied with provisions and water with the greatest promptness and order. The women and children embarked first and the coolness displayed by the passengers, officers and crew was truly remarkable and worthy of all praise. A landing was effected about a mile distant from the ship, and in the course of the morning, all the passengers were landed in safety. Every effort was made to save the ship, but in vain. Had it not been high tide at the time she struck, she might possibly have been got off. During the day the boats were constantly passing between the ship and shore. All the baggage in the state-rooms was saved, and various articles for the comfort of the passengers sent on shore. The baggage which was stowed below was lost.

Soon after the accident, Mr. Butterfield, of this City, at the request of the Captain, went, in a small boat, to Trepassey, about eight miles distant, and telegraphed to St. Johns for assistance, and to New York announcing the disaster.

As the place of landing was eight miles from any habitation, and no conveyance for the passengers could be procured before the next day, preparations were made for passing the night on shore.

Tents were made with sails, which afforded shelter for the women and children, but most of the men passed the night in the open air. The next day the steamtugs

Dauntless and *Blue Jacket* conveyed all the passengers to St. Johns, about eighty miles distant

The conduct of all, throughout this trying occasion, was commendable. The officers of the ship did every thing in their power to alleviate the sufferings of the passengers, and make them as comfortable as the circumstances would admit. The ladles, in particular, deserve much praise for the cheerfulness and courage with which they bore their perils and suffering.

During the day, the fishermen, in their boats, came in crowds around the wreck, and seemed waiting, like harpies, for their prey. It is true, in some instances, they assisted with their boats, but not without pay. Before night they had commenced their disgraceful work of plunder on the ship, and a hundred or two of them were to be seen stripping her of everything they could lay hands on.

As to the cause of the loss of this fine ship, various absurd and unfounded rumors have been afloat, as to the carelessness on the part of the Captain and his officers. At the time of the disaster, and for sometime before, all the principal officers were on deck, and among them an experienced coast pilot.

The loss of the ship must be attributed to the fog, some local attraction affecting the needle or particularly the force of a current which at times sets into Trepassey Bay with great power. Many ships have been wrecked near this place, and their loss has been ascribed to these causes.

The agents of the line, Mr Shea of St Johns and Mr Butterfield, were unremitting in their attentions to the passengers, and did everything to make them comfortable, 'The *Glasgow* has been sent to St Johns, and will take over the *Argo's* passengers. Some five or six of them returned in the *Adelaide*, which arrived at the port this morning.'

EXPANSION

As Mare's firm moved into the second half of the nineteenth century it prospered and expanded. At its height it was a 30-acre prime industrial park, split into two sites on either side of Bow Creek. It was more than capable of undertaking the largest contracts up to a capacity of 25,000 tons of warships and 10,000 tons of first-class mail steamers at the same time. Orchard Place remained the company's registered address until 1903 and was linked to the main shipbuilding base in Canning Town by a chain ferry. At the zenith of its development this mechanism was capable of transporting 200 men at a time across Bow Creek, evidencing that the company was a major employer in the area.

Mare was fast building a reputation for inventive maritime design and development. He built the first screw-driven ship for the Royal Navy, Queen Victoria's Royal Yacht *Fairey*. The propeller drive of the *Fairey* was far less noisy than the paddle steamer it replaced and avoided the vibration formally experienced in the Royal apartments. The Queen showed her relief and gratitude by offering Mare a knighthood, but he was reported to have 'modestly declined'. This was an odd reaction, particularly during this period in Britain's class history when the distinction of a knighthood would have opened many doors to Charles Mare. Of course there are a number of reasons why he might have spurned aristocratic recognition, his politics or religion for instance, but it is more likely that the young monarch may have acted a little too spontaneously for the taste of her political advisors. Victoria was not long into her reign and deeply influenced by her consort Albert who, being of German origin, may not have been as limited by class distinctions as his English cousins. Little is known of Charles Mare's background, but he does appear to have come from an artisan class, perhaps with Irish connections. As such, his 'modesty' may have been a convenient response for those who wished to preserve Royal favours for a certain class or 'type' of person.

For all this, and maybe partly because of it, Thames Ironworks continued to capture lucrative and prestigious contracts, although the company was not without competitors on the Thames. Millwall Ironworks were involved in a number of the same markets as their neighbours in Canning Town. Millwall smelted their steel from iron ore and rolled it. Thames Ironworks reconstituted scrap and hammered it. As such there was a rivalry between West Ham and Millwall that pre-empted their infamous enmity premised on the beautiful game. This said, the ancestors of the 'Lions', Millwall Rovers, were not in fact Ironworkers, but a group of mostly Scotsmen employed at jam and marmalade makers

J.T. Morton's at West Ferry Road on the Isle of Dogs. As such it is perhaps not surprising that West Ham have had Millwall on toast so many times!

The P&O transport ship, *Himalaya*, was very much a milestone in the history of Thames Ironworks. With a displacement of 4,690 tons she was, at that time, the biggest merchant ship in the world. Her construction was an outstanding achievement for the yard, showing the potential that Thames Ironworks had to build ships on the most grandiose scale.

HIMALAYA

Following on the heels of *Argo*, in 1853 the Peninsular and Oriental Steam Navigation Company (P&O) ordered the single screw passenger steamship SS *Himalaya*. She was laid down in 1852 and launched on 24 May 1853, at which point she was the world's largest steamer. The *Illustrated London News* of 28 May 1853 reported the event:

'Launch of the *Himalaya* screw steam-ship'
This leviathan screw steam-ship, which in the course of her construction, has excited very considerable interest, more especially among the visitors to Blackwall, was launched on Tuesday afternoon (the Queen's birthday anniversary), from the premises of her builders, Messrs. C. J. Mare and Co. The spectacle was witnessed by the Duke of Leinster, Lord and Lady Naas, Lord and Lady de Tabley, Miss de Tabley; Mr. T. Russell, M.P., Sir James and Lady Matheson, Lord Alfred Paget, M.P., Col. Boldero, M.P., Mr. O'Brien, M.P., Mr. Wyndham Goold, M.P., Sir James Emerson Tennent, M.P., Mr. A. Hastie, M.P., Mr. B. Wilcox, M.P., Mr. James Allen, and other Directors of the Peninsular and Oriental Company, for which this splendid vessel has been built.

The ceremony of naming the *Himalaya* was performed by Lady Matheson, wife of Sir James Matheson, chairman of the Company. The arrangements were very complete, and reflected the highest credit on all concerned with the establishment of her eminent builder. On a given signal, at half-past two o'clock (shortly before high water), when the axe fell, the lowering vessel glided gently and smoothly into the water, amid the cheers of the numerous spectators; and by an excellent arrangement of ropes attached to the eastern bank of the creek, which were made of sufficient strength to turn her a little to the eastward at the moment of the launch and then break, the launch was most satisfactorily effected.

The *Himalaya* was designed and built under the inspection of Mr. F. Waterman, jun., at Messrs. Mare's establishment, at Blackwall. The vessel was commenced in November, 1851, and her length between perpendiculars is 340ft; breadth, 46ft 2in; depth of hold, 34ft 9in; and she is 3550 tons burden, with engines of 700 horse power, by John Penn and Son. She was originally intended to have paddle-wheels, with engines of 1200-horse power, but subsequently, and before she was too far advanced, it was decided that she should be fitted with a screw propeller and engines of 700-horse power on the most approved principle. Thus will her efficiency for ocean steaming be proportionately increased; carrying, as it is intended, some 1200 tons fuel, with accommodation for 400 cabin passengers, 500 tons measurement goods, and ample space for mail rooms, &c.

In regard to strength of build and form for speed, the *Himalaya* is unrivalled; having six water-tight bulkheads, and otherwise fitted with every appliance to safety. She will be provided with an entire outfit of 'Trotman's improved Porter's' anchors, the excellency of which have been fully proved in numerous instances on board the Peninsular and Oriental Company's extensive fleet; and affirmed also by the 'Committee's Report on the merits of Anchors of all Nations,' to possess 132 per cent superiority over the Admiralty anchor in respect to holding power and strength. The bower anchors will be respectively 48 and 50 cwts, in lieu of ordinary anchors, of five tons each. Thus a saving equal to that enormous weight upon the bows will be effected.

The cabin arrangements of this vessel with regard to ventilation are most effective, combining elegance and simplicity in its application. The merit of the invention is due to Mr. J. Robinson, under whose auspices the plan is in course of application to fourteen other new steam-ships now constructing for the Peninsular and Oriental Company.

We understand it is intended, on Saturday week next, to launch the *Jason*, 2600 tons; and successively, on completion, three others of like tonnage, rendered necessary by the increasing development of screw-steaming under the auspices of the General Screw Steam Shipping Company.

Sir James Matheson, whose wife, as the above report details, launched the *Himalaya*, was born on 17 October 1796 at Shiness, near Lairg in Sutherland, Scotland. He was one of the founders of the Jardine Matheson trading empire. His father had been a trader in India and James, after leaving university, followed in his father's footsteps. In 1828 he went into partnership with his compatriot, William Jardine, establishing the trading company Magniac and Co., which proved to be highly successful and on 1 July 1832 they formed Jardine, Matheson and Company Ltd. with the aim of trading opium, tea and other goods to and from China, working closely with the British East India Company. In 1833 the British Parliament revoked monopoly rights of the British East India Company to carry trade between Britain and China, and Jardine Mathesons swiftly took their place as the most important British trading firm in Asia.

By 1841, Jardine Mathesons had nineteen clipper ships, while their closest rivals in the intercontinental carriers business had just thirteen. They also owned hundreds of more modest ships, junks and smaller craft. Key areas of business included carriage of opium from India to China, trading spices and sugar from the Philippines and tea and silk from China. The firm also acted as shipping and insurance agents as well as operators of port facilities. When the Chinese tried to stop the flow of opium into their country because of its serious impact on the population, William Jardine (with support from many other British traders) persuaded the British Government to declare war on China to enforce the resumption of the trade. The war lasted from 1839 to 1842. Ultimately the British won, and the surge of opium into China resumed, and with it the flow of profits to the trading companies. This was perhaps the first drugs war and Jardine Mathesons can be regarded as the first big-time pushers – a primal narcotic cartel with state sanction and backing. It was the First Opium War that led to the colonisation of Hong Kong by the British and the consequent occupation of that area until 1997.

In February 1843 Jardine died and Matheson succeeded him as MP for Ashburton in Devon. On 9 November 1843 he married Mary Jane Percival. The following year he purchased the Isle of Lewis for £190,000. By the standards of the day, Matheson proved to be an enlightened landlord, who invested heavily in the island and introduced a number of schemes to provide work and ease poverty including road building and drainage schemes. This helped to ease the impact on the island of the potato famine by creating much needed employment. By 1850 he is said to have spent £329,000 on the island. Between 1851 and 1855 he also assisted 1,771 people to emigrate: these departures seem to have been more genuinely voluntary than most of Scotland's clearances.

Between 1847 and 1851 Matheson built Lews Castle, described as a Tudor Gothic mansion, which still overlooks Stornoway today. In 1851 he was rewarded for his efforts by being made Sir James Matheson, 1st Baronet of Lewis. He ceased to be MP for Ashburton in 1847, and from 1852 to 1868 served as the MP for Ross and Cromarty, being eventually succeeded by his nephew Sir Alexander Matheson. In 1878 Sir James Matheson died without a direct heir in Menton, France at the age of 82.

As indicated above, *Himalaya* had been planned as a paddle steamer but, such was the pace of nautical development at the time, the design was becoming outdated before she was completed. As such the ship was altered to screw propulsion while she was still on the stocks. She was fitted with a single two-bladed propeller, 18ft in diameter. The *Himalaya*'s sails were hoisted on three masts. *Himalaya* could carry 200 first-class passengers and required a crew of 213. She was almost twice the size of any other ship in the P&O fleet, capable of 14 knots using her 2,050hp steam engine alone and about 16½ knots under engine power and a full spread of sail. She was not exceeded in size until the SS *Australia* of 1870.

However, *Himalaya* proved to be a larger vessel than the passenger traffic demanded, in an era when coal was becoming more expensive with the advent of war in the Crimea. The ship almost immediately ran at a loss, so when, in July 1854, the Admiralty made an offer of £130,000 to procure her services as a troop ship it was soon snapped up. This was equivalent to her cost price.

In service for her country HMS *Himalaya* would have carried many more passengers per trip than in her civilian role. As a naval ship she carried Armstrong guns.

In the 1840s the Royal Navy had built smaller vessels, frigates, which had served as troopships, iron warships having been discredited by live-firing trials. *Himalaya* was purchased as the Crimean War created an urgent need to transport troops. The acquirement of the *Himalaya* was viewed with suspicion by many naval experts. For example, General Howard Douglas is reported to have predicted that she would have a short career, but he was proved wrong. After the end of the Crimean War *Himalaya* served as a troopship for almost four decades, supporting operations during the Second Opium War, and carrying servicemen to India, South Africa, the Gold Coast and North America. She gained battle honours in New Zealand 1863–66 and in Ashantee 1873–74.[2]

She was retired from trooping service in 1894 and became a coal hulk at Portland Harbour – she was given the new but less imposing name, HM *C60* in December 1895. She was sold out of the Navy on 28 September 1920 to a private owner, E.W. Payne, and continued to be based in Portland Harbour, probably still operating as a coal hulk. She met her end on June 1940 when German Junkers 87 dive bombers sank her in Portland Harbour.

During periods when there were no major emergencies in the British Colonies, and so no requirement for rapid, large-scale transport of troops, HMS *Himalaya* would have been employed mainly in the scheduled ferrying of regiments to and from Malta, Egypt or India for their tours of duty. When the ship was in port the crew would have had a chance to sample some of the exotic (and other) attractions of such destinations.

In January 1854 the *Melbourne Morning Herald* reported from Southampton:

The magnificent screw-steamship *Himalaya*, Captain A. Kellock, belonging to the Peninsular and Oriental Steam Navigation Company (the arrival of which from the Thames was reported in *The Times* of Saturday last), since her appearance in the Southampton Docks has been the object of great interest and attention to numerous visitors of all classes of society who have been permitted to go on board to make an inspection of the wondrous triumphs of enterprise and skill displayed in this gigantic ocean steamer. The *Himalaya* is the largest ocean steam ship in the world.

The engines, of 700 horse-power, by Messrs. Penn, of Greenwich, are on the trunk principle, similar to those supplied by that firm to the *Agamemnon* and other vessels. Their splendid performance cannot be exaggerated; they work like the mechanism of a chronometer, and propel the ship through the water with incredible smoothness and ease of motion. The cylinders of the engines are of 84in diameter, with a 31ft stroke, and the revolutions per minute are from 50 to 60. The screw is a two-bladed one, on the old principle, of 18ft diameter, with a 28ft pitch, and weighs nearly seven tons. The vessel is full ship-rigged, and the masts, spars, and sails Captain Kellock assures us, from the experience he has already had of the qualities of the vessel, that in a heavy breeze there would be no difficulty in getting 18 knots or 20 miles an hour out of the ship by using both steam and canvas. Passengers by this magnificent steamer will revel in every luxury and comfort that can be comprehended in a sea-voyage. The saloon, nearly 100ft in length, will dine 170 persons; the bed cabins are the largest and most roomy ever yet appropriated.

---

2. The Anglo-Ashanti Wars involved four conflicts between the Ashanti Empire, in the Akan interior of the Gold Coast (modern day Ghana) and the British Empire. These episodes continued from 1824 to 1901. They were chiefly concerned with Asantehene, the ruler of the Ashanti (or Asante), establishing definite control over the coastal regions. However, the inhabitants of these areas (the Fante and the inhabitants of Accra, who were mainly Ga) became reliant on British protection in the face incursions by the Ashanti. The Ashanti were impressive in their defiance of the British, but ultimately the Ashanti Empire was made a British protectorate.

There is in the various suits of apartments accommodation for 200 first and second cabin passengers, besides the usual mail-rooms, baggagez-rooms, store rooms, water-tanks, &c. The ship will carry 1,000 tons of measurement goods on freight, and in her bunkers can stow 1,200 tons of coals. The spar deck is flush from stem to stern, and it is when setting foot upon this part of the vessel that her immense size produces an extraordinary effect upon the spectator. An uninterrupted promenade of 375ft, or 125yd, is here provided. To walk round the spar-deck precisely one-seventh of a mile has to be traversed. The possession of such a stupendous steam-ship as the *Himalaya* must be a matter not merely of local, but national interest. If, unhappily, the threatened war should break out, there is no telling the uses to which, upon emergencies, this vessel and other steamers of lesser size belonging to the great steam companies might be applied. 3000 men could be embarked at Southampton, and conveyed by the *Himalaya* in 11 days to Constantinople or the Black Sea; while steamers such as the *Colombo*, *Plata*, *Atruto*, *Jason*, *Argo*, *Cranus*, and many others, might be despatched with proportionate numbers … employing temporarily the great steamers usually congregated at Southampton, a small army might in fact be rapidly thrown upon any particular point of the European or Asiatic coast, where the exigencies or unexpected hazards of war should render such succours necessary. For rapidly transporting immense supplies of provisions, ammunition, artillery, or men to the Black Sea, in the Mediterranean, or in the Baltic, it is difficult to say what enormous services might not, on emergency, be rendered by a few steamers such as these, should the Admiralty at any time find it desirable to employ them. Armed with long Paixhan guns, manned with a sufficient force of seamen trained to gunnery, such a ship as the *Himalaya* would laugh to scorn the efforts of any ordinary ships-of-war to capture her, with her steam-power of 701 horses, she could escape from and outrun any craft that might confront her. At the same time she could, in a running fight, reek substantive damage to an assailant.

The *Duke of Wellington*, according to accounts recently received from Lisbon, is as easily handled at sea as a Cowes yacht; and, if we rightly interpret the intelligence which has lately reached us, the Admiralty are determined to try, on a more extended scale, the principle of screw line-of-battle-ships. Instead of ships of 40,000 tons, 800-horse power, and carrying 131 guns, there is nothing to prevent the construction of ships 500ft long, of 10,000 tons burthen, and capable of mounting 200 or 250 pieces of ordnance of the largest size. Line-of-battle ships would then be turned into moveable fortifications of the most tremendous and destructive character, capable of being transported with incredible rapidity from place to place. If this principle be once admitted – and there seems nothing to prevent its feasibility – no land fortifications will hereafter be enabled to resist the gigantic naval forces which may be appointed for their reduction.

Warlike operations on the ocean will assume an entirely new character, and the time may come when these formidable fortresses of the sea will have classed in military operations as floating citadels, and when the destruction or loss of one of them will be considered as a disaster equal to the fall of a land fortress …

The origin of the *Himalaya* is, perhaps, one of the most interesting features connected with the progress of steam enterprise. Three years since the postal contract of the Peninsular and Oriental Steam Company was on the eve of expiration, and powerful competitors were understood to be preparing to contest the commercial supremacy of the Indian route with that association. The *Himalaya* was, therefore, designed, and it was determined that she should be fitted with paddle-wheel engines of 1200 horse power, which it was estimated would give a speed of 20 miles an hour, and enable the run from Southampton to Alexandria to be effected in eight or nine days. Five other ships of equal, if not superior size, were to be built and employed on the other side of the Isthmus. If this project had been brought to perfection, the communication between England and our Indian empire would have been facilitated to an extent that can even now be hardly realised, and Calcutta brought within 25 days of Southampton. The idea of building five ships of equal size to the *Himalaya* was, however, abandoned, and, the screw principle just at that time having been tried with favourable results on a small scale by the Company, it was decided to fit the *Himalaya* with screw engines of 700 horse power, instead of machinery on the paddle-wheel principle. The great success of the *Himalaya* was shown by the extraordinary speed attained at her trial-trip in the Channel last week, viz., 14 knots, or 16 miles an hour.

The same edition of the *Illustrated London News* that reported the launch of the *Himalaya* included the following piece that tells the reader about the nature of European commerce of the time and in particular British interventions with regard to the same:

'Commencement of the Lisbon Railway'

There is a plethora of English capital seeking profitable investment, and judicious railway undertakings offer so reasonable an assurance of pecuniary success, that nothing but the indifferent reputation of the Governments of Spain and Portugal has prevented English capital from flowing like a fertilising stream into those countries. We have to offer them not only money, engineering skill, and the thews and sinews of our sturdy labourers, wherewith to construct their railways, but we can even supply them with large portion of the passenger traffic which would make them pay; for Italy and Germany are beaten ground for our tourists, and thousands would gladly penetrate into the picturesque recesses of Iberia and Lusitania, if the large cities of the Peninsula were connected by railways. But what can be done for Governments which evade their most solemn obligations? If they repudiate the fair claims of the public creditor, they cannot wonder if the committee of the London Stock Exchange refuse in any way to recognise their attempts to obtain English capital for constructing the railways which are so much needed to develop their resources.

Nevertheless, the inhabitants of Lisbon are, it seems, to have a railway; and, more wonderful still appear likely to be largely indebted to English enterprise and skill for the means of constructing it. In order to give the greater éclat to the event, her Majesty the Queen of Portugal condescended to turn the first sod. The ceremony took place on Saturday, the 7th instant, in a quinta belonging to Lieut. Cunha, at Beato Antonio, about two miles from Lisbon, on the margin of the Tagus. The day was observed as a gala, and a large assemblage of the rank, fashion, and beauty of Lisbon was collected. The Queen, on her way to the scene of the day's proceedings, passed under three triumphal arches – the first at the Grillo, where a number of children, dressed in white, with garlands of flowers round their heads, stood, with baskets of flowers, with which they sprinkled her Majesty and the King Consort. At Alto de Grillo, a second triumphal arch, of gorgeous character, was erected, at the expense of an English gentleman, (Mr. Kerr). Here a regimental band of music was stationed; and on the approach of the Royal escort, their Majesties were covered by little fairies, dressed in white, with roses, carnations &c. Having passed through a third triumphal arch at Beato Antonio, their Majesties arrived at a few minutes before eleven o'clock at the quinta; on entering which the Royal cortege ascended a hill, where a magnificent tent was erected, containing seven divisions.

This was part of the beginning of Portugal's massive investment in its transport infrastructure that went on into the first decades of the twentieth century. The ongoing project came close to bankrupting the country. The value to British industry and the extent it took advantage of the situation was stoked by Edward VII's celebrated visit to Lisbon in 1903 (you can visit the Eduardo VII Park in the city that commemorates the event).

Thames built a number of warships for the Portuguese Navy in this period but also other craft for non-military use. For instance, in 1903 a 39-ton twin-screw tug was produced for the Portuguese Government. She was fitted with engines of 150hp.

CROESUS

It seemed as soon as one great ship rolled off the Thames Ironworks production line another was being readied to follow. By the end of June 1853, the 1,897-ton *Croesus*, 280ft long and over 41ft wide, was launched by one of Peter Rolt's daughters. *Croesus* was the better part of 32ft in depth. Her twin cylinder, 400hp engines (augmented by three masts) made by G. & J. Rennie, were the first of their kind. Her three decks were built of iron.

Croesus, which was originally intended to be called the 'Jason', had a crew of eighty in 1853; a couple of years on a further forty men were added to this number. She was used for regular runs to Australia, carrying a range of cargo and passengers. On 14 December 1854 she arrived at Southampton with £284,344 in gold dust, which was a massive sum in those days. That same month she became a transport for the British Government and was the first ship to enter the New Graving Dock at Southampton for a complete overhaul and fitting as troop transport. It was on 16 March 1855 that *Croesus* sailed from Portsmouth, carrying the Wiltshire Militia contingent for the Crimea, to be disembarked at Corfu. A month later she was destroyed by fire off Portofino, in the Gulf of Genoa, while conveying troops from Sardinia to the Crimea. However, just five or six lives were lost. She was insured for £57,000 but had cost £99,000.

ROLT

By 1856 Mare was in charge of one of Britain's leading civil engineering concerns, but he ran into some considerable financial difficulties due to miscalculations on a contract for a number of gunboats. These were exacerbated by problems involving some bridge work. After a brief struggle the firm was on the point of bankruptcy. Peter Rolt, a timber merchant and Mare's father-in-law (Mare was married to one of Rolt's two daughters) stepped in and suggested that the company should be turned over to him. The firm would retain the name Thames Ironworks but Rolt wanted to add 'shipbuilding and engineering' to the company title. Mare readily agreed and Rolt, who was also Mare's major creditor, purchased the assets and assigned them to a new 'limited liability' company established under the then recent Limited Liability Act passed by Parliament. This action prevented one of the largest employers on the Thames from being broken up.

In 1858 the French Navy launched *La Gloire*, a wood-and-iron hulled ship. At this time all British naval vessels were totally wooden-hulled. Although there were many iron-hulled merchant ships at this time, the Navy had been cautious about the use of iron. In tests, when hit by shellfire, ships girdled in metal would splinter, threatening to inflict fearful and complicated injuries to the crew. However the French advance obliged Britain to respond and an order was then placed with Thames Ironworks to build the world's first all iron-hulled warship that would also be the biggest fighting vessel ever to sail the seas. Rolt's company won the order against stiff competition because of the quality of its own wrought-iron plate and the firm's experience of building ships in this material.

The 9,000-ton plus ship was given the name *Warrior*, epitomising her practical and psychological purpose. She was launched on a bitterly cold day. The shipyard workers had been up all night keeping the ways clear of snow and ice. Lord Palmerston, the Navy surveyor, performed the launching ceremony at 2.30 p.m. The *Warrior* was then pulled by tugs into Victoria Dock where she spent a year being fitted out and having her engines installed. The engines themselves were supplied by Penn and Sons of Greenwich, who were world leaders in the development and design of nautical engines.

3

THE *WARRIOR*

THE TRANSITION OF THE BRITISH NAVY

As the *Warrior* took to the seas, the British Navy was very different from what it had been in Nelson's time. In the years between, the old enemy, the French, had avidly adopted any technological advance that might give them the upper hand. Every few years throughout the Victorian period, despite its entrenched conservatism, the British Admiralty was jolted into a response, and the service was forced through the biggest physical and social changes of its 1,100-year history. The first of these was the coming of steam. By 1840, the French were challenging Britain's hitherto undisputed naval might with small, manoeuvrable steam vessels mounting the latest guns. Inevitably, French boasts and repeated rumours of invasion stung the Admiralty into building several large paddle frigates armed with a small number of heavy guns. But paddles were vulnerable to attack, and took up the space that could have been usefully used for guns.

These frigates were eclipsed at their zenith by the screw propeller, more powerful than the paddle and less restrictive on gun space. Developments came thick and fast, for with screw propulsion and new horizontally-driven engines which were safe below the waterline, even battleships could be steam propelled.

However, advances in propulsion were matched by improvements in firepower, and better protection became urgently needed. In the past, wooden-hulled ships had been more than a match for round shot. During Trafalgar not one English ship had been sunk, as victories were usually won by dismasting and boarding, but now the French had come up with explosive shells capable of destroying any ship within their admittedly limited range. These shells became standard in the French fleet in 1837, the British reluctantly following suit two years later. Stronger ships were needed, and experiments with iron vessels began. However, the iron plating was brittle and shattered like glass when hit by cannonballs. The lethal, razor-like shards that shot through a ship with iron plating conjured up a bloody scenario in the collective imagination of the Admiralty and tests were abandoned in 1851. It was the Crimean War that proved the turning point. Shells from a Russian squadron wiping out the wooden Turkish fleet at Sinope hammered home the new situation. The French answer was to build long armoured gun barges with 4in iron plate backed by thick wood. These proved instantly successful at Kinburn in 1855, but yet again the Admiralty proved stubborn, and battleship design remained unchanged; however this was not to be the case for much longer.

Late in the 1850s relations with France, never very cordial, deteriorated. In 1858 a new French fleet was commenced. The first ship was *La Gloire*, a 256ft long, wooden-framed frigate, clad in iron. It had a displacement of 5,618 tons, thirty-six guns and a top speed of 13 knots. *The Times* called it, 'the most perfect and formidable vessel ever built' and it was the most advanced warship of its day. Launched in 1858, she was manoeuvrable and well armoured. Alongside her planned sister ships, she caused Napoleon III to face the possibility of war with confidence. And further truly iron-hulled ships were planned, when industrial capacity permitted. After a royal visit to Cherbourg, Prince Albert was fuming, 'The war preparations of the French are immense,' he said, 'ours despicable. Our ministers use fine phrases but they do nothing. My blood boils within me!' He was to ask the Admiralty, 'What have we got to meet this new engine of war?'

Many others shared his view and a vigorous campaign was mounted demanding that the Admiralty restore Britain's naval prestige. Their Lordships' timid first response was to suggest following the French in building an ironclad. By good fortune the new First Lord, Sir John Pakington, decided on a much bolder scheme, destined to snuff out the French threat at a stroke – the building of the world's first iron-hulled battleship.

When, in March of 1858, the French Navy ordered the ironclad *Gloire* and her sister ship *Invincible*, public and private British opinion demanded a thoroughly British reply. The possibility of French seagoing ironclad warships brought swift action from a normally conservative British Admiralty.

GRISDALE

In 1857 Joseph Grisdale was born, the son of a sailor, Matthew, and his wife Sarah, in the Liverpool docklands. When it was time for Joseph to start work, he and then his younger brother Lowther, entered the shipbuilding industry as apprentice coppersmiths. In January 1878 Joseph married Annie McKenzie, a sailor's daughter, in Everton.

Following the loss of his father that same year, Joseph relocated from Liverpool to West Ham, finding employment as a coppersmith with Thames Ironworks and Shipbuilding and Engineering Company. As a coppersmith, it is likely that Joseph carried out skilled work on the boilers and pipes used in ships and their engines at that time.

THE *WARRIOR* IS BORN

The reply to the French was ordered in 1859 and the keel of a thirty-six gun, armoured, iron steam frigate, the ship that what was to become the *Warrior*, was laid down on the 25 May 1859 on the authority of Admiral Baldwin Walker, Controller of the Navy.

Warrior was made to the design of the Royal Navy's Chief Constructor, Isaac Watts with Scott Russell contributing his knowledge and intelligence to the project. She was built at a time of rapid change and would quickly be overtaken by new designs in a matter of just a few years. *Warrior*'s active service life as a first line battleship lasted just twelve years. However, she did so much better than her counterparts across the channel.

Because French industry was not capable of manufacturing an iron hull, the *Gloire* had to be built of wood protected by 4½in of iron. She was a poor sea ship in comparison to *Warrior*, with a metacentric height of 7ft. Her two sister ships were built with rotten timber and had to be scrapped after just a decade of service.

Walker and Watts developed a concept of an iron-framed ship with unbeatable speed, unmatched firepower and impenetrable protection. To achieve the necessary speed in all conditions, steam power was needed.

As the new ship took shape, crowds of onlookers gathered to view her being built. Unlike today's world, where warship construction is treated with the utmost secrecy, Victorian Great Britain wanted the whole world to witness her might. The only companies able to build such hulls were commercial firms. The Royal Dockyards were not equipped to build iron ships and, given the swiftness of French naval expansion, there was no time to bring these yards up to speed. Not until the twentieth century, with the construction of such giants as the HMS *Dreadnought* and the Imperial Japanese Navy's *Yamato*, did nations become more 'modest' about major naval projects. In the autumn the great iron-hulled beast growing on the banks of the Lea received her name, inherited from a venerable ship-of-the-line recently broken up: The *Warrior*.

By the spring of the following year, 900 men were swarming over the huge vessel as it rose above the rooftops that surrounded the Canning Town yards. The aim was to launch her in the summer of 1860, but because of the innovatory nature of her design and Admiralty indecision, particularly about what guns should be fitted, delays and huge cost over-runs occurred. Reaction in the newspapers swung between flag-waving patriotism and morbid doubt as to whether *Warrior* would ever touch the water. However, she was completed on 10 October 1860. *Warrior* was launched on 29 December of the same year by First Lord Sir John Pakington and towed downstream to be fitted out at the Victoria Dock. By 1 August 1861, only a year behind *La Gloire*, *Warrior* was ready for her first commission, the largest, fastest and most powerful ship in the world. She was built almost exactly 100 years after Nelson's Flagship HMS *Victory* that now lies just a short distance away from *Warrior* in Portsmouth dockyard.

At first glance *Warrior* appears to be remarkably similar in external appearance to *Victory* and other ships that went before her. She would have been immediately recognised by generations of seamen, from Drake to Bligh to Cook, Hardy and Collingwood. Like *Victory*, *Warrior* carries a bowsprit and three masts, foremast, main mast and mizzen and is fully square rigged for sailing. However, closer examination reveals the impact of a century of technological change. *Warrior* was built of iron, had heavier guns on a single gun deck (technically she is a frigate although rated as a battleship), steam power as well as square-rigged sails.

Warrior's overall length was some 380ft and her beam was 58ft. She weighed 9,137 tons. She had a top speed, with the sail assistance, of 17½ knots, a record *Warrior* held for several years. This high speed was made possible partly because of the ship's innovative hull design – iron tongue-and-groove plating making a smooth, clean hull that cut through the water. The armoured plates on the side of the ship ran for 213ft of her 420ft long hull. Each armoured plate measured 15ft long by 3ft wide and weighed 4 tons. This was the first layer of Watt's 'citadel', designed to protect the guts of the ship from bombardment. In effect the guns, boilers and engine were situated in an iron box sealed at each end with strong bulkheads and doorways. The armoured citadel was constructed of 4½in wrought-iron plate, made from hammered scrap and puddle iron, bolted to 18in of solid East India teak, mounted on the 5/8in thick plating of the ship's hull and framework, with an internal finish of pine. The citadel was tested against the most powerful guns of the day and none were able to pierce the armour, even at point blank range.

Warrior had a fifty-seven section double bottom for 240ft of her length. She was subdivided into a further thirty-five watertight compartments amidships. This was an impressive ship that led the world technically and provided a symbol of Britain's determination to take the lead in nautical warfare design. HMS Warrior transformed concepts of naval warfare when she first joined the fleet in 1861 as part of Britain's response to an uneasy peace with France – and concerns over French maritime ambitions. She was revolutionary – at a stroke all existing ships were rendered obsolete. Warrior housed all her main guns, engines and boilers within an armoured iron hull, and could be driven by both steam and sail. The combination of iron hull, armour-plate, breech-loading guns and powerful steam screw propulsion meant that she could outrun and outgun any ship afloat.

HMS Warrior never fired a shot in anger. This was probably partly due to the fact that there was not a ship on the seas capable of facing her. She never blockaded a hostile port or had any active part in open hostilities, yet she played a famous part in naval history. Built during the 'Pax Britannica', she served at the beginning of a revolution in technology and, like the HMS Dreadnought and USS Nautilus, Warrior brought existing ideas forward by leaps and bounds. Her construction employed the first use of iron instead of wood for a ship's hull, the first use of watertight compartments, and the first use of heavy armour-plating on a ship designed to receive such weight. She was also by far the longest and largest warship ever built. Upon launching, it was claimed that she could have fought any known ship in the world and come away with little real damage to show for the effort. I'm biased, but looking at the top ten ships in the world at the time of her first weeks of service on the high seas, I'd say, even if they had all come at her at once, she'd have sunk the lot, single handed. Warrior was an awesome phenomenon; a great and overwhelming weapon in her own right that encompassed the might of British ingenuity and determination at the height of the nation's power. She was, and remains, staggering. Dickens described her as:

A black vicious ugly customer as ever I saw, whale-like in size, and with as terrible a row of incisor teeth as ever closed on a French frigate.

Warrior was the most important ship produced by Thames Ironworks and Shipbuilding Company. Unquestionably, she ruled the seas, a living embodiment of Britain's pride in her industrial, territorial and military superiority. She was faster, better armed and better protected than any other ship in the world. The success of Warrior as a deterrent contributed to the reduction of a French invasion threat and these were quiet times for the Home Fleet. However, within a year of her first commission, events were taking place on the other side of the Atlantic which were destined to make Warrior's rule as 'Monarch of the Seas' very short lived.

The rapid evolution of warship design in the 1860s meant that in a few short years the previously mighty *Warrior* was overtaken by more advanced vessels. Just a year after *Warrior* entered service, the success of a grotesque ironclad, the *Monitor*, fighting in the Civil War on the other side of the Atlantic, was to have a dramatic effect on the thinking of naval architects. *Monitor* was short, sail-less and very manoeuvrable, with all guns concentrated in an armoured turret on the upper deck. By 1866 the Royal Navy had ordered its first ocean-going turret ship, HMS *Captain*, although this ship still relied on auxiliary vessels.

After a number of mundane assignments, in 1902 *Warrior* took on a new lease of life as she was fitted out to become mother ship to the Portsmouth flotilla of small torpedo boats. But this role was a brief one. In 1904 she was converted to become part of HMS *Vernon*, the Royal Navy's floating torpedo school, which was moored in Portchester Creek. She was transformed into a floating workshop under the name *Vernon III*. All her original machinery was now gone and she was equipped with just a single funnel, boilers, generators, lathes and other machinery as well as offices, classrooms, a chapel and on the upper deck a gymnasium.

In 1923 Vernon moved ashore, having outgrown its sea-borne accommodation and, once more, *Warrior* was paid off. But again she survived at a time when her sister ship *Black Prince* and many others went to the scrap yard. She was offered for sale, but there were no takers. Finally, because the hull was still in excellent condition, *Warrior* was converted and, in 1929, towed to Milford Haven, Wales for use as a floating oil jetty at Llannion Cove, Pembroke Dock, cruelly renamed *C77* in 1945. She performed this undignified task for fifty years, ships loading and unloading oil alongside her. When in 1960, HMS *Vanguard* submitted to the cutting torch, *Warrior* remained as Britain's last surviving battleship.

A full restoration program was initiated during the 1980s under the administration of the Maritime Trust. Every detail has now been attended to in order to restore HMS *Warrior*, and she appears today just as she did at the height of her career. Her permanent mooring is at Portsmouth Historic Dockyard. Go and see her. She is more than worth the effort; built in West Ham, to the ring of cockney hammers – she has a lasting effect.

HMS *WARRIOR*: FACTS AND FIGURES

Ordered:	11 May 1859
Launched:	Canning Town, London 29 December 1860
First Commissioned at Portsmouth:	1 August 1861
End of service as first line warship:	15 September 1871
Commissioned as ship of First Reserve:	1 April 1875
End of active service:	31 May 1883
Commissioned as stationary depot ship:	16 July 1903
Commissioned as *Vernon III* at Portsmouth:	December 1904
Paid off as HMS *Vernon*:	31 March 1924
Arrived as fuelling hulk at Pembroke Dock:	16 March 1929
Handed over for restoration at Hartlepool:	12 August 1979
Restoration begins:	3 September 1979
Returns to Portsmouth:	16 June 1987

HMS *WARRIOR*: SPECIFICATIONS

Length overall:	420ft
Length inside:	380ft
Deck length:	380ft
Beam (width):	58ft
Displacement:	9,210 tons
Draught:	26ft
Maximum speed:	13 knots (Sail)
	14½ knots (Steam)
	17½ knots (Sail and Steam)
Cost:	£377,000
Armament (originally armed with):	26 x 68lb muzzle loading guns
	10 x 110lb Armstrong breech loading guns
	4 x 40lb Armstrong breech loading guns
	2 x 20lb Armstrong breech loading guns
	1 x 12lb Armstrong breech loading gun
	1 x 6lb muzzle loading gun
Ships complement:	
Officers:	42
Warrant officers:	3
Seamen and boys:	455
Royal Marine officers:	3
Royal Marine NCOs:	6
Royal Marines:	118
Chief engineers:	2
Engineers:	10
Stokers and trimmers:	66
Total ships complement:	705 men and boys

HMS *WARRIOR*: CHRONOLOGY

At the time of her completion *Warrior* was the most powerful ship-of-war in the world.

1859 May 25:	Laid down at the shipyard of Ditchburn & Mare (Thames Ironworks & Shipbuilding Co), Canning Town.
1859 December 29:	Launched.
1861 October 24:	Completed.
1864 November 22:	Paid off and taken to the Portsmouth Dockyard for a refit.
1867:	Re-commissioned.
1881:	Paid off.
1901 May to 1902 July:	Served as a hulk, stationary training ship and torpedo stores.
1902 August:	Served as a depot ship for the Portsmouth destroyers and was renamed *Vernon III*.
1904 April:	Served as a floating workshop at the Naval Torpedo School, the HMS *Vernon*, Portsmouth.
1923 October 1:	Given back her original name.
1923 October 23:	Converted to a mooring hulk for oil tankers at Pembroke Dock.
1979 June 12:	Handed over to the Maritime Trust.
1979 September 2:	Towed from Milford Haven to Hartlepool.
Today	Still among the most beautiful and awe-inspiring ships ever constructed

With the success of the *Warrior*, orders came in from navies around the world. The impact this ship made cannot be underestimated. She made the Thames Ironworks one of the most famous shipbuilding and engineering companies in the world.

Around the same time *Warrior* was paid off, Thames Ironworks supplied the last paddle steamer to P&O. *Nyanza* was 2,032 tons and took on the job of carrying 143 first-class and 34 second-class passengers from Southampton to Alexandria.

She served P&O for nineteen years before being purchased by the Union Steam Ship Company. In January 1875, while carrying mail from the Cape of Good Hope to Plymouth, *Nyanza* rescued the only three survivors of a fire on the New Zealand migrant ship, *Cospatrick*. The loss of life amounted to 474 souls, including all of the 429 migrants who had left Gravesend the previous September.

Nyanza saw service in Zanzibar, before being scrapped in 1904 in Bombay.

THE LIFE OF THE RIVER

The river surrounding the Thames Ironworks was a lively area in the company's developmental years. Many of the local people earned their living from London's main waterway. Their combined skills, generated from working in a collection of industries, were used to convert former lifeboats, whalers and other antiquated craft into suitable vessels for use on the river, ferrying goods and passengers to and from wharves up and down the banks. At the mouth of the Thames the waters were harvested for whitebait, shrimps and cockles and transported up to Billingsgate fish market for sale. 'Toshing' was also a profitable pursuit. The swift-running tide near the entrance of Bow Creek, close to Orchard Place, would sweep into Bugsby's Reach and carry ashore baulks of timber and other salvageable materials, together with items that had fallen from the huge amount of traffic that plied the Thames in those times, from lifeboats to gold watches (which were known as 'yellow kettles': kettle means gun metal and watches were commonly made out of gun metal). According to the law, anything salvaged had to be delivered to Dead Man's Wharf at Deptford to await reclamation, but the prize for honesty was so negligible and slow to materialise that most of the fruits of the tosher's labours were 'recycled' locally.

As Thames Ironworks took on more and more projects, building ships in wood and iron and later steel, the company began to expand both in terms of the expertise it commanded and also its product. The reputation embodied in the *Warrior* generated demand and the yard built the first iron-hulled warships for Spain, Russia, Portugal, Greece, Turkey and Denmark. In 1870 the company completed an order for the first iron-hulled ship to serve in the Prussian Navy, the *Konig Wilhelm* that was very similar to the *Warrior* in dimension and design. She became Germany's longest serving warship, fighting the cause of the Fatherland through the First World War and beyond, up to 1926.

The importance of the Thames Ironworks to the area in which it is located can be seen in the coat of arms of the County Borough of West Ham (adopted in 1886). This included crossed hammers – the symbol, and nickname, the football club adopted later.

4

'HOW HE PLOUGHED THE RAGING MAIN'

As a new century began to rise above the horizon of time, management and workers from all the major maritime nations came to Canning Town to share in the latest advances in shipbuilding.

Thames Ironworks continued to do business whilst the yards around them were collapsing – shipbuilding in the East London area had been in decline since the end of 1866. Early in 1867 *The Times* reported that 30,000 unemployed were seeking poor relief in Poplar, many of these coming from the shipbuilding industry that, just a few months earlier, had employed 15,000 men and boys. Thames Ironworks probably had their penchant for quality, product diversity and reputation to thank for their continued prosperity.

YAVARI AND THE YAPURA

In 1861, the Peruvian Government of Ramon Castilla ordered two small cargo-passenger 'gunboats' for Lake Titicaca. The lake was the main route between Puno, Peru, and La Paz, Bolivia. Already profiting from the guano industry on the coast, the Peruvian Government looked to exploit the natural resources of the southern highlands or Altiplano region around Lake Titicaca. Here lay the potential for trading Peruvian copper, silver, minerals, wool, timber and the riches of the rainforest from Bolivia with manufactured goods from Europe.

Through the agency of Anthony Gibbs & Sons, the government commissioned the James Watt Foundry in Birmingham, England (where steam was first harnessed for industrial use) to build the ships that would collect goods from around the lake. Mules had to carry all cargo up to the lake, as there was no rail link at the time. Therefore, the ships were built in kit form, with no piece weighing more than 3½cwts, the maximum carrying capacity of a mule.

The Thames Ironworks and Shipbuilding Company were subcontracted to build the iron hulls of the *Yavari* and the *Yapura*. It is interesting to speculate on how this contract might have linked with one-time major shareholder and eventual owner of Thames Ironworks, Frank Hills (father of Arnold), and his interest in guano and mineral extraction.

On 15 October 1862, the *Mayola* docked at Arica, having rounded the Horn, bearing eight British engineers from London. At that time Arica was a Peruvian port before Chile took control of the city in the 1879–83 War of the Pacific. She discharged the packing cases and pieces of the *Yavari* and the *Yapura*. The Peruvian Navy then faced the daunting task of getting 2,766 pieces and two crankshafts transported to Lake Titicaca, 12,500ft above sea level.

Originally, the *Yavari* and *Yapura* were going to be gunboats, as well as cargo and passenger ships, to establish Peru's sovereignty in the waters. The guns, however, never reached the lake. They were snatched in Arica by the Peruvian Navy and used for defence against the Spanish when the former colonial power threatened to invade Peru.

The ships were transported 40 miles north to the Peruvian city of Tacna, using one of the earliest railways in South America. In Tacna the unassembled parts, weighing a total of 210 tons, were unpacked and arranged in the order that was needed for construction. They were then carried by mules and llamas 148 miles across the Andes to Puno on Lake Titicaca. Local muleteers and porters, who were to carry the crankshafts, competed for the work. The route, though only 225 miles in all, would take them across the moonscape of the driest desert in the world, mountain passes higher than the highest European peaks and the sub-zero windswept wastes of the Altiplano. However, the successful hauler quoted a delivery date of six months. Buoyed by this prospect, the British engineers who were to help assemble the ships went on ahead to build a jetty, slipway and machine shops in preparation.

Six months later, the contractor, hopelessly defeated by the task, was fired, leaving pieces of ship scattered between Tacna and Puno. Outside events seemed to conspire against the project as grumbling muleteers, an earthquake, an Indian rebellion ('peasants revolt') and the threat of a second invasion of Peru by the Spanish, brought the expedition to halt.

That was not the end of the project. Five years on it received fresh impetus when requests were sent out for more muleteers and around 1,000 Indians to help with the task. By 1 January 1869 enough pieces had arrived for the keel of the *Yavari* to be laid. Although a number of the British engineers had passed on during their wait for the ships to arrive, survivors and local workers painstakingly put the *Yavari* together bit by bit until the first lady of the lake finally made her maiden voyage at 3 p.m. on Christmas Day in 1870. She was 100ft long and powered by a 60hp, two-cylinder steam engine. The amazing journey from the centre of the British Empire to the spiritual heart of the Inca Empire was finally complete. The *Yapura* was launched into Puno Bay in 1873.

So began the life of these little ships, plying the deep blue waters of Lake Titicaca high in the Andes, carrying passengers and supplies, such as minerals, coffee, cocoa, coca leaves, wool and livestock, to the numerous communities along its shores. They helped to link the Bolivian and Peruvian towns and ports that formed important agricultural and commercial centres of the area. Vestiges of the Lake's prosperity dating back to the colonial period can still be seen in churches with elaborate gold-leaf-covered altars, that were found in many of the towns that were visited by the *Yavari* and the *Yapura*.

Because of a lack of more conventional fuel, the ships boilers were fired by dried llama dung. The *Yavari* was also equipped as a two-masted sailer. In 1914 her original engine was replaced with a Swedish Bolinder, four-cylinder, semi-diesel engine. *Yavari* still has its Bolinder and this engine has the distinction of being the oldest of its kind in the world.

The *Yapura* has since been renamed BAP *Puno* and converted by the Peruvian Navy into a floating hospital that still serves lakeside communities.

A military government nationalised the entire Lake fleet in 1972. The *Yavari* became property of the National Railroad Co. in 1977 and was then turned over to the Peruvian Navy, which retired the aging vessel. British archaeologist, Meriel Larken, who had been conducting research in the area, bought it as scrap.

Today, over a third of a century after the ship was grounded and left to rust, Larken has brought her back to life. She is the oldest working ship in the Americas, offering bed and breakfast accommodation to tourists who are visiting not only the world's highest navigable lake, but also the centre of the Tiwanaku and Inca civilizations as well as other thriving pre-Columbian and colonial-period communities. Increasingly, tourism is providing a source of income for Puno, Copacabana, Huatajata and Puerto Suarez supplementing the commerce that continues to provide an important source of earnings for the hundreds of thousands of Aymara Indians who live along the lake's shores.

Tourists can enjoy the Victorian wheelhouse, the library, narrow sleeping quarters, and a dining room surrounded by the ship's mementos and documents depicting the iron vessel's history.

—⁓—

Many of the Ironwork's employees must have counted their blessings in the hard winter of 1867. For the third time in twelve years there were bread riots in the most hard hit districts; there were even problems in areas hitherto thought of as lower middle class in nature.

This was the social milieu of contradiction and the industrial foundation on which Thames Ironworks Football Club was to be built and developed. It is also the background of the first years of West Ham United. However, people had been kicking balls to rules in and around the fringes of London's East End docklands long before Charlie Mare had dreamt of building ships in Canning Town.

GETTING THE NEEDLE

In March 1877, Thames Ironworks Company were contracted to build the vessel that was destined to carry the name *Cleopatra*. It was designed by Benjamin Baker to be towed, by either animals or a ship. Five months later the wrought-iron cylinder, 15ft in diameter and 92ft long, pointed at both ends with a vertical stern, was ready for use. Her job was to get to Egypt and bring an ancient obelisk (over land and sea) back to London. The monument was a gift to the British government in 1819 from Mehemet Ali, the Pasha and Viceroy of Egypt in recognition of British triumphs at the Battle of the Nile and the Battle of Alexandria in 1801. However, it had remained under the Egyptian sands as the cost of transportation was seen as prohibitive.

Cleopatra made the outward journey without much incident, but on the return voyage, following a dreadful storm in the Bay of Biscay, the craft, which was really a type of pontoon with a rudder, two bilge keels and a mast with balancing sails, was cast adrift, with the loss of six lives before the she was rescued by the *Fitzmaurice*.

On her return to Gravesend in January 1878 crowds gathered to greet *Cleopatra*'s arrival. She was broken up as soon as the obelisk had been unloaded (6 July 1878). The obelisk was placed in its designated position, on 12 September 1878, close to Westminster Bridge, where Cleopatra's Needle can still be seen today.

FRED CORBETT

Fifteen years after the obelisk was set in place on the banks of the Thames Fred Corbett was born. As a man he was employed as a labourer at the Thames Ironworks, and made three recorded appearances for the company football team in the 1899/1900 season. Fred went on to play a single season for West Ham United before a starting a longer career at Bristol Rovers. Fred, who got himself something of a reputation as a goal scorer with Rovers, is often referred to as the first black player to turn out for West Ham. This is based on a poor quality team photograph and a trade card wherein Fred looks slightly swarthier than his pallid peers. But given the deficiencies of photography of the period (even in 1923 the grey horse at the first Wembley Cup Final has been remembered as white) and no claims by Fred himself or any commentator at the time that he was 'black', West Ham's first black player (and the first black player to represent England) must remain John 'Charlo' Charles from the Hammers 1960s/70s era (see Belton, 2003).

CASTALIA

In the early 1880s a smallpox epidemic put London hospitals under pressure. To create more bed space the Metropolitan Asylums Board (MAB) chartered the old wooden warships, *Atlas* and the *Endymion*, from the Admiralty.

These vessels were supplemented during 1884 with the *Castalia*, an extraordinary twin-hulled paddle steamer built by Thames Ironworks. Her design had not taken off, but she was able to accommodate five ward blocks on her deck, which gave her the appearance of a floating road.

The ships were ultimately moored at Long Reach, near Dartford, where the permanent Joyce Green Hospital was completed in 1903. Consequently the floating hospitals were scrapped.

ROBERT WHITING

It was in 1883 that Robert Whiting first saw the light of day in Canning Town. He was 7 years old when his mum passed away. Bob went on to find work as a dock labourer and later was employed in the ship-building industry located in London's docklands. After taking up a post with Thames Ironworks, he joined the company football team (by this time the side had taken the name West Ham United), playing in goal.

However, Bob found it hard to get into the side, but after relocating to Kent he turned out for Tunbridge Wells Rangers and in 1906 signed for Chelsea. When the Blues regular 'keeper was injured in the first part of the following season, Whiting was given an opportunity he made the most of. He played fifty-four matches for Chelsea prior to 1908. At that point he moved on to Brighton and Hove Albion, running out 320 times for the Goldstone Ground lads.

Bob was known to supporters and fellow players as 'Pom Pom', the same nickname as that given to the heavy machine guns used by the British Army in the early years of the twentieth century. These were scaled-up Maxim machine guns, firing a 1lb-round and made a characteristic 'pom pom' sound. Whiting's goal kicks were said to be so forceful they reminded folk of this noise.

Following the Battle of Mons in late August 1914, as it began to be recognised that the First World War would not be over by Christmas (as had been popularly predicted), the first 'Pals' units were initiated to advance recruitment into the forces. This approach encouraged men to join up together with friends and associates from their town, company or profession. One such was the 1st Footballers' Battalion. This was later known as the 17th Battalion, Middlesex Regiment. 'Pom-Pom' at the age of 30 joined their ranks on the day the Battalion came into being in December 1914.

In May 1916, Whiting was sent back to Britain (after six months on the Western Front) as unfit – he was suffering with scabies. Nellie, his wife, was able to stay in Brighton where he was convalescing and there the couple conceived their third son. However, when faced with being sent back to the front, Bob deserted, starting a 133-day absence from his unit. He was subsequently given nine months hard labour and demoted from Lance-Sergeant to Private.

However, in 1917 his sentence was suspended and he returned to his unit in time for the start of the Arras offensive in April. He is among the 1,969 British and Empire warriors that fell on the same day (28 April 1917) who have no known graves. They are among the 35,000 men commemorated on the Arras memorial.

After Bob's death gossip had it that he had not been killed in battle but shot for cowardice. However, Nellie sent a Sussex newspaper copies of letters from his officers and the unit's padre telling of her husband's honourable death by shellfire near Vimy Ridge. It seems, like my own great grandfather, and many other working boys, Bob had been blown to pieces courtesy of the capitalist arms manufacturers that, unlike its victims, endure today.

In 2010 on the anniversary of the dedication of the Tomb of the Unknown Warrior, a memorial was created in Westminster Abbey for soldiers whose graves were never found. Bob Whiting is one of those remembered on that memorial.

THE LIFE OF A COPPERSMITH

Among many other ships, coppersmith Joseph Grisdale would probably have helped to build the HMS *Sans Pareil*, a 10,470-ton battleship launched in 1887.

By 1881 Joseph, his wife Annie and their daughter, Frances, were living at 14 Lennox Street, along with Annie's mother, Catherine McKenzie, and her other daughter, Mary (Lowther's future wife).

Annie gave birth to seven more children by Joseph prior to her death in 1901. The following year Joseph remarried, by which time the family had moved twice, first to nearby Newman Street (1891) and then to Barking Road (both addresses being close to the Ironworks).

Lowther and his new family had joined Joseph in London by 1891; the two brothers and two sisters lived and worked together.

MATCHGIRLS AND MAHATMA

In July 1888, around 1,500 workers, mostly women and girls, went on strike at the Bryant and May match factory in Bow (the factory can still be seen, on the north-western edge of the Olympic Park, although ironically it has been converted into expensive apartments).

Obliged to labour twelve-hour days, the 'Matchgirls' were incessantly fined for trivial transgressions but perhaps more seriously, they worked extensively with white phosphorous. This was known to be harmful at the time but has since been understood to be deadly poisonous to humans continuously exposed to it.

The industrial action received massive support from the working-class population of East London and achieved a level of success in terms of improving working conditions at the factory. However, probably as important with regard to this history of industrial relations, the women set the precedent for the Great Dock Strike soon afterwards. Although this strike action was not protracted, it did much to change worker–employer relations. As you will read later in this book, it could be argued that this was part of the motivation that led to Arnold Hills taking a relatively philanthropic attitude towards his workforce and, ultimately, in the creation of West Ham United.

It was also in 1888 that Mahatma Gandhi, soon to be leader of the Indian Independence movement and thought of as the 'Father of the Indian Nation', arrived in London to study law. A vegetarian, he was to take up with the London Vegetarian Society. The headquarters of this leguminous organisation was in Farringdon Street and, as a consequence of his numerous visits there, Mahatma was soon sitting on its Executive Committee (a famous image shows Gandhi attending a London Vegetarian Society meeting in Portsmouth during May 1891). This is where he rubbed shoulders with the Society's President and the owner of Thames Ironworks, Arnold Hills. Gandhi was later to write of Hills:

> The President of the Society was Mr Hills, proprietor of the Thames Iron Works. He was a puritan. It may be said that the existence of the Society depended practically on his financial assistance. Many members of the Committee were more or less his protégés.

It seems Hill had his own veritable allotment of veggies growing in mutual admiration of their own abstemiousness! Gandhi was taken by Arnold's definite attitude to temperance, frugality and chastity. These 'qualities' and related principles might be understood to have played a major part in shaping Gandhi's political philosophy. The Hills view of the world would have almost certainly have aligned with Gandhi's 'Seven Deadly Sins':

> Wealth without work
> Pleasure without conscience
> Science without humanity
> Knowledge without character
> Politics without principle
> Commerce without morality
> Worship without sacrifice.

However, Hills might have fitted this in with a more ardent world view, premised on a sort of extreme aesthetic version of 'muscular Christianity'. It is the latter that would be seminal in his perspective on the social aspiration of his work force at the Ironworks and thus the formation of its football club.

Gandhi returned to London in 1931, and chose to lodge in the East End rather than the more salubrious hotels on offer in central and West London. Legend has it he was a Hammers supporter and enjoyed a cream soda in the Boleyn pub, chatting politics with the local radicals and football with anyone who might listen. One could write a weighty article on Gandhi and football, but this is not the place for that, but Poobalan Govindasamy, president of the South African Indoor Football Association, gives an idea of his interest in the game:

> What fascinated Gandhi in particular was the notion he had of football's nobility. At that time, the idea of team play was much stronger than the idea of individual 'star' players, and this is something that greatly appealed to him.

Hence his likely approbation of the 'noble' Irons of the early 1930s.

HMS *BENBOW*

There have been a series of three ships in the British Royal Navy named HMS *Benbow* in honour of Admiral John Benbow, born in 1653, the son of a tanner. His story is a fascinating one. From a butcher's apprentice, John Benbow rose to be Vice Admiral in command of the West Indian Fleet in 1702. When he led the engagement with the French Fleet under Admiral du Casse, he was outnumbered seven to four, but only Captain Waldon of the *Ruby* agreed to fight alongside Benbow's flagship, the seventy-gun *Breda*. The five captains who refused to face the foe were later court-martialled, and two of them executed. The *Ruby* was disabled early on, so *Breda* was forced to chase the French unaided. During the action John Benbow was mortally wounded by chain-shot. He died in Port Royal on 4 November 1702. He was buried at Kingston, Jamaica where his grave can still be seen.

The first HMS *Benbow* (1813) was a wooden-hulled, seventy-two gun Vengeur third-rate ship of the line. The Royal Navy's rating system was devised to classify ships according to guns, gun decks, men and displacement. Under that system, a 'third-rate' ship had seventy-four guns or less, two gun decks, 500 to 650 men, and displaced about 1750 tons. The first *Benbow* used sails for propulsion. In 1892, after 79 years of service, she was sold out of the Navy, and was broken up in 1895 at Castle, Woolwich.

The contract for the second HMS *Benbow* (1895) was awarded to Thames Ironworks, and stipulated delivery within three years. Built at a cost of £764,000 (equivalent to about £100 millon today) this *Benbow* was laid down on 1 November 1882 and launched on 15 June 1885. She was fitted out at Chatham Dockyard and commissioned on 14 June 1888 for the Mediterranean Fleet. Her two-shaft, three-cylinder inverted compound engines produced 10,850hp. She was 330ft long with a beam of 68½ft. Her displacement was 10,600 tons and draught 28ft. *Benbow* carried a complement of 523 and was capable of 17½ knots. She was a twelve-gun twin-screw battleship, the last of the four Admirals Barbettes built for the Royal Navy in three groups in the early 1880s. They differed from other British battleships of the period as their main guns were mounted in open barbettes. This system kept the weight of the revolving mass low, but this was much criticised for offering little protection in battle. However the Admirals were quite well protected, with an armour belt and transverse bulkheads 18in thick at the heaviest, surmounted by a 3in deck.

Benbow's largest guns were two 16¼in calibre Barbettes in single fittings. At 110ft they were so heavy that she could mount only one forward and one aft, instead of the original pairs.

At the time of *Benbow*'s construction, and indeed for many years afterwards, the limiting factor in battleship construction was the great length of time taken to manufacture heavy artillery, and it was recognised that the gun of 13½in calibre, scheduled to be installed in the other ships of the class, was and would remain in short supply. The shipyard was therefore faced with the choice of either reverting to 12in calibre guns, which were available but seen as inferior to guns mounted in contemporary foreign ships, or mounting the new Elswick BL 16¼in gun.

Although contemporary guns with a calibre of 12in were well able to destroy any ship afloat, the larger guns were chosen. With the exception of the 18in armament mounted in HMS *Furious* and in some monitors, these were the largest guns ever mounted in a ship of the Royal Navy. One of these pieces nevertheless weighed less than a pair of 13½in guns, and the weight saved was used to increase the number of 6in guns in the broadside battery. The big guns were not a wholly satisfactory substitute for the armament of Benbow's sister ships. They were slow to load, the rate of fire being only one round every four to five minutes so the chances of hitting the target, being a function of the number of guns in use, was reduced. There was also a tendency for the muzzle to droop and the barrel liner lasted only some seventy-five rounds – replacing it was a difficult and time-consuming operation.

Benbow had an unexceptional career, serving in the Mediterranean until October 1891. She was then held in the Reserve until March 1894, with two short commissions, returning to home waters, where she took part in summer manoeuvres until being sent to the Clyde to serve as a guardship from 1894 to 1904. Thereafter *Benbow* remained in the Reserve until she was sold for £21,200 on 9 July 1909 and scrapped.

HARRY GRENFELL

Harry Tremenheere Grenfell (who was to become Vice Admiral Sir Harry Tremenheere Grenfell, KCB, CMG) was born in 1845, the fifth son of Admiral John Pascoe Grenfell of the Brazilian Navy and his wife, Maria Dolores Massini. He became captain of the *Benbow* in 1894. He was a keen sportsman of notable strength, being reputed to be able to carry a small pony under one arm and walk about with it (although why one might want to do this is a mystery!). During his command he was said to have gallantly jumped overboard to rescue a boy who was in danger of drowning.

Respected for his strapping personality, he was also very fond of cats – his cabin was crowded with Siamese felines. They could be fierce and were disliked by the galley's crew, which looked after the cabin. The 'top-cat' was called Satan (and was said to have looked and acted at bit like his namesake). One day the creature vanished, but was eventually found some weeks after his disappearance, locked in a drawer. He had not survived his internment and it was thought the feline monster had been the target of a revenge mission by one or more of the galley's crew whom Satan had serially bullied.

Grenfell also had glass tanks in his gun-ports full of frogs and strange fish. For these, and for the cats, the cabin was kept at a temperature of about 95°F, and stunk to high heavens. Grenfell also liked to hold luncheon parties when, despite the complaints of the ladies, he would refuse to open any skylights or scuttle to allow some fresh air to alleviate the stench.

HMS *Benbow* (1913) was an *Iron Duke*-class battleship, the third ship of that particular class, which was the last group of dreadnought battleships. She measured over 622ft in length and displaced 25,000 tons. Propulsion was by four shaft Parsons steam turbines, driving four propellers. Top speed was 21¼ knots. Her crew complement was between 995 and 1,022 men. Her armaments included ten 13½in/forty-five guns in five twin turrets and four torpedo tubes.

The third HMS *Benbow* was launched in 1913 and commissioned in October 1914 after the outbreak of the First World War. She served as part of the Grand Fleet, and led one of the squadrons of the Fleet in the Battle of Jutland in 1916, one of the major naval engagements of that war. She spent the rest of the war in home waters, but was dispatched to the Mediterranean after hostilities ended and then to the Black Sea. Here she carried out a number of shore bombardments in support of the White Russians in the Russian Civil War, until their collapse in 1920. She remained with the Mediterranean Fleet until 1926, when she returned to the Atlantic Fleet. She was decommissioned in 1929, disarmed under the terms of the London Naval Treaty in 1930, and was sold for scrap in 1931.

THE LIFE OF A SEAMAN

As Thames Ironworks began to produce ships of significant size and impact, the lives of those who served on such vessels were changing. Prior to 1853, a new recruit to the Navy would sign on to a ship of their choice for a single tour of duty (a commission), likely to be for a period of a couple of years. After this one was paid off and possibly be out of work until one found another commissioning ship.

However, in 1853 (the time of the Crimean War) the Admiralty saw this tradition as inefficient for the demands on the service, particularly in terms of developing trained sailors at short notice and, as a consequence, introduced Continuous Service (CS). This involved volunteer seamen serving for a continuous but fixed number of years (initially seven) but those who did not want to commit in this way could join as previously. The advantage of the new system for the seaman was a guaranteed job and a better pay scale. A possible disadvantage was that they could no longer choose their ship, they went where they were sent. This was at a time when some captains still believed that an occasional flogging encouraged a crew to work harder and promoted discipline.

If joining or leaving dates of their last ship could not be provided, no credit could be given for this alleged service. After the CS system was introduced many seamen would have grabbed the opportunity, volunteering to serve for a seven years term, likely looking to their pensions, even if the prospect might be some considerable time away.

In the second half of the nineteenth century, on reaching retirement, a career sailor could qualify for the Navy's Long Service Award with gratuity and pension if they had completed 21 years of satisfactory service.

Many seafaring traditions date from the second part of the nineteenth century, particularly those of the Royal Navy. The lower deck uniform was established in 1857 not only in the Royal Navy but eventually (with minor adaptations) by the majority of other navies. Pressing (abducting men for service) peaked in the eighteenth century and was still going on as late as 1850 but the press-gang was to disappear not long afterwards.

Men-of-war had remained much the same over the hundred years up to the 1860s, although iron and steel had started to replace oak. However, the latter part of the nineteenth century saw the breechloader replace the smoothbore and boilers were drawing the curtain on the age of sail. As a consequence, gunnery and engineering expertise started to displace seamanship on board ship. The crew was once a body of men who 'knew the ropes', each individual being able to man one of sometimes many dozens of guns. The ship's company was now becoming a collection of a broad range of specialists, largely trained ashore and messed by rating at sea.

While the working life of seamen gradually improved overall, steam ships were even more overcrowded than was the case under canvas. According to Captain Milne of the screw sloop *Plumper*:

The space allotted to them (the ship's company) is miserably small and confining. There is not room to hang up more than 56 Hammocks without using space over the Engine room … and when steam is up, it is impossible for the men to sleep there. In consequence of the confined space on the lower deck the men are obliged to sleep on the Deck or where they best can.

Towards the end of the nineteenth century, the Royal Navy introduced social and technological change during a time of unprecedented expansion. In 1865 there were 70,000 seamen. This figure dropped to 60,000 in the 1870s and 1880s, but the numbers of enlisted men doubled between 1888 and 1902. This growth was not a consequence of war but the result of the arms race leading up to the First World War.

In order to meet the demand for manpower, recruitment became more formalised and systematic. What might be thought of as the first attempt at a recruitment drive/career promotion was the use of the *Calliope*. She was a gunboat designed to patrol the far-flung borders of the Empire, but she was reassigned to the coast of Britain to show the flag, conduct training and what we might today call creating an 'interface' with the public. Around the same time 'middy' and 'Jack tar' suits became fashionable for boys and sometimes ladies, which also acted as an early sort of 'product placement'. The image of the seaman as a courageous adventurer was deployed to sell anything from soap to tobacco. All of this effected a make-over of the sailor from the rough seafaring barbarian type of former times; pre-empting Hetty King's contention, 'All the nice girls loved a sailor'.[3]

As the Navy became a modern organisation in the twentieth century, further changes were made as a result of successive waves of inventions and innovative practices. Thus, in the space of a few dozen years, the role the seamen, while not completely altering culturally, was subject to dramatic social and technological transformation as nautical history leapt forward.

> Come all you seamen bold, landed here, landed here
> It is of an Admiral brave called Benbow by his name
> You shall hear, you shall hear.
> (Admiral Benbow from Chappell's *Old English
> Popular Music*)

---

3. The song, written and composed by A. Mills and Bennett Scott, was performed first in 1905 by 'The Immaculate' Hetty King (1883–1972), who was well known around the music halls as male-impersonator, Winifred Emms.

5

1895/96: THE FIRST SEASON

In the last part of the nineteenth century, Thames Ironworks was arguably coming close to its zenith as an industrial and nautical enterprise. The shipyard was visited by many of the crown heads of Europe including the Kaiser, who arrived in England aboard the Ironworks ship *Konig Wilhelm* for Queen Victoria's Silver Jubilee (1887) – 'Vicky' was his grandma. During his stay, the *Konig Wilhelm* was placed in the hands of Thames Ironworks for dry dock hull inspection.

The next decade produced a great deal that resonates with us today. In December 1887 the character of Sherlock Holmes made his first appearance in a story Arthur Conan Doyle published in the magazine, *Beeton's Christmas Annual*. At the end of August the following year, Jack the Ripper's first victim was discovered in the East End of London. This probably helped the interest in crime fiction no end, and on 25 June 1891, Sherlock Holmes appeared in *The Strand Magazine* for the first time. Thomas A. Edison finished building his first motion picture studio during February 1893 in West Orange, New Jersey,[4] while ten months later the British public was outraged when Arthur Conan Doyle published a story ('The Final Problem') in which Sherlock Holmes seemingly died. On 22 June 1894, Pierre de Coubertin organised a meeting which led to the creation of the International Olympic Committee and eventually the Olympic Games.

IRON RULES THE WAVES

In 1895 the British government decided to finance a colossal expansion of the Gibraltar docks. The contract to provide the massive caissons (watertight retaining structure also used, for instance, to work on the foundations of bridge piers, in the construction of dams or for the repair of ships) went to Thames Ironworks. The impermeable retaining structures allowed work on the docks while holding back the seawater.

The preliminary construction was well received and Thames got more work on the second phase, creating employment for the civil engineers up to 1906. The three major

---

4. The 'Kinetographic Theater', because of its somewhat dour design, came to be known as the 'Black Maria' – the slang term for the dark, cramped and uncomfortable police wagons.

docks Thames helped to construct continue to be used today, providing a base for the Royal Navy. Thames produced similar structures for Hong Kong and Keyham (Plymouth).

Towards the end of the nineteenth century, the Thames Ironworks and Shipbuilding Company Limited was one of the biggest and most important shipbuilders in Britain. At the height of its activity the Thames yards had eight slipways grouped in the two locations. The three lower slips faced almost due south down Bow Creek at Canning Town, while the five upper slips lay at a north-west, south-east angle further up stream.

Orchard Yard, situated just across the river to where the Millennium Dome would squat over 150 years later, wrang, almost non-stop, with the sound of a gigantic orchestra of riveting hammers. As you walked into the Thames Ironworks the first thing you would notice would be the density of the air, filled with smoke from the forges. You would have already heard the dissonance of the seven giant Nasmyth steam hammers forging the wrought-iron plates, but if you made your way inside, the noise would be almost deafening. Your sight would be struck by several forges, burning metal for the British Navy or any one of an abundance of other customers.

It took the expertise of more than a score of trades to give shape and form to a ship, but it was the riveters, who were always regarded as the backbone of the shipyard, binding the great iron hulls together in the dark, hard environs of the yards. Come torrential rain, steely cold or stifling heat, they laboured, machine-like, in units of five.

It would be the role of the apprentice to bring the rivets from the rivet-heater or rivet-boy (even if this person was well advanced in years) and heave the hundredweight sack of 200 panhead rivets up as high as eight or nine dozen feet to a work station.

When the rivets finally reached the site of their intended use, they were placed over coals in shallow pans that would also be used to heat up a brew when required. With the energetic pumping of bellows, the rivets, like malicious fireflies, would glow white hot. At this point the phosphorescent bolts were passed with long tongs to the catch-boy or putter-in who would, with smaller tongs, place the still fluorescent but reddening pins, into holes previously driven in the steel plate. No sooner had the cooling, but still blushing rivet reached its designated place, the 'older-on would wield a 16-lb sledgehammer with sweet accuracy to flatten the head of the nail. When the rivet had been smashed home as hard as possible the 'older-on would press on the head of the rivet with his hammerhead. The catch-boys and the 'older-on operated inside the hull, whilst the riveters laboured on the outside, braving the cruelties of the weather. Two riveters, one left-handed, the other right-handed, would wait on the toil of the 'older-on. Their weapon of work was a more subtle foil, a species of mallet, with a relatively slim, elongated head. These sleek but powerful riveting hammers would one day symbolise football in East London and become a distinctive element of the club crest to be worn on the heart of every player to take the field in the cause of West Ham United down the generations. They were swung with unfailing precision to conclude the riveting process, which signalled the start of a repeat performance of the whole sequence, thousands and thousands of times until the trussing of iron to iron had melded another gargantuan hull, destined to enter into life through the birth canal of the Lea.

Many hundreds of riveting teams worked side-by-side in the industrious yards that blistered from every estuary, brook and creek along the eastern Thames in the last quarter of the nineteenth century. As evening drew on and the rest of London town quietened, the 'tink' and 'tank' of these men's toil, at Canning Town, Blackwall and Limehouse combined with an unremitting industrial percussion beating forth in a brooding bass thunder from the Millwall Ironworks, rolling out steel, and the satanic rhythm of the huge steam hammers that banged and thumped on what seemed like each spit, reach and wharf. This chaotic timbre would, in strange collisions of place and time, achieve a harmony with the hoots, toots and bellows of the collective horns of the plethora of craft that bustled on the watery highway of the 'Smoke' – the bobbing, chugging and steaming children of the Thames.

When the early darkness shrouded the metropolis in the grey metallic winter, this devil's chorus was illuminated by a cavalcade of 'firefalls' – hot fragments of metal showering in sheets that flowed down the shear face of mighty hulls, skipped over bulkheads and 'drenched' decks. This incandescence, which would have been reiterated by the reflection in the mirror of water, was the product of a thousand burners knitting iron and steel (welding didn't come to shipyards until 1940), ignited and fanned by regiments of charred imps who were employed to stoke the collective inferno of the yards. Rivet fires punctuated the prospect like smouldering lava pools.

The awesome prospect of industry bathed in the night, every night, as men, boys and women[5] blasted, wove and moulded iron, bashing, banging, beating so breathing form and life into gracefully grotesque, maritime monsters and their accompanying outriders. As the smoke-shrouded moon glowered down on the infant years of a century, and the stars looked on with jealous blinking, these creations of immensity, forged by the multitudes of races, creeds, cultures and ethnicities that was the East Londoner (the splendidly rambunctiously ribald, rebelliously crazed, brutally convivial and ingenious bastard progeny of empire) ruled the very waves.

On 29 June 1895 the *Thames Iron Works Gazette*, the company newspaper, told its readers that, 'Mr Taylor, who is working in the shipbuilding department, has undertaken to get up a football club for next winter and I learn that quoits and bowls will also be added to the attractions of the Hermit Road ground … '

Dave Taylor, who was a foreman in the shipbuilding yard and also a local referee, spent the summer of 1895 planning the new club's first season. Workers were invited to join the club and membership cost half a crown, about 30 per cent of a riveter's weekly pay. It was planned that the side would use a nearby football ground for practice and matches and that member subscriptions would help finance the new club. It was accepted, however, that in the first instance, much of the money needed to run the team would come directly from the coffers of Arnold Hills, the owner of the Thames Ironworks.

---

5. There are indications that women did the work of catch-boys and the 'older-on in shipyards. Although this is reliant on limited photographic evidence from the early twentieth century, logically, given the Ironworks existed through protracted periods of labour shortages, there is little reason to suppose that women would have been totally excluded from such employment. To needlessly and purposely preclude the contribution of women from this part of shipbuilding history would be clearly misogynistic and almost certainly incorrect.

Initially Taylor was looking to organise four teams but when just fifty applications for membership were received it was clear that this number could not adequately supply personnel for more than two sides. Taylor accordingly arranged fixtures and affiliated the Thames Ironworks Football Club to the Football Association. He also entered both teams in local cup competitions and arranged friendly matches.

At first Thames did not join a league. It is not known if this was a conscious decision – such arrangements were not seen as 'form' by the class elite that controlled the game at the time. However, Thames' first timetable of matches was much closer to the schedule of a professional club than that of a typical works team. It included matches against one First Division team and two teams from the Southern League.

With Thames now ready for their first season of football, Dave Taylor stood down from his position to concentrate on refereeing and was replaced by A.T. (Ted) Harsent, another Thames Ironworks employee who lived nearby in Mary Street, Canning Town. Harsent became the first secretary of Thames Ironworks Football Club. Francis Payne worked as a company secretary in the Ironworks and became the chair of the new club. Payne was involved in several of the other works associations, most notably as vice president of the Temperance League. This, alongside Arnold Hills' commitment to alcoholic abstinence, might go some way to explaining why the first Ironworks teams were teetotal and also non-smokers. Five years later, when Thames Ironworks FC had become West Ham United, the *East Ham Echo* still referred to the team as 'the Teetotallers'. Such a tradition would have been very strange to some other generations of West Ham players – as John Charles told me (see Belton, 2003) when referring to the side of the mid/late 1960s, 'win or lose, we were on the booze'.

From the very beginning of its history Thames was an ambitious side. Not content with testing itself against local amateur teams, the club entered the FA Cup. This represented a relatively swift recognition by the Tsars of late Victorian football and was probably facilitated through the influence and connections of Arnold Hills. The club secretary explained, 'Having some good men in the club, we somewhat presumptuously considered it would be wise to enter the English Association Cup.'

Thames would have had no realistic chance of winning the FA Cup, but the competition would test the team's ability and publicise the new club, and if they were lucky enough to be drawn against a good professional side this would also have added considerably to their funds.

Thames played their first match on Saturday 7 September 1895. The game was played on their home ground, Hermit Road, known locally as the 'Cinder Heap'. This location had previously been the home to Old Castle Swifts. Thames took over the tenancy when the Swifts dissolved into the annals of East London football. Royal Ordnance were the visitors that late autumn day. They were what might today be known as a 'nursery club' for Woolwich Arsenal. There is no record of the eleven names of the Thames team that took to the field for this football baptism, but there must have been a number of players who were employed at the Ironworks, if the recollections of the manager of West Ham in 1906 and former Thames player Syd King were near accurate. He wrote in the *Book of Football*, when explaining the early formation of club policy:

In the summer of 1895, when the clanging of 'hammers' was heard on the banks of Father Thames and the great warships were rearing their heads above the Victoria Dock Road, a few enthusiasts, with the love of football within them, were talking about the grand old game and the formation of a club for the workers of Thames Ironworks Limited.

There were platers and riveters in the Limited who had chased the big ball in the north country. There were men among them who had learned to give the subtle pass and to urge the leather goalwards.

No thought of professionalism, I may say, was ever contemplated by the founders. They meant to run their club on amateur lines and their first principle was to choose their team from men in the works.

The iron workers acquitted themselves well in their first outing, pulling off a commendable 1–1 draw against experienced opposition. The *Kentish Mercury* reported:

The home team won the toss and elected to play with the sun and the wind at their backs. Despite this advantage, however, it was not until about 30 minutes from the start when their outside-left (Darby of Plumstead) received the ball just upon the 12yd line and promptly sent it passed Henshall who had no chance whatsoever of saving the shot.

Royal Ordnance equalised in the last twenty minutes after a scramble in the home goalmouth.

Following their first official match the *Kentish Mercury* correspondent observed that not a few Thames players had been with other East London clubs the previous season. These were the 'good men' referred to by the secretary and were indeed mainly recruited from leading local clubs including Anchor and Old Castle Swifts. Swifts were a company club sponsored by the Castle Shipping Line. They were reputed to be the first professional club in Essex, but folded as Thames Ironworks FC came into being. Thames also won players from the parish side St Luke's, who like the Ironworks side took on players that had formerly turned out for the Swifts, creating a kind of informal merger between the two former rivals.

J. Lindsay was probably among those who played against Royal Ordnance. He was an inside-forward and one of those recruited from Old Castle Swifts. Lindsay played in a number of early games for the Thames. Winger G. Sage was also likely to have taken the field for that historic opening encounter. Like Lindsay he joined Thames after the break-up of Old Castle Swifts. Sage was to turn out for the Ironworks side in their first FA Cup tie against Chatham and also the floodlit friendly against Old St Stephens ten days before Christmas 1895. Another probable member of the first Thames side would have been John Thomas Archer Wood, who also played cricket for Essex. He was a cousin of the champion jockey Fred Archer.

From their earliest days Thames was quick to attract talent from outside the immediate catchment area and on 20 September 1895, the *Kentish Mail and Greenwich & Deptford*

Observer noted that, 'Robert Stevenson the late captain of the Arsenal team is coming from Scotland to play for the Thames Ironworks.'

Stevenson was yet another former Castle Swifts man to join Thames. Able to fill a full back role or any of the three half back positions with equal effectiveness, Bob would, at a push, also play centre forward for Thames. He was the first player of real note to wear a Thames shirt, having previously been the skipper of Woolwich Arsenal (at that point a Division Two club, as were Manchester United and Liverpool). Born at Barrhead, Glasgow in 1869, Bob joined the Swifts from the Gunners in March 1895 but returned to Scotland following the break-up of the club. However, he was brought to Hermit Road for Thames' initial campaign and was promptly installed as club captain and assistant trainer, working alongside the 42-year-old guru of East London Football, Tom Robinson, the Malcolm Allison/José Mourinho of his day.

Bob moved back to his Caledonian roots after his time with the Irons, joining Arthurlie. His decision to return to Scotland for a second time was recorded in *Association Football and The Men Who Made It*:

> Robert Stevenson, a full-back of merit, who captained the Arsenal team in their early Second Division struggles, was among those who helped to build warships when the suggestion of a football club was made at the Thames Ironworks, and he was the first captain of the team ... There was not much of him in the way of physique, but he was a wonderfully good player and invaluable as an advisor to the fathers of the club ... He remained with Thames Ironworks until the second season, when they were located at Browning Road, East Ham. About halfway through their campaign at this enclosure, Stevenson returned home to Scotland and played for Arthurlie. (Gibson and Pickford, 1905)

Stevenson's alliance with trainer Tom Robinson was something of a dream team. Robinson was well respected in East London, having previously worked with both St Luke's and the Castle Swifts in the 1880s. Robinson, distinguishable by his huge moustache and trademark cigar, who also worked with East End cyclists and boxers, convened his training sessions in a room in Trinity Church School, Barking Road, in the recognisable trainer's attire of roll-neck woollen jumper and cloth cap. Robinson could be regularly spotted marshalling training along Turnpike Road (now Beckton Road).

The second game, against Dartford 'A', brought Thames their first victory, the *Thames Iron Works Gazette* commenting that the Kent side were given, 'a licking of 4 to nil'.

Results continued to improve and on 28 September Thames played their first away game, taking on Manor Park. It was a runaway 0–8 victory. However, all too often in their first season Thames found themselves involved in games like this, playing against sides that did not have the ability to stretch them, but the committee was looking forward to sterner, more rewarding tests and so continued to strengthen the playing squad.

The first real test and truly competitive match for the club came in October when they made their debut in the FA Cup. Their opponents were Chatham, a Southern

League side with a growing tradition. Thames had been drawn at home, but conceded this advantage, consenting to the tie being played at Chatham following, it was said, the Kent club's request, due to the 'unsuitability' of the Hermit Road ground. Of course the prospect of better gate receipts might also have been an unforeseen but welcome consequence for both clubs. Thames managed to compete well in the first half, but during the second period they were overrun and the game ended in a 5–0 victory for Chatham. The *Sportsman* noted that, 'goalkeeping and defence of the visitors was the best part of their play.'

Aside from the result, this first FA Cup adventure had been a resounding success. The club had earned extra revenue as a result of switching the tie to Chatham and the game had helped raise the profile of the Thames Ironworks Football Club.

By November the committee's efforts to improve the team were paying dividends. Thames took on Reading from the Southern League, considered to be one of the South's top club sides and, although they lost 2–3, the Londoners emerged with credit after dominating much of the game. This excellent display was followed by more impressive results during the winter of 1895/6, including a victory over St Luke's, who were still a potent force in the East End. After these performances, it was widely speculated that Thames would be elevated to the Southern League for the 1896/7 season.

During this first season Thames attracted much interest and a certain amount of notoriety by their experimentation with floodlighting. The lighting engineers from the Ironworks were given permission to rig up lights so that kick-off times could be put back. This would allow men from the works to attend games played during the week. The first match to enjoy this rudimentary illumination was a friendly against Old St Stephen's at Hermit Road on 16 December 1895. The fact that the game was refereed by Lt William Simpson, who was to take charge of that season's Cup Final (The Wednesday[6] v. Wolves) underlined the status of the match. Twelve lights, each of 2,000 candle power, were mounted on poles. The results were far from perfect. The precarious supports for the lights posed a constant threat to players and spectators alike. A Christmas tree effect was probable and not wholly conducive to flowing football. The huge bulbs blew at random and had to be replaced as the game continued. There were also a number of periods when the pitch was plunged into total darkness due to a collective failure of the lighting system. One reporter commented that he heard members of the Old St Stephen's team complaining that, 'the lights always went out just when the Thames Ironworks men had a shot at goal'.

However, the lights were gradually improved, though the ball still had to be regularly dipped in whitewash to make it visible. At the end of January a report of a friendly against Barking Woodville (the fourth 'illuminated' game) in the *Sportsman* noted that, 'the company (Thames Ironworks) have spared no expense … ' and that, 'the light gave a good view'.

---

6. Later to be known as Sheffield Wednesday.

A report by *West Ham Herald* indicated that the innovation was popular with supporters:

> Boys were swarming up over the fences for a free view when I put in an appearance. And what a smart man the Ironworkers have at the gate. He seemed to think my ticket was a real fraud until he had turned it upside down and inside out, and smelled at it for a considerable time. But he graciously passed me at last.

Thames won 6–2 with the help of a Charlie Dove hat-trick.

In March 1896, Hermit Road played host to Second Division Woolwich Arsenal and West Bromwich Albion from the First Division of the Football League. Albion fielded the legendary Billy Basset. Thames were beaten by both big clubs; going down 3–5 to the Gunners and 2–4 at the hands of Basset and co., but results were very much a secondary consideration in terms of these matches, which were all about getting Thames Ironworks club noticed and recognised as a footballing force in East London.

By the end of the 1895/6 season, Thames were a match for any amateur side. The overall record for that first season stood at, played 46, won 30, lost 12. The Hermit Road team had scored 136 goals, conceding only 68 in the process. Secretary Harsent told the Gazette that this was, 'a record to be proud of'.

Thames had rounded off their inaugural season by winning the West Ham Charity Cup, their first ever trophy. Thames beat Park Grove 1–0 in the semi-final at Plaistow, but following protests about a technicality from Park, the tie had to be replayed. Thames went through to the final, 3–0 winners at Becton Road.

It took three games to decide the destination of the cup that year. Following a 2–2 draw at the Old Spotted Dog ground at Upton Lane, Forest Gate, the replay at the same venue ended in another draw, 0–0. In the second replay Thames went away 2–1 winners before a crowd of more than 3,000. Thames were now widely known as 'the Irons', a reference to the hammers used to rivet ships together in the Ironworks Yard, just a short walk from their Hermit Road home. They clearly needed to find a regular, more demanding competitive football routine for the 1896/7 season, something more than what had been provided thus far by the Charity Cup and Essex and London Junior Cups. Before the start of the 1896/7 season the *Gazette* announced:

> With reference to the forthcoming season, it has been decided to enter for the English Cup, London Senior Cup, West Ham Charity Cup, South Essex League senior and junior and if possible, one or two others. There will be very few dates left open for 'friendly' matches, so it ought to be a good thing for the club financially.

The Irons were quite literally meaning business.

6

THE *FUJI*

In December 1895 Alfred Nobel, the inventor of dynamite, arranged in his will for his estate to fund the Nobel Prize. In the spring of the subsequent year the first modern Olympic Games were held in Athens, Greece.

In the late 1890s the world was taken aback with swiftness of the build-up of Japanese naval power. In 1897 *The Engineer*, focusing of the *Fuji*, the first battleship Thames Ironworks built for Japan, told its readers, 'that it is within the lifetime of the present generation, or the last quarter of a century, that the Empire of Japan – the Island Kingdom – has placed itself, by the marvellous energy of its ruler and people, well within the ranks of the Great Powers of the civilised world'.

The article continued, 'Due to her weight, very substantial launching ways and cradle had to be provided. The sliding ground ways used were 300ft and 400ft respectively.'

The *Fuji* (the lead ship of the Fuji-class of pre-dreadnought battleships, named after the sacred mountain of Japan – an instantly identifiable symbol of Japan around the world) was ordered by the Imperial Japanese Navy in 1894. It was designed by Mackrow to a modified *Royal Sovereign* design, very similar to the British Royal Navy's Majestic-class ships. The story of the construction of this ship is a tribute to the ingenuity of engineers of the time, both British and Japanese.

Fuji's coming into the world followed a thirteen-year study by the Japanese government into two heavy armament vessels. Her keel was laid on 1 August 1894 and she was delivered in 1897. She was 412ft long, with a beam of 73ft 6in. Her full-load draught was 26ft and she usually displaced 12,533 tons.

Fuji had a crew of 637 and was powered by two Humphrys Tennant vertical triple-expansion steam engines, using steam generated by ten cylindrical boilers, these rated at 13,500hp, using forced draught. The design offered a top speed of approximately 18 knots but she managed 18.5 knots during sea trials. *Fuji* carried a maximum of 1,180 tons of coal. This meant that she was able to steam for 4,000 nautical miles at a speed of 10 knots.

In the late nineteenth century, it was not unusual for shipyards to commission detailed builder's models of their creations as promotional tools. One of the Fuji-class battleships can be found at the Royal Hospital School, Holbrook, England. The record of the construction of these ships is unusually complete.

Fuji was launched on 31 March 1896 and completed on 17 August 1897. Her construction was supervised by more than 240 engineers and naval officers from Japan, a group that included the future Japanese Prime Ministers Saitō Makoto and Katō Tomosaburō. *Fuji* was the heaviest ship of her class to be set afloat from a building slip in a dockyard. She was around 2,000 tons heavier than preceding battleships.

While fitting out at Portland, she took part in the fleet review at Spithead, celebrating Queen Victoria's Diamond Jubilee on 26 June 1897. Thereafter she sailed for Japan by way of the Suez Canal.

Fuji's main battery was made up of quartet of 12in guns. These were mounted on a couple of twin turrets – one forward, the other aft. The secondary battery was ten 6in quick-firing guns; four of these were mounted in casemates on the sides of the hull, while the other six, protected by shields, were mounted on the upper deck. Smaller guns were carried for protection against torpedo boats, including fourteen 1.9in 3lb guns and ten 2½lb Hotchkiss guns of an identical calibre. *Fuji* was also equipped with five 18in torpedo tubes. Her waterline armour and Harvey armour belt had a thickness of 14–18in. Fuji's gun turrets carried 6-in thick armour, while her deck was 2½in thick. During 1901, sixteen of Fuji's 1.9in guns were replaced with the same number of QF 12-lb 12cwt guns. As a result of this, the number of crew was raised to 652, with 89 more crew members allocated to the ship later.

As Japan's first modern battleship, *Fuji* received an enthusiastic reception on her arrival in Japan. In 1898, during her sea trials off Kobe, the Emperor Meiji came aboard, as she roared along at just under 20 knots, demonstrating her main armaments with some notable salvos. After the embarrassment of the Tripartite Intervention of 1895,[7] the Emperor and his advisors resolved never again to be obliged to give way to European powers, planning a decade of naval expansion from 1896. As a consequence, armoured battleships under the Japanese flag were able to equal the best of what Europe could put to sea, able to warn off avaricious imperialists, defend Japan's trade and send a signal to the Russians making clear Japan's determination to protect its interests in China and Korea.

In 1896, Japan was building or arranging the finance for four more pre-dreadnought battleships in the UK, together with a fleet of modern cruisers, armoured cruisers, and torpedo boats. Japanese naval officers and architects were working with the Royal Navy and the Royal Dockyards, creating the means for Japan to build its own warships. The first two Fuji-class battleships were relatively small vessels, scaled down versions of Britain's 1892 model, however the other four were to be full-size battleships of 15–16,000 tons, the equal of anything the British Navy had.

---

7. The Tripartite Intervention or Triple Intervention was a diplomatic intervention by Russia, Germany and France on 23 April 1895 over the terms of the Treaty of Shimonoseki signed between Japan and the Qing Dynasty, China that ended the First Sino-Japanese War. The Japanese had reluctantly acceded to the intervention, being in no position to militarily resist three major European powers simultaneously.

    To Japan's astonishment, Russia moved almost immediately to occupy the entire Liaodong Peninsula and especially to fortify Port Arthur. Germany secured control over Shandong Province and France, and even Great Britain took advantage of the weakened China to seize port cities on various pretexts and to expand their spheres of influence. The Japanese reaction against the Triple Intervention was one of the underlying causes of the subsequent Russo–Japanese War.

Japan was intent on vengeance and tempering what they saw as Russian arrogance and greed. Japan broke the peace with a surprise torpedo assault that ultimately anticipated the later attack on Pearl Harbor. So started a war that sought to regain the fortress of Port Arthur in Manchuria, which had been captured by Japan in the 1895 war with China, but had subsequently been ceded to Russia by the Tripartite Intervention Treaty, which was signed under what the Japanese elite saw as little more than naval blackmail by the Russians and their French ally. Many of the Japanese Navy's actions centred on the blockade of Port Arthur, fortified by the Russians as their main naval base and home port to seven battleships. However, even with the Russian battleships being bottled up in port, blockade duty could be hazardous.

Fuji was involved in the Russo–Japanese War (1904–5) from the very start of hostilities, one of six battleships deployed in that conflict. With Captain Matsumoto Kazu (a man with a chequered and ultimately ignominious future) in command, she was consigned to the 1st Division of the 1st Fleet and on 9 February 1904 fought in the Battle of Port Arthur, when Admiral Tōgō Heihachirō led the 1st Fleet in an assault on the Russian Pacific Squadron, anchored outside Port Arthur.

Tōgō had anticipated that his surprise destroyer night attack would be more successful than it turned out to be. He had expected to find the Russians poorly organised and swiftly weakened. However, the ships of the Pacific Squadron rallied to the challenge, being ready to repel the attack. The fact was that the Japanese armada had been seen by the Russian cruiser *Boyarin* during an offshore patrol, so the Russians had been alerted.

Tōgō had decided to attack the Russian coastal defences using his main armament and to engage his enemy's ships with his secondary guns. Dividing available fire in this way turned out not to be the best idea, given that the Japanese 8in and 6in guns did little damage to the Russians, as the defenders, with some effect, focused their fire on the Japanese. While a relatively large number of both Russian and Japanese ships were hit, the Tsar's Navy suffered just seventeen casualties, while the Emperor's Navy came out of the fight with sixty killed and wounded. When Tōgō disengaged *Fuji* had been hit by two shells. Two hands were lost and ten were wounded.

On 10 March, *Fuji* and her sister ship *Yashima* (an ancient poetic name for Japan, which had been built by Armstrong Whitworth at their Elswick Works) commanded by Rear Admiral Nashiba Tokioki, from Pigeon Bay, blindly bombarded the harbour of Port Arthur, on the south-west side of the Liaodong Peninsula. At a range of 6 miles they fired 154 12in shells but failed to inflict much damage. Twelve days later, involved in much the same exercises, the Japanese took fire from Russian coastal defence guns, which had been moved to that location by the new Russian commander, Vice Admiral Stepan Makarov. At the same time *Fuji* and *Yashima* were attacked by a number of Russian ships in Port Arthur, directed by observers overlooking Pigeon Bay. Before the Japanese ships disengaged *Fuji* had taken a 12in shell.

On 13 April Tōgō drew out some of the Pacific Squadron, including the battleship *Petropavlovsk*, Makarov's flagship. On spotting the half-a-dozen 1st Division battleships, which included the *Fuji*, Makarov turned back for Port Arthur. But the *Petropavlovsk* struck a Japanese mine which had been laid the previous night. In less than two minutes the Tsar's battleship sank. Makarov was among of the 677 lost.

Buoyed by this success, Tōgō recommended long-range bombardments. This provoked the Russians to lay more minefields.

In August 1904, during the course of the Battle of the Yellow Sea, *Fuji* avoided being hit because the Russians focused their attack on the battleship *Mikasa*, Tōgō's flagship and as such the leading ship of the column.

Fuji was hit twelve times during the Battle of Tsushima on 27 May 1905. The most severe damage was the result of the penetration of the hood of the rear barbette, which ignited some exposed propellant charges and killed eight men and wounded nine. After the ammunition fire was put out, the left gun in the barbette resumed firing and played a significant part in the sinking of the battleship *Borodino*. Eight of *Fuji*'s crew were lost at Tsushima, while twenty-two were wounded.

Two years after Japan's 1905 victory, *Fuji*'s cylindrical boilers were replaced by Miyabara water-tube boilers and her fighting tops removed. On 23 October 1908, she hosted a dinner for the American Ambassador and the most senior officers of the Great White Fleet[8] during their circumnavigation of the world. Two years later she was overhauled, her Armstrong guns being replaced by Japanese-built weapons.

Leaps in technology and the huge number of more advanced ships being built in Britain and, soon, Japanese dockyards, resulted in *Fuji* becoming obsolete. She was reclassified as a first-class coast defence ship and was used for training duties in various capacities. She spent the whole of the First World War based at Kure, south-west of Hiroshima in southern Japan. Under the terms of the Washington Treaty for Naval Disarmament[9] she was disarmed and on 1 September 1922 reclassified as a training hulk and barracks. *Fuji* was decommissioned in 1923. Her propellers, main turrets and all guns were removed. Large wooden deckhouses were added to the superstructure and flat drill platforms covered her main deck. She was stationed at Yokosuka. From 1944, *Fuji* was also used as a development centre and observation post to test the effectiveness of various camouflage schemes on 1m-long models of Japanese aircraft carriers. This was ironic because all of Japan's carriers had been sunk by this time, and no new ones could be completed before the end of the War. She was hit several times in American air raids, but remained afloat.

After the war, any sign of Japanese militarism was viewed as a menace by the occupying authorities; apart from this, Japan needed all available sources of raw materials to rebuild its shattered infrastructure. The *Fuji* was broken up for scrap at Uraga Dock Company in 1948.

----

8. The nickname for the United States Navy battle fleet, which completed a circumnavigation of the globe (16 December 1907 to 22 February 1909) following the order of US President Theodore Roosevelt. It was made up of sixteen battleships in two squadrons, along with various escorts.
9. Also known as the Five-Power Treaty, this was a treaty among the major nations that had won the First World War, which agreed to prevent an arms race by limiting naval construction. It was negotiated at the Washington Naval Conference from November 1921 to February 1922, and signed by the governments of the United Kingdom, the United States, Japan, France and Italy. It limited the construction of battleships, battlecruisers and aircraft carriers by the signatories. The numbers of other categories of warships, including cruisers, destroyers and submarines, were not restricted but limited to 10,000 tons displacement.

ALL THINGS BRIGHT AND BEAUTIFUL ...

ARNOLD HILLS

Frank Clarke Hills, the first 'Hills' to own the Thames Ironworks, had always been determined that one of his three sons would inherit the company. He died in May 1895. Arnold Frank Hills was educated at Harrow (where he captained the school football team) and University College, Oxford and, in the early 1890s, joined the board of directors of his father's ship building business, the last surviving major shipbuilding company in London. Subsequent to his father's death he took over the leadership of the firm.

From the start of his career Arnold Hills showed a strong interest in the living conditions of the workforce. At the age of 23, like other young industrialists of the time working in the East London area, he decided to take a house near to his place of business. For five years he owned a small property in Canning Town, on the East India Dock Road, just a short walk from the Ironworks.

In his younger days Arnold had been a successful footballer – he represented Oxford University in the Varsity match. This match, during the period Arnold was turning out for his university, was equivalent in terms of talent, to a top European club match today. Arnold went on to don the colours of Old Harrovians, one of England's most powerful sides in that era and won an international cap, playing for the England team that defeated Scotland 5–4 at Kennington Oval in 1879. The young Hills was not content to restrict his sporting achievements to the confines of association football, he was also a star of the athletics field, gaining the coveted blue ribbon of the track when he became the English mile champion in 1878.

THE RICH MAN IN HIS CASTLE ...

In January 1895 Arnold Hills, now the owner of Thames Ironworks, began to publish his *Thames Iron Works Gazette*. This periodical was a combination of a technical journal, propaganda instrument, company newsletter, popular history magazine and local newspaper, but Hills saw it as primarily providing a channel of communication between the workers and the management of the firm, that would address resentment and bad feelings following recent industrial strife. Much of this antipathy had its root in Hills' decision to take on 'black' labour, casual workers from outside the firm, during the withdrawal of labour. As he stated in the *Gazette* of June 1895, he wished to create, 'a fresh link of interest and fellowship between all sorts and conditions of workers in our great industrial community'.

For Hills, the *Gazette* was a potential direct line to his employees, a mouthpiece through which he was able to advance his own world view, including the idea that the common interests of all those involved with Thames Ironworks were intrinsically tied to the prosperity of the firm. Under the headline, 'The Importance of Co-operation between Workers and Management' he wrote:

> But thank God this midsummer madness is passed and gone; inequities and anomalies have been done away with and now, under the Good Fellowship system and the Profit Sharing Scheme, every worker knows that his individual and social rights are absolutely secured.

This illustrates that the publication was used to inform employees about and promote support for changes in company policy that Hills had initiated, one of which was the co-ownership scheme mentioned and another being the introduction of the first recorded eight-hour working day for his employees in 1894.

The *Gazette* also advertised corporate facilities such as the range of worker associations and clubs that Hills had set up within his organisation. In the evenings he would often visit these societies which included cricket, rowing, athletics and cycling clubs, a science society and a drama group. Hills saw music as being particularly important, so drawing on members of the Thames Ironworks Temperance Society, a temperance choir was created. This existed together with an operatic group, a string orchestra, a military band and a brass band, that would play at the home matches of Thames Ironworks FC. There was a Thames Ironworks Ambulance Corps and a surviving image of the stalwart body (produced in 1899) provided evidence of East London's long multicultural heritage.

As well as promoting these extracurricular activities the *Gazette* kept workers informed about the progress of the various clubs, providing a results service and reporting on performances and events.

The *Gazette* appeared for over twenty years, until Hills was paralysed by arthritis. The lead article was almost always written by Hills and often took the form of a kind of sermon, focusing on issues that attracted his interest. Invariably the reader was assailed by a political point, but this was not always overt and sometimes got lost in a diatribe held together by Hills' class perspective and puritan values. Couched in the contradictory blend of Christian capitalist aestheticism, the moral engine of the repressed and suffocated Victorian elite and the bedrock on which the British Empire was built, these writings suggest that the author was a complex and driven soul. However, they also provide a clear understanding of the role of clubs and associations, alongside initiatives like the co-ownership scheme and the eight-hour day, within Thames Ironworks. They embodied the connection that Hills saw between social welfare and the development of his organisation as an effective business enterprise. This gave them a complex character. As illustrated above, Hills set up the societies ostensibly to create a feeling of commonality across wage and status boundaries. This part of the plan aimed to encourage loyalty to the company, in particular amongst his shop-floor employees. Out of this Hills looked to generate a psychological fusion between everybody involved in the company that would create solidarity and a shared interest in the firm's aims, which were mostly defined by him.

In short, Hills wanted those who sold their labour to the firm for a wage to see this as a good investment, in spite of the fact that Thames Ironworks, like all companies within the Victorian capitalist environment, primarily existed in order that owners might make profits by paying workers less than the true value of their labour. Profit straightforwardly being the difference between the sum of money paid in the form of wages to workers, plus the cost of plant and raw materials and the income from what that labour power produces, in Thames Ironworks' case ships and so on. Owners took or, according to Karl Marx, stole it for themselves.

This strategy was complimented by the potential of the clubs to offer an alternative form of fraternity to that found outside the company in the growing Union movement. This movement was seen by late Victorian entrepreneurs as a huge threat to capitalist organisations, by making inroads on the profit margin of capitalist organisations, through pressure for higher wages and better conditions. To this end Hills set up a central council to co-ordinate the efforts of the many new associations. He urged that every club should:

> ... rally loyally around the Central Council ... and thus united ... the social movement which has already done so much will go from success to success ... It will set the seal upon the business prosperity of the firm and crown the labours of the Works with the laurels of the road, the river, the racing track, the field and the public hall.

Without doubt Hills wanted his clubs to be good at whatever they were doing, but he insisted that the council encourage the development of these societies as separate entities. This demonstrates the contradictory cultural imperative of capitalist organisation – the creation of a nexus of co-operation whilst promoting competition within the same. This is not saying that Hills consciously developed this situation, but the 'house' system within public schools and the allegiance to 'college' within the university system prepared upper-class young men well for their destiny – the organisation and maintenance of Victorian capitalist society, its culture and its values. As such, the clubs were much more than a diversion for the participants.

Hills was not the first capitalist in the area to seek to manipulate and ingratiate himself with his workers using company benefits, alongside the carrot of better conditions to motivate the most advantageous environment for production – worker compliance and the resulting industrial peace. When the workers of the South Metropolitan Gas Company 'left work' in 1889 (strikes were illegal at that time) in protest against the company's profit sharing plans, owner George Livesey extended the scheme, making a huge investment in social facilities. The company's Institute and Theatre (in Greenfell Street, which was demolished to make way for the site of the Millennium Dome) were both were built as part of a co-partnership initiative. This extended to a scheme that provided children born to employees of the South Metropolitan Gas Company with work, housing and burial at the company's expense. As will be seen later, the Hills family had a close association with the gas industry and were always quick to learn and benefit from it Arnold, in this respect, was carrying on a tradition. He was a man of his era and true to the tactics of his class, but he was also part of a group of industrialists ahead of their time. Not until the 1960s did the majority of large-scale organisations in the USA and later Japan begin to rediscover the full business benefits in developing paternalistic and philanthropic relationships between themselves and their employees.

ENTREPRENEURIAL PHILANTHROPY, CONSCIENCE AND CAPITALISM

All this should not undermine the fact that Hills was certainly passionate and sincere in his hope that the worker associations and other company initiatives would positively affect worker morale and employment satisfaction of his workforce. His initiatives were not straightforward, cynical efforts to exploit his workers. His puritanical beliefs, aesthetic outlook and moral convictions, including a wish to better those in his employ and his faith in 'the enterprise' of Thames Ironworks as a philanthropic community were deeply set.

Hills was a man steeped in the Protestant work ethic and the Calvinist influence of his time and social position. The making of money was a vulgar enterprise for a gentleman. To be a 'respectable' member of upper class society one certainly needed to command appreciable financial resources, but an individual also needed to have a 'greater end' and a sense of their 'class duties' – the 'white man's burden' in the colonial context – in order to achieve the social high ground. This was the engine of Victorian philanthropy founded on 'good works'. This being the case Hills genuinely wanted to improve the moral and physical condition of those he relied on to keep his company profitable. This evoked in him the paternalism so typical of the elite classes of the time. Hills saw it as his social duty, as well as his personal and class responsibility, to influence and, if necessary, finance the direction of his workers' leisure and the lives of others. At the 1895 meeting of the Vegetarian Federal Union Meeting, Hills, as the first Chair of the Union, gave an 'inspiring' hour-long talk on vegetarianism and its benefits. On a subsequent visit to Birmingham he called together a group of business men and said, 'I would like to see a first-class vegetarian restaurant in Birmingham and if you will start it I will subscribe 10 per cent of the cost.'

Being a militant temperance advocate and a believer in crusading for good causes, he wanted to provide his workforce with opportunities to enjoy wholesome leisure pursuits and so prevent them from spending their spare time on what he saw as the evils of drink and gambling.

Hills was also, at times, to show commendable loyalty to his workforce. For instance, he would have not entertained the idea of moving his shipyards further down the Thames. This would have been more efficient, allowing for greater margins of profit, but at the same time it would have caused tremendous hardship in the area of Essex that was part of the extended east end of London, which included the borough of West Ham. To his credit Hills wished to avoid this. By 1895 the Thames Ironworks and Ship Building

Company was the largest, and one of Britain's most important, shipbuilding yards. The Ironworks had employed 6,000 men in 1860 and at the time of the great docks strike of 1890 it had 7,000 men out on strike. The docks were an important source of work. The Victoria and Albert Docks were the biggest single sources of employment for men in West Ham. A great deal of cheap housing was built in the Canning Town Tidal Basin and Custom House areas of West Ham for this casual labour force that, for the sake of efficiency, needed to live close to the source of work. Although more than 7,000 men worked on the docks in 1904, factory work provided employment for three times as many people in West Ham. A few industrial concerns, like the Thames Ironworks, were associated with the docks, but the majority of the West Ham working population was not composed primarily of either casual labourers or dockers. The largest employers of skilled labour were the repair shops of the Great Eastern Railway. In 1904 there were more than 11,000 men working in the metal and machine trades in West Ham.

In governmental terms, West Ham was not part of London. It was an Essex suburb – a manufacturing centre, containing factories that had moved from London. Many of these were 'offensive' industries, producing dirt, fumes and chemical residues. A survey published in the late 1880s had indicated that 60 per cent of the population existed below the poverty line. Sickness, poverty, pollution and unemployment were rife. In the last two decades of the nineteenth century West Ham suffered serious overcrowding with an average of 6.46 people per house, while the average for England and Wales was 5.21. There were, however, tremendous differences within the borough. Overcrowding was severe in Canning Town, Custom House and Silvertown – areas containing the highest percentage of casual labourers. In Upton Park and Forest Gate comfortable housing was occupied by professional and business families. The northern part of West Ham was described as a dormitory for London, and this increased as one went into the surrounding areas of East Ham, Barking and Ilford. The inner area of West Ham lacked open space and public recreation grounds – football was played mainly on the spaces between factories and industrial areas.

Howarth and Wilson's detailed survey of the social problems in West Ham in 1907 compared its lack of open space with 'planned towns' like Bournville, where it was thought necessary to have undeveloped areas within a five-minute walk of homes. It was impossible to achieve this in West Ham but the report made the point that a lack of open space 'is conducive neither to health nor to morals', and concluded that it 'was not surprising to have bands of young hooligans whose energies are expended in petty larcenies in the streets'. Hills often cited the lack of recreational facilities as one of the worst privations in the lives of West Ham residents. It is true that the borough had inherited most of London's worst problems, overcrowding, impoverishment and filth, but its rates were so low that it could not afford good sanitation and open play areas. Arnold Hills was to note, 'the perpetual difficulty of West Ham is its poverty. It is rich only in its population.'

This would accurately describe many non-industrialised countries in the modern era. In 1895 Hills vigorously supported a plan to bring the borough of West Ham into the county of London. Hills understood that becoming part of London administratively meant that West Ham could effectively be subsidised by the rest of the city to the benefit of the local community. He also grasped that this would improve the quality of the workforce, as regards health and education, and provide an impetus for the general business environment at the lower reaches of the Thames. This recognition of the relationship between social welfare and the health of business was evident throughout Hills' tenure in the East End, as was his awareness of the value of loyalty to his workforce. This is likely to have influenced his decision not to move the Ironworks downstream. He may well have understood that company loyalty to the workforce could motivate reciprocation in the form of working-class/East End solidarity that existed in the West Ham area, harnessing this resource for the benefit of production – what is now often thought of as 'social capital'. His faith was well founded. Arnold Hills was never let down by his workers. Subsequently West Ham United Football Club has always benefited from the same cultural values of the district – those who support the Irons remain Hammers for life; for us iron is in our souls.

There can be little doubt that Arnold Hills had authentic concern for his employees and the wider population of the West Ham community that huddled around the banks of the Thames and Lea. However, these sentiments coexisted within Hills' frame of reference alongside a commitment to the structure of capitalist enterprise and the master/servant ethos. This was the culture that permeated Victorian employment relations and the wider context of the British Empire of which Arnold Hills was very much a product. Indeed, the attitude that Hills and the likes of South Metropolitan Gas Company owner George Livesley displayed towards their employees was similar to the relationship that their class contemporaries, the well-meaning British colonial elite, fostered with the natives of the great swathes of red that then dominated the global maps. Both colonialist and industrialist regarded those they saw as being 'in their charge' as potentially troublesome children. As such, they needed to be educated, gainfully occupied and kept in conditions that, in times of labour shortages, would sustain an efficient, fit, skilled and devoted workforce, free from the enemies of effective production – hunger and sickness.

So, the overall effect of Hills' investment in the free time of his workforce, in his ideal world, would be to raise the ethical and market reputation of his firm together with its capitalist efficiency. At the same time it would play a part in converting his workforce into respectable, decent, God-fearing and, above all, obedient members of society, who knew and were content with their station in life, to produce wealth for the use of their social 'betters', who were the only group capable of using this in a responsible and effective manner. This would achieve the Victorian world symmetry in a class system that the upper echelon of this society saw as being ordained by God – 'All things bright and beautiful … The rich man in his castle, the poor man at his gate, God made them high and lowly, and ordered their estate.'

THE POOR MAN AT HIS GATE … ?

It is not clear how many Thames Ironworks employees took up the temperance advocated by Hills. It does appear, however, that many defiantly braved the moral perils that he saw as so threatening to his workforce particularly in the Old Imperial Theatre in the Barking Road, on the doorstep of the Ironworks.

The Old Imperial started its life as the Royal Albert Music Hall, and was more widely known as 'Relf's', after the owner Charles Relf. Relf's was advertised in *The Stage* as, 'The handsomest and most comfortable (music hall) in East London, entirely lit by electricity'. Despite the efforts of Arnold Hills it was a favourite haunt of many a Thames Ironworks riveter. The hall had its own built-in pub, The Town of Ayr, and at the height of Thames Ironworks' history, the facility engaged acts, at enormous expense. These included Tom Costello, famous for the ditty 'At Trinity Church I Met Me Doom', Charlie Coborn who wowed audiences with his 'Two Lovely Black Eyes' and 'The Man that Broke the Bank at Monte Carlo'. Kate Carney, the voice behind 'Three Pots a Shilling', also trod the boards at Relf's as did Vesta Victoria whose rendition of 'Waiting at the Church' was a national hit. Other favourites at the Old Imperial were Gus Elen who had great success with 'It's a Great Big Shame' and Ella Shields, the original 'Burlington Bertie from Bow'.

The last pantomime to be staged at the Old Imperial over the Christmas period of 1920, was *Aladdin*. One of the big successes of this production was a tableau, based on the famous Pears soap advertisement and the song 'I'm Forever Blowing Bubbles'. Audiences joined in with great gusto and soon the tune was to be heard all over the East End, whistled in streets, sung in pubs, clubs and of course at the Boleyn Ground. The funny melancholic little tune was to become synonymous with the progenitor of Thames Ironworks Football Club, West Ham United.

The question of who was to run Thames Ironworks FC was posed from the very earliest days. There was, almost from the inception of the club, a desire for independence and a level of professionalism. This was illustrated in 1895 when the Thames players decided that the club's governing committee should be made up of non-players. The *Thames Iron Works Gazette* reported, 'A number of gentlemen were asked to fulfil this function, which proved most beneficial to the club.'

This group was made up of clerks, foremen and supervisors at the Ironworks. It would regularly find itself at loggerheads with Arnold Hills and occasionally openly rebelled against his passionate advocacy of the virtues of sporting amateurism. This was a struggle between the committee seeking to actualise their vision for the football club with Hills' abhorrence of the growing tide of professionalism in Victorian sport.

The new club had already shown its ambition by developing an active committee, recruiting top coaching and playing staff and by organising a fixture list with a distinct professional look about it, including entry into the FA Cup. The very first foray into the FA Cup was telling in terms of understanding the future aims of the football club. One of the main reasons for taking part was to raise the profile of Thames Ironworks Football Club. The committee also chose to waive home advantage and that meant extra cash was raised from gate receipts. This strategy emphasised the movement the club was making towards professionalism. The game was not being played for an end in itself, as would befit the amateur code of conduct, so close to the heart of Arnold Hills.

8

THE LONDON LEAGUE: 1896/97

The original Blackwall Tunnel linking Tower Hamlets and Greenwich under the Thames was completed in 1897. My great grandfather worked on the excavation. At that point it was the longest underwater tunnel on the planet. The project was completed using tunnelling shields and compressed air techniques, together with a Greathead shield (taking the name of its inventor, James Henry Greathead).[10] The tunnel shafts, huge double-skinned iron cylinders, were manufactured by Thames Ironworks. They were lined inside with glazed brickwork.

A decade later the Rotherhithe Tunnel was built further east and once more the expertise and craftsmanship of Thames Ironworks was called on.

At around the same time that the Irons were busy entertaining West Bromwich Albion and Woolwich Arsenal, a meeting was held at Finsbury Barracks to discuss the formation of a London League. It was agreed that a league should be formed made up of both professional and amateur teams in three divisions. It was hoped that the new league would help raise the standard of football in London at a time when clubs from the Midlands and North West were dominating the professional game. Arnold Hills was elected as president of the new league and Francis Payne, Chair of Thames Ironworks Football Club and an official of the Ironworks Sports Association, was recruited to a group drafting the new league's rules.

Thames, although strictly speaking an Essex club, were initially placed in the Second Division of the London League, but they were elevated to the top division after the withdrawal of Royal Ordnance. Secretary Harsent declared in the *Thames Iron Works Gazette* that, 'the League will be a new feature in London football next season … it should raise the whole tone of football in the great city.'

As the 1896/7 season approached it seemed that Harsent's optimism was well placed. Club membership had increased, enabling the Irons to field three teams. Thames had

10. He was also renowned for his work on the London Underground railway. In January 1994 a statue was erected outside Bank Station next to the Royal Exchange in the City of London. While Bank Station was being refurbished, a section of the Barlow–Greathead shield was discovered in a passageway between the Underground and the Waterloo and City Railway. The section has been painted red and a brass plate erected as a further memorial to Greathead's achievements.

attracted several new players of renown, these included first-teamers from leading local clubs St Luke's and Castle Swifts and four players from Reading, including Davey, Hatton, Rossitter and Holmes. One player who was prevented from joining Thames at this time was an ex-Middlesbrough man called Wynn. Although Wynn was employed at the Ironworks, he was unable to play for the amateur Irons as he had previously been a professional footballer. Inevitably, rumours circulated that the Thames were preparing to turn professional, a notion that the club committee was quick to dismiss.

With Harsent standing down as secretary, Francis Payne took over the role as Thames kicked off their first full season in serious competition. There were thirty first-team matches scheduled and six cup competitions. The Irons' first taste of League action came against Vampires at the Hermit Road ground on 19 September 1896 and resulted in a 3–0 victory for Thames. Seventeen days later the Ironworks side beat the 1st Scots Guards. The reason for the extended period between games was simply that the inaugural London League First Division comprised of only eight sides.

Despite promising League form, success in the FA Cup was not forthcoming. In a qualifying round, played on 10 October 1896, the Irons were defeated 8–0 at Southern League Sheppey United. Inside-right E.G. Hatton, one of the men who came from Reading in August, was among the unhappy Thames side that day. He was to play in all three FA Cup ties for the Irons during the following season. He and his team mates would have a hard job recovering from this first-hurdle defeat. The sports reporter for the *Courier and Borough of West Ham News* commented, 'I do not understand how Sheppey were able to run around Thames by 8–0. Surely the visitors must have been off colour.'

Thames were also bundled out of the London Senior Cup 2–0 away to Bromley. Kent was not proving a happy hunting ground for the Irons.

The bad news continued for Thames when they discovered that they were to be evicted from Hermit Road in October 1896. The club had rather blatantly violated its tenancy according to the ground agent by, in effect, building a stadium, including a pavilion, on the ground and charging admission.

The home of the Irons was rather eccentric in design. It was surrounded by a moat, to prevent spectators from getting a free view of games. Canvas sheeting had been used for some time as fencing. In those days most matches played by amateur clubs were usually not much more than park affairs. Even the better teams in the district, the likes of Upton Park, marked out the ground with no more than chalk lines around the perimeter of the pitch. Even major FA Cup matches could be watched, for free, by almost anybody. In retrospect Thames' activity on the site, which was rented purely for playing purposes, seems outrageous, but the men involved with Thames Ironworks Football Club were, by dint of their occupation, constructors. Added to this, in their pursuit of engineering and sport they were also innovators and adventurers, possibly with little interest in the finer points of leasing arrangements. Their activity was also consistent with the growing professionalism of the club. Whilst a culture made up of such individuals had its drawbacks, it may be that the same drives were critical in building the foundations of what was to be the biggest professional sporting organisation in the area and one of the largest of its type in London.

For a time confusion reigned. At one point the club believed that it had been granted a new plot at the same site. However, the Irons were obliged to play their next four matches on opponents' grounds. Two London Senior Cup ties proved successful but league points were lost on a visit to the champions to be, the 3rd Grenadier Guards. It was five weeks before Arnold Hills secured a temporary home ground for his team at Browning Road, a side street off of East Ham High Street. The stay in East Ham didn't get off to the best of starts. The Irons got themselves knocked out of the Essex Senior Cup 3–2 by Leyton.

Thames did have a fair run in the London Senior Cup. The kick-off for the third round had to be delayed due to the late arrival of the Wandsworth team. The Irons were leading 7–0 with ten minutes to go when the referee abandoned the game because of bad light. Thames appealed to the London FA, asking to be awarded the tie due to their opponents' belated appearance at Browning Road. The South Londoners argued that the fog that had put a stop to the tie was the same fog that had delayed their arrival at the Irons' home ground. The London FA ordered the tie to be replayed. Although Thames were unable to repeat the former rout they won comfortably, seeing off unhappy Wandsworth 3–1.

The fifth round occupied the next four Saturdays. The first match against Bromley FC was postponed. The second was abandoned in extra-time. The third was undecided after extra time and the fourth went to the London League Second Division club 2–0.

Overall the Irons' first-team enjoyed little luck in the local cup competitions, and were overshadowed by the reserve team who progressed to the club's second consecutive West Ham Charity Cup Final, losing 1–0 to West Ham Garfield before 6,000 spectators at the Spotted Dog Ground in Forest Gate. Bob Heath was the Garfield goalkeeper that day. He must have impressed his opponents. With little delay Thames signed the big, dark, strong keeper known to Garfield followers as 'the black panther'. He is yet another candidate as the Irons first black player, but as previously stated, John Charles of the Bobby Moore era, the first black player to gain England honours, remains the only verified candidate for this milestone.

Thames made good progress in the London League, finishing as runners-up to, although well behind, the 3rd Grenadier Guards. The soldiers put a total of nine goals passed the Irons in the two league encounters with Thames managing just one in reply. Much of the credit for the excellent performance of Thames in the London League was attributed to the generosity of Arnold Hills. *The Courier and Borough of West Ham News* declared, 'Mr Hills is very liberal with the money and the satisfactory position of the club is almost entirely due to his judicial supervision.'

Hills' generosity did not stop with investment in players. In January 1897 he announced that he had found a new home for the Thames Ironworks Football Club and athletic societies. He made his announcement at the Thames Ironworks Federated Clubs Annual Festival, remarking that he had, 'secured a large piece of land for an athletic ground ... ' and that the 'ground would contain a cycle track, with banking equal to any in London'.

This comment was met with applause. He went on to say that, 'it would also be used for football, tennis ... '

That football is mentioned after cycling, and that cycling would provide a major occupation for the stadium, is revealing. Thames Ironworks Football Club was not considered to be the most important of the Ironworks societies at that point. The cycling club seems to have been both more popular and more successful. As a result, the grandstand at the new ground would be positioned to give the best view of the home straight.

The new ground would be situated in Plaistow. In order that it could be opened in June 1897 to commemorate the 60th year of Queen Victoria's reign, the stadium site was turned from a wilderness into an arena equal to any in the country in fourteen weeks. This was a magnificent achievement that would be hard to match in modern terms. The Memorial Ground, named in honour of Her Royal Majesty's anniversary (not, as some recent commentators have claimed, in response to the Albion disaster, that happened at a later date; see below), could accommodate more than 100,000 spectators and was constructed at a cost of more than £20,000. This was a monumental sum before the dawn of the twentieth century. For instance a police officer at the time earned about 28s a week. At the time of writing the average wage (given service and grade) would be around £1,450. While the calculation is not statistically perfect, the latter comparison would suggest that the construction of the stadium cost Arnold Hills the equivalent to over £100 million in today's terms.

The stadium provided a clubhouse and sports complex that included plans to build an outdoor swimming pool that would be over 100ft in length and available for the use of the Thames Ironworks employees. The cycle track, a third of a mile in circumference, skirted a cinder running track, which itself encompassed the football pitch. The opening of the new ground attracted 8,000 people, who came to see a varied programme of events that included polo and cock fighting.

In November 1897 Hills secured an arrangement with the London, Tilbury and Southend Railway (LT&SR) to build a station at Manor Road to allow convenient access to the Memorial Ground. The LT&SR board approved the project three months later and Mowlem was given the contract to build a four-platform station, allowing for the proposed quadrupling of the line – Mowlem was one of the largest construction and civil engineering companies in Britain at the time. Other projects undertaken by them in the second half of the nineteenth century included Billingsgate Fish Market (completed in 1874), Smithfield Fruit Market (finished in 1882), Liverpool Street Station and the Great Eastern Hotel (completed in 1891). Mowlem, taken over by Carillion in 2006, was the owner and developer of London City Airport, situated not too far from the Memorial Ground in Newham.

The station, on the line from Fenchurch Street to Barking which was opened in 1858, was completed in May 1900 but did not open until 1 February 1901. It was originally known as West Ham but from 11 February 1924 to 1 January 1969 it was West Ham (Manor Road).

The Irons made their debut at the Memorial Ground in a friendly against Northfleat, shortly after the grand opening on Jubilee Day. Only 200 spectators turned up. As the rain began to fall on the ragged little band of supporters strung out around the huge ground, Secretary Payne sent out the invitation to every spectator to move undercover in the grandstand. It was a poor showing for a facility that Payne described as being good enough to hold the English Cup Final. Indeed, it was to be considered for the 1901 Cup semi-final, Spurs v. West Bromwich Albion.

Disappointing support was something the Irons were becoming accustomed to. This was surprising given that after only two years Thames had become one of the top teams in an area that was described in *Association Football and the Men Who Made it* (1905) as 'football mad' with 'hundreds of urchins kicking balls in the streets'.

Disappointment that so few men from the Ironworks attended matches was expressed in the *Gazette*, 'The support we have received has not been so large as we should wish for, the gates not totalling near the number we might expect and certainly not so many as the quality of the play of our men should warrant.'

It was hard for the club organisers to understand why so many people went to matches at grounds that were, 'much less pleasing and where the football is nowhere near as good … Things will have to improve when people realise how splendid the ground is and how good the club is.'

These remarks expose what the club had become and account, however subconsciously, for its lack of support. Thames could hardly expect to be well supported by Ironworks employees when its path to professionalism was taking it ever further from being a works team. Workers could gain membership to the club, this allowed them to attend training on Tuesday and Thursday evenings and take part in practice matches, but there was no suggestion that they would be considered for a place in the team. While some of the early Thames teams included men employed at the Ironworks such as Thomas Freeman (ships fireman), Walter Parks (clerk), Tom Mundy, Walter Tranter and James Lindsay (all boilermakers), William Chapman, George Sage, William Chamberlain and apprentice riveter Charlie Dove, as the club developed the absence of such men was noticeable. This situation was masked to some extent by players being taken on as employees of the Ironworks. This was a common practice in many works-based teams with higher aspirations – Woolwich Arsenal had been guilty of much the same scam for instance. As such, Ironworks employees could have little hope of taking an active playing part in the main function of the club, the winning of games against first-class opposition. Thames had incorporated leading local clubs and was winning, but it had no specific constituency to whom it could appeal. It was not representative of any particular area of West Ham and it only had a nominal tie with the Ironworks. The Irons had no trouble defeating their local rivals on the field. They had a long record of remaining undefeated by any amateur team, but this did not ensure success at the gate.

To gain support. the committee had long ago decided to attempt to produce high quality football and this meant becoming more professional. Large crowds would only be attracted if professional clubs came to play competitively at the Memorial Ground, but the club was never going to come anywhere near filling its massive home ground whilst it was converting Thames into a competent professional side that could compete at the highest level. The Irons needed to buy time. This was made possible by the continuing patronage of Arnold Hills. Hills was to supplement the club's income well into its maturation as a professional entity, but it would have been unlikely that he would have been willing to subsidise an openly, fully professional organisation. As such, it was perhaps not surprising that the committee held back on admitting to professional ambitions. What is surprising however is that Hills remained tolerant of the obviously growing professionalism of Thames Ironworks Football Club, the sporting progeny that sprung from the adamantly amateur loins of his puritan paternalism. Why did he continue to nurture the football club long after it had ceased to play the role he had envisioned for it, as a cementing factor within a harmonious 'industrial community', that would help create solidarity and identity with the firm, wherein all would flourish (some more than others of course) united in the pursuit of excellence and purity in the cause of company, capitalism and Empire?

What are claimed to be the original iron gates to the Memorial Ground can still be seen at 302 Grange Road, West Ham, although some say that these are, in fact, the original gates to the Boleyn Ground. The ground Arnold Hills built is still used for football and other sports, which is probably the most lasting and poignant legacy of his efforts in this respect, although when I walk around the area, I wonder how many of the kids running about on Thames Ironworks FC's old ground have any idea who Hills was, what he did and why he did it. History is so often an invisible flame and you can only feel its heat if you look for it. That said, why should anyone know or care about what was? We live in a world wherein what 'is' takes up our emotional, personal and collective horizons; but isn't this just an existential hell? If we don't have roots with the past, not even as a backdrop, what are we other than dust? Those whose existence is trapped in the immediate and no more are by definition simply to be blown away by the successive 'now'; we 'become as sounding brass, or a tinkling cymbal', something less than ethereal that vanishes almost before it begins.

THE *SHIKISHIMA*

Between 1897 and 1902 Thames Ironworks produced two ships for the Royal Navy, HMS *Cornwallis* and HMS *Guncan*. In the same period it produced the *Shikishima* for the Imperial Japanese Navy. Designed by Clement Mackrow, the naval architect who had been involved in the original design of the yard, the *Shikishima* was laid down on 29 March 1897 and was launched on the 1 November 1898. She was finally completed in 1900.

The *Shikishima* weighed 15,483 tons and carried 12in guns; the hull was sub-divided into 261 watertight compartments and she could reach a speed of 18 knots. Like *Fuji* she fought at Port Arthur.

'Shikishima' is an epithet for Japan. 'Shikisima no michi' expresses the 'way of Shikishima' – the composition of waka poetry. A poet, Ki no Tsurayuki, about a thousand years ago wrote:

The poetry of Japan has its roots in the human heart and flourishes in the countless leaves of words. Because human beings possess interests of so many kinds it is in poetry that they give expression to the meditations of their hearts in terms of the sights appearing before their eyes and the sounds coming to their ears. Hearing the warbler sing among the blossoms and the frog in his fresh waters – is there any living being not given to song!

History is a silent human song. Shakespeare saw this; in our relative deafness to what we are and where we come from, what we do and where we go ends with the doing and going. The consequence of this is that the colour and depth of existence drains away and we become merely transient spirits, and:

> Are melted into air, into thin air:
> And like the baseless fabric of this vision,
> The cloud-capp'd tow'rs, the gorgeous palaces,
> The solemn temples, the great globe itself,
> Yea, all which it inherit, shall dissolve,
> And, like this insubstantial pageant faded,
> Leave not a rack behind. We are such stuff
> As dreams are made on; and our little life
> Is rounded with a sleep.
>
> (*The Tempest*, Act 4, scene 1, 148–158)

Launch of the Portuguese corvettes *Rainha de Portugal* and the *Mindello* (1875).

9

THE *ALBION*

At the end of the 1897/98 season the splendid facilities at the Memorial Ground and the enlistment of better players energised the ambitions of the committee of Thames Ironworks Football Club. This, together with the success of their team, boosted their confidence to such an extent that they effectively decided to more openly embrace professionalism in an attempt to increase the sparse population of the vast open spaces of their home ground.

The committee decided to approach Hills with a range of proposals that would ultimately change the amateur profile of the club. Hills, as an advocate of 'sport for sport's sake', must have found the suggestion that players should be blatantly paid a wage, rather than just receive expenses or compensation, quite unpalatable. Following protracted debate he agreed to the committee's propositions but with the greatest reluctance. It is difficult to understand why he compromised his very deeply held convictions but, at this juncture, Hills was recovering from the tragic launch of the *Albion,* a first-class cruiser that had been ordered by the Royal Navy. The Admiralty had commissioned her from Thames Ironworks at the height of the 'naval race' in Europe, as the continent started the slow build-up to war. She had been completed slightly behind schedule, as the yard was suffering from a staff shortage and an engineering union strike centred on the cause of the 'eight-hour-day' was affecting supplying contractors, disrupting delivery dates. The workers at Thames Ironworks had not taken part in the engineers' action; Hills had introduced the eight-hour day some years earlier.

The *Albion,* one of the Royal Navy's last pre-dreadnought battleships, was 800 tons less than her original design had stipulated, due to the failure of government-employed contractors to supply the correct level of armour plating to clad the ship, but at 390ft long, 74ft wide, she still weighed in a massive 6,000 tons.

Launches were not an unusual event at the Thames yard, but the *Albion* was no ordinary ship. She was British, and that was seen as something to celebrate on 21 June 1898, as was the fact that she would be the first Thames Ironworks ship to be launched by royal hand. Although a local newspaper reported that no fewer than 100,000 people attended the launch, probably nearer 30,000 people crammed around the yard to watch the Duke and Duchess of York (soon to be King George V and Queen Mary) give the massive vessel her title.

It was a fine day and the shipyard was covered in bunting and flags. The excitement was mounting as the 3 p.m. launch time approached. Yard workers and local schools were given the day as holiday to attend the event and families dressed in their best clothes. Employees received a special bonus on the day, 1s for apprentices, half-a-crown and a straw hat for shipwrights. The afternoon was bathed in golden sunshine and this exaggerated the festival feeling. Around 20,000 tickets had been given to employees of the yard, but the men on the yard gate were told to let anyone in that looked respectable. Yard management had arranged for seventy policemen to help with crowd control, far too few to have anything but the most minimal impact on the mass of people jostling around and seeking the best view of the occasion.

A narrow workmen's slipway running by the side of the nearly finished Japanese warship the *Shikisima* provided the best view of events. Workers at the yard knew the bridge had not been designed to take the weight of any sizeable number of people. Indeed, they had erected a sign indicating the danger of using it. However, as the afternoon drew on and the crowd grew more anxious to find a good vantage point, the police, who up to this point had kept the bridge clear, allowed over 200 people to squeeze onto it. The *East Ham Echo* described the situation:

> As the time for the ceremony approached the crowd grew denser, and just after the Royal party and the other guests of the company had left the luncheon table, a rush took place for the bridge at the bottom of the middle slip. The temptation was a great one. There was no one there, and the place was clear of scaffolding except on the left, where the towering sides of the Japanese battleship rose many feet in the air. The warnings of experienced workmen and officials of the company were unheeded and, bearing down all opposition, the people swarmed on to the frail bridge. Most of them were women and children.

When the Royal entourage arrived at the yard, which was festooned in a kaleidoscope of colour, they went off to lunch with Arnold Hills, Lady Mary Lyon, Sir Charles Cust, the Venerable Archdeacon Stevens[11], Canon Richard A. Pelly (the Vicar of West Ham)[12] and other dignitaries. The atmosphere was enjoyably tense and expectant.

---

11. Stevens would be the first Bishop of Barking. He then held incumbencies at St Luke, Victoria Docks and was Vicar of St John's, Stratford. He was appointed Suffragan Bishop of Barking in February 1901. He died in 1920.

12. Pelly founded the West Ham Evangelical Trust to promote the teaching of 'the Protestant and evangelical party in the Church of England'. The purpose of the trust was to counter strong Roman Catholic and Anglo-Catholic movements in West Ham (Irish, Italian and other European immigrants would have invigorated this phenomenon). Later it provided poor-relief and prizes for school children. By 1898 Pelly's staff comprised three curates, two lay readers, two women workers, and a parish nurse. During the First World War, Pelly's successor, Canon Guy Rogers, employed four women as curates for everything except the administration of the sacraments. This created a few 'whatever next' questions, and likely some 'soon there'll be women bishops' observations. Pelly Road in Plaistow was named after the Canon and his family in recognition for his contribution to the spiritual life of the area.

As much as anything else the occasion was a rite of passage for Hills. He had never been offered the honour turned down by Charles Mare, the yard's founder, and the completion of the *Albion* was his chance to break into the ranks of the aristocracy, the one privilege to evade his family. This was his moment, the zenith of a lifetime of work in industry and philanthropic activity. He had been a good servant to capitalism, working intelligently with his employees, making every effort to recruit them to the cause of company, capital, Britain and the Empire.

Following hurried consultation with the company's engineers it was decided to bring the launch time forward to 2.50 p.m. as the dogshores supporting the ship looked like they were giving way and a collapse seemed imminent. The royal guests and other dignitaries gathered under a canopy headstage, close to the bow of the great ship. The Duchess sent the champagne bottle hurtling toward the hull but it failed to shatter. Two more times she tried but still not a drop of alcohol touched the *Albion*. It was like she was as teetotal as her yard's owner. In exasperation the Duchess gave up and cut the cord, this was the signal to the workmen to release the dogshores. George Clement Macrow, the shipbuilding manager, had expected the *Albion* to move into the water at speed and it did, creating a massive surge of water. As she hit the water the *Albion* displaced a tidal wave that smashed the slipway into a thousand pieces. With no time to escape spectators on the crowded gantry alongside the *Shikisima* were thrown into the muddy, churning waters around the *Albion*, their screams of panic and cries for help drowned by the cheering of the thousands that saw the *Albion* descend into Bow Creek. At that point few people had any idea of the tragedy that had occurred. The Duke and Duchess certainly did not. From the royal grandstand at the bow of the vessel, nothing could be seen of the starboard side of the *Albion*, the site of the calamity. As soon as their task was completed the royal party quickly returned to the launch, completely oblivious to the desperate struggle that was taking place in water just 10ft deep and 5yd from shore.

Many of the thirty-eight people who died were trapped underneath timbers, concussed by floating baulks or other debris that had fallen into the water from the slipway. Others were trampled by groups of people desperately trying to reach safety. Almost immediately nearby spectators and shipyard workers did their best to rescue people in the water, diving into the creek to drag out survivors, or jumping into whatever small craft was at hand to do what they could, but it was more than ten minutes before the shipyard managers knew anything about the disaster. As soon as they did Thames Police in rowboats were dispatched to bring victims ashore where the Metropolitan Police and the Fire Brigade were doing their best for the injured and dying and to prevent further chaos.

At first nobody realised that people had died but the reality soon became horrifyingly clear. Sub-Divisional Inspector Dixon of the Thames Police was to tell the inquest, 'for a time officials thought everyone had been safely recovered … then one, and another, and another body came to the water's surface.'

An hour or so after the accident, workmen began to drag the river and the shipyard diver, Bill Hodgson, was lowered into the dark water to check for bodies trapped in the mud. The body count was twenty-four by 5.30 p.m. A mortuary was set up in an engineering department shed. The St Katherine's Homes nurses and Dr Humphries checked for signs of life. The nurses covered each cadaver with a sheet, washed the bodies and replaced wet and damage clothes with clean outfits that had been swiftly brought to the yard. The suits and dresses that the victims died in were left in a bundle at the feet of each corpse to aid identification by relatives. PC Lambert took descriptions of the victims before they were covered with canvas.

A more suitable mortuary was soon required. The shipyard workers quickly erected wooden benches in an old galvanising shed while electrician Fred Wilson installed lighting. By 7.00 p.m. the bodies were moved from the engineering shed. When the light was turned on in the makeshift mortuary, Wilson's eyes fell upon the lifeless form of his sister Matilda, who had recently married and just returned from her honeymoon. Not far from her, Fred found his dead mother.

When news of the tragedy spread, a crowd gathered outside the Ironworks but only relatives and friends of the deceased were allowed in. The search for victims went on as darkness fell over the dark waters of the Thames. By midnight twenty-nine victims had been identified by distressed relatives and three others awaited recognition.

The day after the accident, West Ham Council opened a fund to help survivors and the bereaved. The Canning Town area and most of those directly affected by the disaster were desperately poor. Some of those who had got away with little more than a drenching had seen what few good clothes they possessed ruined.

Hills was overcome with grief and in the days and weeks following the disaster he visited bereaved families and promised to meet funeral expenses that would have otherwise financially crippled many. He was to write, 'I went out to the homes of those who had lost dear ones and shared with them of the grief that filled our hearts. I found the sweetest solace for all. For I met with no shadow of bitterness – no tone of complaint.'

He went on to express his feelings of personal responsibility:

I represented the Company at whose doors the responsibility of this great accident lay; but none the less the mother weeping for her child, the husband heartbroken for the loss of his young wife, clasped my hand, and in broken accents told me how sorry they were that this terrible accident should have marred all the joyous festivities. I can make no fit recompense, but I pray to God that so long as He may spare me I may be enabled to do something for the well-being and happiness of Canning Town.

Within twenty-four hours Hills had purchased a large plot in East London Cemetery. He planned a grandiose memorial, involving a rolling wave and an angel, but the Disaster Fund Committee felt that the money that had been collected for the families of the victims should not be spent on stonework. The grave was marked by two engraved tablets, set apart from the surroundings by an anchor. It can still be found in the cemetery today, the last resting place of twenty-eight victims. Others were buried in individual graves in different parts of the cemetery or interned at other graveyards.

The *Albion* had been launched on the Tuesday, the dead were buried on the following Saturday, Monday and Tuesday. Scenes at the funerals were harrowing. Huge crowds lined the routes that the different funeral cortèges took. Mrs Eliza Tarbox, at 64 years of age, was the oldest person to lose her life in the catastrophe. She was the first to be buried. Mrs Isabel White, who was 30, was next to be interned. She was found in the water with her two small daughters still clutching at her skirts – both the little girls lost their lives.

The police received a deal of criticism for having insufficient officers on duty at the launch, although the inquest later heard that the number of police needed had been calculated by the management of the Ironworks. However, 15,000 officers attended the Saturday funeral. On the Monday 7,000 turned up, whilst the Tuesday service saw around 5,000 on duty. Clearly the authorities were more careful about the need to control and deter possible protest than they were in taking responsibility for the policing of community events.

The disaster was a huge news event at the time, which shocked the nation and the Empire. William McGonagall, reputedly the 'worst poet in the English language', penned an ode to 'The Albion Battleship Calamity'. It is a something of a rambling dirge, extending to what seems like a never ending series of stanzas, but the following lines might give you a taste of the 'quality' of the work:

> The launching of the vessel was very well carried out,
> While the guests on the stands cheered without any doubt,
> Under the impression that everything would go well;
> But, alas! instantaneously a bridge and staging fell.

A couple of short film clips of the *Albion* launch exist. One, by pioneer film-maker Robert William Paul (he designed and constructed Britain's first film studio in Muswell Hill, North London) recorded something of the festive character of the day but also the immediate aftermath of the disaster. After releasing the footage, probably the first disaster to be caught on film, Paul was hounded for a range of reasons.

HMS *Albion* went on to serve in operations against German South West Africa in 1914 and the Dardanelles campaign, supporting the landings at Gallipoli during the First World War. She was scrapped in 1920 but her name would forever be associated with the tragedy of her launch day.

There is no plaque or monument to those who lost their lives at the launch of the *Albion*. Surely this constitutes an awful oversight on the part of the local authority and the football club that arose out of the Ironworks. Arnold Hills was never to be the same man he was before the disaster. Perhaps this explains why he didn't put up more of a fight against the professionalisation of Thames Ironworks Football Club. Maybe the disaster had caused him to develop his perspective on life and see that sport was of relative insignificance in the scheme of things.

ONWARDS AND UPWARDS!

Whatever the case, the Thames committee were determined not to rest on their laurels. With the London League title not yet dry from the celebratory champagne, the committee secured a place in the Second Division of the Southern League, where the likes of Fulham and Watford, as well as their recent sparring partner Brentford, awaited them. They also entered the Thames and Medway combination for the 1898/99 season. Elevation to the Southern League meant that the club required an even more professional approach but the team was still struggling to attract big crowds. The Memorial Ground had always been difficult to get to and the Irons had continued to fail to appeal to any particular constituency or community that was capable of supplying the necessary core support for a professional club. All too often the committee had been forced to go cap in hand to Arnold Hills. A letter to the *Thames Iron Works Gazette* from the club secretary summed up the situation:

> I regret to say that from a financial point of view it has been a hard struggle. We are much indebted to the kindness of our President, who from time to time has assisted us in paying our debts, but it is very discouraging to us to feel that we have little or no support from the Works and that among the many admirers of football in Canning Town, so few attend our matches.

A lack of support, however, would not get in the way of the committee's ambition to reach the First Division of the Southern League at the first attempt. Although Walter Tranter remained as skipper, he was one of only three players (out of thirty) who were retained from the victorious London League campaign. Twenty-seven new players were engaged, many of them professionals. Although the administrative and financial connections with the Ironworks were maintained, this overt leap towards total professionalism as good as severed any remaining community links with the Ironworks.

The new players were attracted from far and wide, amongst them were four Scots and a Welshman, so the side were also losing their East End associations. There are no records of player wages but it would be naïve to think that they were attracted from professional clubs as far away as Middlesbrough, Aberystwyth and Inverness just to take in the sights, sounds and smells of Canning Town. Amongst the new recruits was David Lloyd who, at 6ft 4in and 13st came along with three others from 3rd Grenadier Guards. Lloyd was to bag twelve goals in fourteen games during his one season playing in the FA Cup and Southern League, making him Thames' top marksman in 1898/99.

As they marched into the professional ranks Thames relied on a very young team by modern standards. In that first season in the Southern League the average age of those that played in the first team was around 22. Nevertheless, the youthful Irons set about their task with no shortage of confidence.

10

THE BOYS FROM THE MEMORIAL GROUND: 1897/98

Just before the new season the Thames Ironworks Football Club committee took the bold step of insuring players against loss of earnings resulting from injuries, thus taking yet another crucial step towards full professionalism. However, club officials were still denying that they were totally committed to the professional road. It might have been that they were merely looking to keep the financial support of Arnold Hills flowing until the club was able to be self-sufficient, but it is more likely that they were taken by the course of events and history than any purposeful, focused ambition to totally depart from amateur values or Corinthian codes of conduct. Social events are much more probably the result of the former than the latter. While we don't have to be corks on a social sea, we can determine our courses via metaphorical rudders and sails, to think we can control the social oceans equates to the dream of a veritable Canute (which apocryphally turned out to be a wet one for the grandson of Harald Bluetooth).

Six new players were signed for the 1887/98 season, five of these were from the Greater London area, but none of them worked for the Ironworks. The single local player to break into the side was 'keeper George Furnell. Once associated with Old Castle Swifts, Furnell was to stay at the Memorial Ground for just the 1897/98 season but played in all three of Thames' FA Cup ties that season and was a regular in the London League side. He was transferred to Hammersmith Athletic. Other new names included Henry Hird from Stockton. Like many players of his time, the precise number of games he played and goals he scored is disputed. But he recorded at least twenty-two outings for Thames between April 1898 (some records claim 1897) and October 1899, scoring three times in the 1898/99 season (there are sources that say that he hit nine goals). George Neill who came in from West Norwood at the age of 22 and could play at wing-half or wing-back. He is credited with appearing twenty-six times for Thames claiming four goals. Like most other players at this time, George would have probably played more than records show as match statistics were not attended to at the end of the nineteenth century with the same precision as would be the case a few decades later. It is known that he first appeared in a Thames XI in the London League and played regularly from his recruitment in 1897 until the end of 1898.

The Irons sported a new kit when they kicked off their first competitive season at the Memorial Ground. The strip consisted of royal Cambridge blue shirts, white knickers (as the shin-length shorts were called in that era), red cap, belt and stockings. The *Thames Iron Works Gazette* commented that, when the new colours were worn on the field, 'the contrast supplied by the delightful green turf is very pleasing.' From time to time Thames would also play in an all-Harrovian blue strip (a sort of mid to dark blue).

Thames also gained some pleasing results. In September the Irons limited Millwall, a strong professional Southern League side then, to a 2–0 margin. Tommy Moore played in goal for the Lions in that game, and his esoteric skills were to serve Thames in the following two seasons. Moore guarded the Thames goal sixty-one times, coming in to the side as cover for Hughie G. Monteith on four occasions during West Ham United's first season in the Southern League. Moore was known as the 'Dancing Dervish', because of his unconventional methods in evading challenging forwards – games were pretty much 'open season' for the aggression of the opposition attack at the tail end of the 1800s. Moore was not without his critics, but he managed to attain a fair level of consistency during his time at the Memorial Ground, missing only two Southern League matches in that period. Tommy was to be exiled to the backwater of Grays early in 1901 and seemed destined to disappear from the limelight, but in the FA Cup of the following season he gave an inspired display of goalkeeping. He was largely responsible for the Essex village team's shock 2–1 second qualifying round win, on a foggy November afternoon at the Memorial Ground.

Hugh Monteith started his playing days with Wellington Thistle, Parkhead Juniors (Celtic's 'nursery' side) before signing for Celtic. Born in New Cumnock, East Ayrshire, Hughie joined Loughborough Town in 1895 for whom he played close to sixty games. He had a seventy-game spell with Bristol City (the side finished runners-up in the Southern League in the two successive seasons between 1897 and 1899 under his watch) before coming to East London, where he stood between the sticks on fifty-three occasions. The Irons conceded just twenty-eight goals in his first season with them, seven during Monteith's five-game absence. Hughie was with Bury for three years from 1902, turning out for the Shakers around eighty times. He was in the Bury side that won the FA Cup for the second time in three years. The 1903 victory at Crystal Palace was achieved without Bury conceding a single goal throughout the competition, including the record FA Cup Final win, 6–0 v. Derby County on 18 April. This is still the biggest victory in any FA Cup Final.

Hughie returned north of the border first to Kilmarnock (ten games) and then Beith, Greenock Morton and Dundee Hibs.

In the second game of the 1897/98 season Leyton were given a 4–0 beating at the Memorial, following which, football correspondent TAM wrote in the *Morning Leader*:

Nearly 2,000 spectators saw the match, which was commenced by the Ironworks in real earnest. Twenty-five minutes after the start the Ironworks, who so far had the best of matters, obtained their first point in the following manner: Hatton secured about 50yd from goal and after dodging and wriggling through the whole of the Leyton defence, tested Sterling with a stinger that was only partially cleared and Hatton, pouncing on the ball again, promptly rushed it through.

Three minutes later, Gresham scored a second, so enabling the Thames to cross over with a deserved lead of two goals. For the best part of the game it was Thames forwards v Leyton's defence and although beaten twice before the finish by Reid and Edwards, they were in no way disgraced.

Hatton was the most conspicuous of the Ironworks forwards, while Dove, Neill, Dandridge and Chisholm all played well in defence with goalkeeper Furnell having a very easy task. (Wednesday 6 October 1897)

By November the East Londoners topped the London League having won their first six games.

The first FA Cup tie played at the Memorial Ground was a preliminary round match that brought a 3–0 victory over Redhill. Simon (Peter) Chisholm from Inverness got two of his total of three goals for the club that day. Chisholm was to be with Thames until the spring of 1899, recording twenty-two appearances.

After beating Royal Engineers Thames Battalion in the second qualifying round the Irons were eliminated 2–0 at Southern League St Albans. It was the third season in succession where it took a Southern League club to better Thames in the competition.

A 1–3 defeat at the Memorial in a local derby against Ilford in the third round of the London Senior Cup was the last real low point of the season. Thames had scored seven in two games against Ilford and had been expected to go through. It was a shock result, causing fear in some quarters that this might be the start of a Thames decline.

James Reid, an inside-forward from Reading and formerly with Petershill and Hibernian, was one of the Irons' XI that started the game. He was born in1879 in Bellshill, North Lanarkshire. Jimmy was to record nineteen appearances for Thames between 1897 and 1900, notching up twelve goals. He played in West Ham United's first season taking the field nineteen times for the Hammers, getting on the scoresheet five times in that initial Southern League Division One term. He went on to play for Fulham before joining Gainsborough Trinity in 1901. After more than thirty games and eight goals Jimmy moved on to Worksop Town and between 1903 and 1904 turned out sixteen times for Notts County (claiming a couple of goals). His playing career continued with Watford, Spurs, Reading and New Brompton before he finished his playing days by returning to Worksop.

Thames switched their focus to the London League. The Irons faced high flying Brentford at Shotters Field in their penultimate game of this competition. It was a crucial encounter between the two main contenders for the Championship. Just before the match the *East Ham Echo* published a feature entitled 'Football Sketches – 1 Charlie Dove (Thames Ironworks)'. The anonymous author wrote:

If not absolutely the finest right half back in Essex, the subject of our sketch is undoubtedly one of the most brilliant men in the country in that position.

Born just over 19 years ago, Charles Dove first began his football career with Park School – a team that has always been classed as one of the finest schoolboy combinations. There he figured at full back and just by way of encouragement won two medals when playing in this position.

Leaving school life he migrated to Forest Swift Juniors as a centre forward and subsequently captained Plaistow Melville.

He also figured in the lines of Upton Park and South West Ham and three seasons ago joined the ranks of Thames Ironworks and has played with them ever since.

Even when joining his true position was not apparent. He played centre forward and full back and it was not until he had occupied nearly every place – with the exception of goal – that his worth as a right half was demonstrated.

In this berth he plays a brilliant game, full of resource and the Thames Limited combination sadly missed him in their opening matches. However, he is expected to be fit and able to turn out on Saturday against Brentford, when he will considerably strengthen the team.

Charles Dove was one of only two Thames players from the side's early days at Hermit Road who had retained their places in the first team. He had joined Thames at the age of 16 in 1895, having served as an apprentice at the shipyard. Standing near 6ft in height and tipping the scales at 12st, Charlie was popular with the supporters, representing home grown, local talent. In a winning game against Maidenhead on the final day of 1898 he played in goal and kept Irons in the Southern League Division Two championship. Dove was transferred to Irons' great rivals of the Edwardian era, Millwall, in September 1901, but a knee injury in the 1902/3 season ended his first-class career. He was to record forty-one matches for the Irons and scored three goals in the 1898/99 term. Dove played sixteen games in claret and blue.

The other long term Iron was inside-forward George Gresham (also known as 'Jim'). Born in Liverpool in 1875, he started out playing for Lincoln City. After a spell with Doncaster Rovers, returned to the ranks of the Imps in 1892, playing twenty-two games and scoring five goals, before moving to Rossendale. He was back with Lincoln by 1894 before moving to another Lincolnshire club Gainsborough Trinity. Just 23 years of age at the end of the 1897/98 season, George was the first of many players to join Thames (and West Ham during their first half-century) from Gainsborough Trinity, turning out fifteen times in the Irons' first season. He scored twice against Woolwich Arsenal in the 'floodlight friendly' of 3 March 1896 and is another player to figure in the three FA Cup ties of 1897/8. In the 1898/99 Southern League Division Two campaign George battled through eighteen matches in Thames colours, notching up five goals in the process.

When Thames were beaten 1–0 by Brentford it was their first defeat of the season. So, everything depended on the final games of the season. Thames faced the 2nd Grenadier Guards, whilst Brentford lined up against Barking Woodville. If the Bees won their match against the Essex boys the championship would go to West London no matter what the Irons did, but Thames had to make sure they defeated the Pongos. The Irons won well, sending the soldiers back to their billets and barracks on the end of a 3–1 thrashing. News didn't travel too fast at the latter end of the nineteenth century but it wasn't too long after the game that Thames found out that Barking and Woodville had done their Essex neighbours a good turn and beaten Brentford. The Irons were, by a single point, champions, pushing Brentford into the runners-up spot. Thames had only surrendered five points out of a possible thirty-two in sixteen games, averaging just under three goals per game.

Thames had achieved some excellent performances during their highly successful London League campaign. Bromley had been beaten 7–3 and 5–1, ample revenge for the previous season's London Cup defeat and the boys from the Memorial Ground had also 'done the double' over the 3rd Grenadier Guards, thus reversing the previous season's fortunes against them.

The club captain of the title-winning side was Teesider Walter Tranter. He had a reputation for rushing in 'where others fear to tread'. Wally was left-back in the Thames team that won the London League Championship in 1897/98, losing only one match in the process. Amid the celebrations at the League's presentation concert to honour the triumph, Wally, 'by mistake' carried off the Dewar Shield, another major trophy but not rightfully the property of the Irons or Wally. The Middlesbrough-born defender was to lead Thames twenty-five times in their championship-winning Southern League Second Division campaign the following season, but surprisingly joined Chatham at the start of the 1899/1900 term. He returned to the Memorial Ground for the 1900/01 campaign, wearing the Hammers over his heart on six occasions. Tranter later went on to play in Northern Ireland for a Belfast club. Wally was to gain representative honours, playing for the London League against the London Football Association alongside teammate George Neil in December 1897 at Kilburn. Jimmy Reid was also selected as a reserve for that game. These appear to be the first Thames players to receive any kind of representative recognition.

In April 1898 Thames rounded off a glorious season with a friendly against Woolwich Arsenal, who were then highly placed in the Football League Second Division. There has never really been such a thing as a 'friendly' between these London clubs and this was confirmed when Arsenal took the field with nine of their regular League side plus two new signings. Following a hard fought eighty minutes of play, Thames found themselves leading their illustrious opponents 2–1. In desperation, the Gunners, almost recklessly, threw everything at the Irons defence and, as would so often be the case in the future with 'lucky Arsenal', they saved their blushes with a last-ditch effort.

11

PROFESSIONALISM AND THE SOUTHERN LEAGUE: 1898/99

When the Irons took to the field at Sheerness for the first game of the season on 1 September 1898 in the Thames and Medway Combination, Sheppey United faced a fully professional team. Arthur Marjeram, the 22-year-old former Aston Villa amateur who had joined the Irons from Swanscombe, played at left-back that day. However, the Irons lost their first five games in that competition. A hitch in the fixtures saw Thames playing just one home game in the first six of the season, and this was a friendly, against 1st Coldstream Guards.

Marjeram kept his place for the inaugural Southern League Division Two fixture against Shepherds Bush nine days later. The Irons hit the Bush Babies with three goals without reply on their own turf. Frank Bret, another lad from Swanscombe, was to make his only Southern League appearance for Thames that historic day. It was his 21st birthday.

The game also marked the debut of Roderick MacEachrane in a Thames shirt. Roddy was one of a number of players who Tom Robinson, the Thames trainer, would invite to breakfast with him at his home in Benledi Street, Poplar, a sort of a forerunner of the West Ham Cassettari Café academy of the 1950s. MacEachrane was one of the club's first professionals and the first player to reach an Irons/Hammers combined appearance tally of 100 games between 1898 and the end of the 1901/02 term. In all, he played sixty-three games in Thames colours and sixty in claret and blue. A creative half-back, MacEachrane scored four goals for Thames and five for West Ham. Coming to the capital at the age of 20, the witty Scot was one of a select band who could lay claim to working in the East London shipyard (Orchard Yard, Blackwall).

Roddy started his footballing career with his local side Inverness Thistle. He stood barely 5½ft tall, but could tackle like a tractor and his consistency made him a favourite at the Memorial Ground. He was ever present in 1898/99 and 1899/1900 seasons, marking the transition to West Ham United with a further 100 per cent appearance record in 1900/01. Another fine season in 1901/02, in which he missed only five Southern League outings, caused Woolwich Arsenal to come in for him. At Plumstead, MacEachrane impressed even more than at West Ham and was soon joined by other ex-Hammers, James Bigden and Charlie Satterthwaite.

Rod played an important role in the Gunners' promotion from the Second Division in 1903/04 but major honours eluded him. Whilst he was with them, the South Londoners fell at the semi-final stage of the FA Cup in 1906 and 1907. Roddy made his last appearance for Arsenal during their 1913/14 schedule, just after the club's move to Highbury and the dropping of the Woolwich prefix, setting a then record number of appearances for the club. His place in the team went to another Scot, Angus McKinnon, who, according to an extract from an Arsenal club history by Bernard Joy, 'was bigger and more robust but lacking McEachrane's constructive ability.'

Roderick passed away in 1952.

The Irons first home debut in the Southern League was a victorious one. Brentford were slaughtered 3–1 on 24 September – Sam Hay got a couple, his first and last for Thames. Charlie Dove also got his name on the scoresheet. Hay, from Renfrewshire, Scotland, had joined Thames from Victoria. He was a strongly built inside-right. He had been a regular in the Irons side during their first season at Hermit Road, but he was to get just seven outings in 1898/99.

On 6 October Chatham were the first visitors in the Thames and Medway Combination. Both this competition and the Southern League expected their member clubs to field their best elevens, but the better class of club in the Combination made that the most prestigious target for the Irons.

Back in the Southern League, following a 2–1 defeat at Uxbridge in the next game, the Irons travelled to Wycombe on 29 October and were given a 4–1 hiding in a continuous downpour. The Buckinghamshire side had lost their previous five matches. Thames arrived at Loakes Park an hour late after missing their train. Jim Aldridge put the Blues two up in the first quarter of an hour and got his hat-trick on the stroke of half-time. Wycombe made it 4–0 before inside-forward Jimmy Reid pulled one back for the visitors as evening was falling in the eighty-eighth minute. It was to be the Irons last defeat of the season. The next time the two teams met, at the Memorial Ground on 14 January 1899 when the scoreline was reversed, Thames were well on their way to the championship. This time Wycombe had trouble with transport. Their keeper Ernie Wheeler missed his connection and arrived at the tail end of the match. The Bucks boys kicked off with just ten players, full-back Henry Turner took up the role between the posts. His career betwixt the sticks didn't get off to the best of starts – one of his own defenders headed the Irons in front. A fan, who was apparently a bit of a regular when Wycombe were short handed, was conscripted to defend the visitors' goal. However, this was not going to be a dream come true for him either, as became obvious when he was well beaten by a low shot from Thames centre-half McEwan. David Lloyd spurned two opportunities before grabbing a brace to send the Irons in at the break 4–0 up. Lloyd almost got his hat-trick but sent a penalty wide. Fred Keen scored Wycombe's only goal from the spot.

In between the two matches with Wycombe, Charlie Dove played in every position for Thames.

In the FA Cup, the Royal Engineers Training Battalion had waived home advantage and the Memorial Ground presented a double bill that afternoon by staging the tie and an athletics meeting against the Sappers. The Irons met the Royal Engineers three times in 1898/9 and won every game. In the FA Cup, Thames got through with goals from Gresham and MacEachrane. A crowd of 2,000 people saw them hold Brighton United to a goalless draw in the next round. Many of these were Irons supporters who had paid the 4s 2d fare to travel from Plaistow to the seaside town. Brighton, from the Southern League's First Division, found Moore, Dove and Tranter outstanding for Thames, but in the Memorial Ground replay the Irons were outclassed and lost 1–4. This was the last game Alf Hitch was to run out for Thames. Playing in a number 5 shirt he was a particularly fine header of the ball. He was to have just five chances with Thames, but continued to develop his talents to the extent that he took part in an England trial match two years later, having played for Grays United, Queens Park Rangers, Nottingham Forest (two goals in thirteen outings) before returning to QPR and finishing his playing days with Watford. Alf, who was from Walsall started his football career with Walsall Unity and joined Thames from Wellington Town. He died in 1962, aged 84.

By the start of 1899 Thames were out of the FA Cup and had registered only three wins in nine Combination outings. However, in the Southern League Division Two they had a 77 per cent success rate. As such, Thames readjusted their sights and priorities and, in a spirit of determination, strengthened the squad starting with the signing of full-back Thomas Dunn from Chatham as the year was turning. Dunn was born in Falkirk in 1872. He had played for the Wolves 1896 FA Cup Final side that were defeated 2–1 by The Wednesday at Crystal Palace and made seven appearances for Burnley in the 1896/7 season. He was to appear thirteen times for Thames in the last part of their South League Second Division crusade, his first sortie being a 4–0 win at Maidenhead on the final day of 1898. At home, in either of the full-back berths, Tom was a consistent feature in Thames' Southern League and Cup campaigns of 1898/9. He returned to the side for the opening match of the following season in a 1–0 defeat at Reading. He donned the number 2 shirt twenty-nine times that term, missing just seven games. Tom left the club before the decision was made for the Ironworks to transform into West Ham United and fully embrace professionalism.

In February 1899 the Warmley club of Bristol folded and Francis Payne, the Ironworks Secretary, secured the services of three of their leading players. This group included Henderson, who scored eight goals for Thames in the last ten games of the 1898/99 season, Peter McManus and George Reid. McManus, a 26 year old from Edinburgh, was serving a two-week suspension when he signed for the Irons. He had won a Scottish Cup winner's medal with Edinburgh St Bernard's in 1895, when they defeated the formidable Renton team at Ibrox Park. He broke into the Thames side in mid-March 1899, playing in six games over the following half-a-dozen weeks. He was back in the side for the opening game of the 1899/1900 season, but following nine outings up to December 1899, scoring his first and last goal for Thames in the first qualifying round of the FA Cup against Grays United, he was not to figure in the side again. Pete was short for a centre-half, standing just 5ft 7in in height. Previously with West Bromich Albion, the stocky defender was said to 'play a cautious and waiting game'.

George (Geordie) Reid had formally been with Reading. Geordie was not related to Jimmy Reid, but they played in the same eleven for the Berkshire club and they took to the field for the Irons together in the first five games that George played for Thames.

He was most at home at inside-left, but he did play one of his six games for the Irons at centre-forward. He scored just one goal in the Southern League, breaching the Southall defence on 25 March 1899. Geordie went on to play for Middlesbrough in the early 1900s and was in Scotland for the 1906/07 term with Johnstone (Renfrewshire). However he returned south to ply his skills with Bradford Park Avenue the following season.

After Tom Dunn took up his place in the Thames defence they dropped not a single point and took the Southern League Second Division Championship, their second title in consecutive seasons. They won the final eleven matches in that competition, which culminated in a splendid 10–0 win over bottom club, Maidenhead United. Their Combination results also took an upturn and only one defeat in their last seven games enabled the Irons to gain a respectable position in that competition. All together Thames went through a run of seventeen successive wins.

For all this, the secretary still had an unhappy response to the *Gazette* at the end of the season:

> The only thing needed to make this a success is more support from the men inside the Works. Up to the present we have received very little indeed and can only regret that so many followers of the game prefer to patronise other clubs to the disadvantage of their own. I hope, that next season will see a different state of things.

However, as outlined above, by this time the club was not the Ironworkers 'own', but this, together with the club's lack of an identifiable fan base in the community, does not fully explain why the Irons failed attract the support their performances and success might be thought to warrant.

SPECTATORISM

Although he had built the Memorial Ground at such great expense, Arnold Hills was, along with others of his class and background, a vociferous opponent of what was then known as 'spectatorism'. The case against the same was put most strongly by the London Playing Fields' Committee, an influential group by the turn of the twentieth century, consisting mostly of ex-public schoolboys committed to extending facilities for playing football and cricket in the Metropolitan area:

> The English love of sport, perverted by want of opportunity for active exercise, produces the gambler and the loafer. Men who, under better conditions, might have developed into active and healthy English people, degenerate into mere spectators at athletic contests, which might almost be compared to gladiatorial shows held by professional giants for the idle amusement of a puny crowd.
> ('The First Report of the London Playing Fields Committee – April 1891'. Also cited in Mason (1980) *Association Football and English Society 1863–1915*.)

Canon Barnett was the founder of Toynbee Hall, the university settlement in Whitechapel. This institution's youth workers encouraged football in the many clubs founded by the settlement in East London in the late nineteenth century. Canon Barnett saw the positive aspects of games founded in forms of rational recreation, but objected to a man, 'exciting himself over a match or race where he does not even understand the skill ... ' (Barnett and Barnett 1915, p. 78).

His wife, who agreed with him on most issues, disapproved of 'the football matches, which thousands watch, often ignorant of the science of the game, but captivated by the hope of winning a bet or by the spectacle of brutal conflict ... ' (ibid. p. 91).

It was Upton Park FC that has set the trend for 'spectatorism' in the East London area. Young boys from the large working-class population that built up around the club from the 1870s onwards had an opportunity of seeing the top players of the day in action in their local park where Upton Park played. With no more than a chalk-mark around the perimeter of the pitch, even major FA Cup matches could be viewed free of charge. This probably motivated many boys to take up the game and almost certainly the spectacle and entertainment these contests offered would have cultivated a taste for watching matches amongst the large numbers of youths and adults attracted to these contests.

However, 'old boy' clubs, like Upton Park, made up of former pupils of public schools, had an ambiguous attitude towards those who came to watch matches. In line with university settlement and the public-school mission attitudes, they saw the potential of football as a contribution to improving working-class life and the character development of young men. For the privileged classes this potential for the 'betterment of the lower orders' lay in playing the game rather than watching it. For all this there were contradictions. Upton Park did not turn away the crowds that came to West Ham Park to cheer them on in their notable FA Cup campaigns. Mason has noted that even though the club successfully objected to Preston's professionalism, following their drawn FA Cup game in 1884, the Upton Park club did not decline to take and keep their share of the proceeds of the gate money paid by the large crowd who had come to watch the match (Mason 1980, p. 80). However, it was perhaps a reassessment of this liberalism and realignment with their Corinthian attitude that led to the final demise of Upton Park FC.

Following problems with spectators encroaching on to the pitch early in the 1884/5 season, it was reported in the local press that the club's committee was, 'considering whether it will not be advisable to play as many matches as possible on other grounds than their own ... ' (Stratford Express, 25 October 1884).

Rather than take such an extreme step, a local supporter wrote to the Stratford Express the following week suggesting that the club should have the ground roped-off for important matches, as was done elsewhere. However, in the end Upton Park decided to play its home matches on an enclosed ground not too far away at Wanstead. The club lasted just three more years and was disbanded in 1887.

In line with the prevailing elitist attitudes of his class peers, Hills created the Thames Ironworks Football Club in order that his men could play football rather than watch it. At the same time football culture in the East End of London and the west of Essex was not really associated with Canning Town in terms of site. The hotbed of the game in the district was the Forest Gate, Upton Park and East Ham areas. This is where the game was first played in the East End vicinity in an organised manner, and where it was developed in the mid-nineteenth century by former public school boys, of the type that played for Upton Park FC, who turned out in what is now West Ham Park. Clubs of this type were to give way to teams made up of local artisans and middle-class players, sides like Barking, Dreadnought, Ivanhoe and Romford. This was followed by the more professional model of the ambitious Clapton FC who in 1887 moved into the Old Spotted Dog Ground in Upton Lane, situated a few 100yd from Upton Park FC's abandoned pitch. From their first game in September of that year, Clapton began to attract large crowds. Fixtures against the top London amateur teams drew gates of more than 2,000. Contests with professional clubs, like the 1888 encounter with Nottingham Forest, could attract more than 4,000 spectators. Clapton introduced season tickets in 1890 at the cost of 4s. This gave admission to the club's twenty-four home matches and was accompanied by the promotional information about friendlies against professional clubs like Nottingham Forest, West Bromwich Albion and Notts County at the Spotted Dog.

It is clear that a culture of paying to watch good quality football had been firmly established in the area by 1890, something that was to continue with Clapton as it established itself as one of the leading amateur clubs in the country over the following twenty years. Thames, and later West Ham, failed to attract significant crowds to the Memorial Ground because there had been no tradition of spectatorism in that area. From 1904 the Hammers succeeded in attracting larger numbers when they moved to East Ham, taking advantage of the tradition of watching top class football that had been established around that district by Upton Park and carried on by Clapton. Upton Park FC could thus be seen, albeit unwittingly, as having laid the foundations for an appreciation of the quality of football that people would, literally, pay to watch.

From the modern perspective it is hard for us to appreciate that in football, spectators preceded fans and supporters. In the late nineteenth century football was essentially an athletic event – in its professional, working-class incarnation it was close in spirit to the Powder Hall sprint competitions in Scotland and the local athletic events familiar to northern working-class towns and villages. Watching a game was not an end in itself as is the case today. If you were working class you went to a dog or cock fight, a boxing match, a cycling, running, horse or dog race or a football match to take in a spectacle (to 'spectate'). However, this would be enhanced by the opportunity to speculate on the outcome of any competition by way of a wager (a monetary 'speculation', the Latin 'specere' means 'to look'). As Mason, citing the statement made in 'The First Report of the London Playing Fields Committee – April 1891', in *Association Football and English Society 1863–1915* pointed out (see above).

So it can be understood that it was not by accident that the Irons found a temporary home in East Ham and that West Ham United eventually moved from Canning Town to the Boleyn Ground. The club moved to an area attuned to spectatorism and away from the moral imperatives of Arnold Hills, who was against watching football (eating meat, imbibing alcohol, smoking and much more besides) on principle and was appalled by gambling. This ethos that West Ham United moved into is exemplified in the design of the first Boleyn Ground, in particular the character of the old 'chicken run'. The design of the structure was reminiscent of something you might associate with a circus and a racecourse. Indeed, early greyhound and whippet tracks often included such enclosures. Like all buildings, the chicken run told its own story.

The ancestor of the original working-class motivation to watch sport is still with us, the Football Pools, which now has its own history. But what the bookmaker offers us in terms of 'football odds' at the ground or in the High Street might be seen as the living root of working-class spectatorism. The modern-day fan is closer to the 'house boy' at public schools, who cheered on this team, loyal to the last, in the 'play up boys' tradition that was carried on to latter-day university life. As Sir Henry Newbolt had in 1892, in his 'Vitai Lampada' (Relay the Torch):

> This is the word that year by year
> While in her place the School is set
> Every one of her sons must hear,
> And none that hears it dare forget.
> This they all with a joyful mind
> Bear through life like a torch in flame,
> And falling fling to the host behind -
> "Play up! play up! and play the game!"

This sentiment got carried into the carnage of the First World War, a point when most involved got to see it for the utter nonsense this kind of sentiment promulgated, as Wilfred Own was to illustrate in his poem, 'Dulce et Decorum est':

> Behind the wagon that we flung him in,
> And watch the white eyes writhing in his face,
> His hanging face, like a devil's sick of sin;
> If you could hear, at every jolt, the blood
> Come gargling from the froth-corrupted lungs,
> Obscene as cancer, bitter as the cud
> Of vile, incurable sores on innocent tongues,
> My friend, you would not tell with such high zest
> To children ardent for some desperate glory,
> The old Lie; Dulce et Decorum est
> Pro patria mori.

The same old lie – 'it is sweet and right to die for your country'.

Thames failed to attract crowds because the club existed in a geographical and moral environment that didn't support the culture of spectatorism that included gambling. If it was just success that was needed to attract supporters then the Memorial Ground would have been well attended for much of the time. The fact that this superb stadium was never full to half of its capacity demonstrates the public-school ethic that Hills wanted to inspire, the wish/desire to support the side, to create a sense of loyalty to a name and ideals associated with that name, had not kicked in. However, interestingly, contemporaneously that ethic is fully developed in the form of fan loyalty. What we see today as supportership, something steeped in working-class mythology, actually has its roots in the ambitions that a ruling/privileged elite had for those they wished to control or exploit.

As I write, I just took a telephone call from my 81-year-old mum. She has just returned from the twelve minute or so walk from Upton Park to my family home. She had bought West Ham shirts and shorts for two of her great-grandchildren as Christmas presents. This woman, living off a widow's pension, whose father fought throughout the First World War and stood as a fire-fighter in the face of Nazi bombing of his family's East London dockland home, whose brother was a Japanese prisoner of war in South East Asia, who lived as an evacuee throughout the Second World War, who worked incredibly hard all her life, was obliged to pay £180 for the gifts. It is doubtful if those garments cost more than a few pounds to make somewhere in the non-industrialised world. This, as such is double-bladed exploitation. History is important if we are even going to come close to understanding what is happening right now.

CHAMPION IRONS

A measure of the Irons superiority in the Southern League Second Division is indicated in a report of a match in April that noted, 'Moore [the goalkeeper] had so little to do that he often left his goal unprotected and played up with the forwards.'

The Irons completed their fixtures nine points ahead of their nearest rivals, winning nineteen, drawing one and losing just two of their matches. However, Thames still had to take part in a play-off to decide the title. A little publicised six-club section of the Southern League, representing the south-west, had produced equally decisive champions. Cowes, from the Isle of Wight, had won all of their ten games but they could hardly have been pleased when the neutral venue for the play-off turned out to be at Millwall's East Ferry Road ground – 100 miles from the Solent and 3 from Canning Town. The crowd was nearly all Cockney and were well pleased when Lloyd put the Irons ahead. Cowes, who had scored fifty-eight goals in their ten League games, pulled one back, but second-half efforts from Henderson and Patrick Leonard gave Thames the victory.

Winger Leonard joined the Irons in 1898. The former Manchester City man scored an impressive eight goals in twelve appearances for Thames, but he caused a sensation when he banged home a hat-trick on his first game for the Irons in a friendly against Upton Park. He also scored twice on his second Southern League game, a 4–3 win at Wolverton, which was one of a run of sixteen consecutive victories for the Irons in the Southern League Second Division. Pat hit four in the 10–0 win over Maidenhead in the last match of the season at the Memorial Ground and also scored in the 3–1 championship decider with Cowes. By the following season he had returned to Manchester City after only five months in Canning Town.

In the end the play-off was rendered meaningless. Winners and losers qualified for the Test Matches. Ironworks were sent to take on Sheppey, who finished twelfth out of thirteen clubs in the First Division of the Southern League. The first match, staged at Chatham, ended in a 1–1 draw, Lloyd scored for the Irons. This was to be the final game that the interesting J. Reynolds was to play for Thames. He was a right-winger signed from Gravesend early in the season. Reynolds had scored five goals for the Irons in his previous thirteen appearances for the club. The tricky flanker, who started his career with Leicester Fosse, was somewhat ahead of his time, being able to fire in 'screw-shots' and bend dead balls, much to the confusion of opposing keepers. He was never on the losing side whilst with Thames, being in the winning team in all but this, his last game for the Irons.

Before a replay with Sheppey could take place it was decided to expand the top division and both teams were admitted, along with Queens Park Rangers and Bristol Rovers from outside the League.

It had been another season of glory for Thames. The heady heights of the Southern League now awaited them, but they still had problems. The biggest crowd they played in front of during the season was the 4,000 that saw the 0–2 away win at Southall. There were two 3,000 gates at the Memorial Ground for the games against Southall and Maidenhead. However, the average Irons home crowd was little more than 1,700. Although the top flight of the Southern League was 'big time' football in the final years of the nineteenth century, this paltry support could not sustain development to the next level, which was the Football League. Something had to be done, the question was, 'What?'

12

THE END OF THE BEGINNING: 1899/1900

All seemed to be well for the Irons as they looked to reconcile their place in the professional sphere. According to the club secretary, speaking to the *Thames Iron Works Gazette*, 'nothing succeeds like success'.

However, nothing fails like failure and beneath the surface, arguments about professionalism continued to simmer. It seemed that the president still had views on this issue. In June 1899, Arnold Hills disapprovingly told the *Gazette* in his article entitled 'Our Clubs':

> But in the development of our Clubs, I find another tendency at work which seems to be exceeding dangerous. The Committees of several of our Clubs, eager for immediate success, are inclined to reinforce their ranks with mercenaries. In our bands and in our football clubs, I find an increasing number of professionals who do not belong to our community but are paid to represent us in their several capacities.

That's the trouble with communities – they define who is 'of' them and who is not, and as such are places of discrimination. At the same time the tighter the boundaries of any given community the less information about the outside world gets in, and information about what is happening in the community is censored and/or restricted. This makes them inherently prejudicial and a sort of factory of conformation bias – 'we' good, 'they' bad – hence the solving of most problems involves getting rid of 'them'. Here one can see Arnold's class culture being premised on what George Orwell was to call 'smelly little orthodoxies'; a 'Little England' perspective, intrinsically suspicious of 'outsiders' that produces little more than paranoiac desperation.

In a way, the committee running the football club could have seen these comments as complimentary. They were looking to build a competitive football club in order to attract supporters. In his article Hills was implying that the club should represent the community of the Ironworks and look to find its players and supporters there. However, if he really believed that, why had he provided a ground that could hold as many as 120,000 people and sponsor the club in the recruitment of players that would enable Thames to participate at a level that made professionalism inevitable?

Echoing and, to some extent, repeating the disgruntled sentiments of his class contemporaries in 'The First Report of the London Playing Fields Committee – April 1891' (see above), Hills went on:

> Like the ancient Romans, in their period of decadence, we seem to be willing to be artists and sportsmen by proxy; we hire a team of gladiators and bid them fight our football battles … Now this is a very simple and effective method of producing popular triumphs. It is only a matter of how much we are willing to pay and the weight of our purses can be made the measure of our glory. I have, however, not the smallest intention of entering upon a competition of this kind: I desire that our Clubs should be spontaneous and cultivated expressions of our own internal activity; we ought to produce artists and athletes as abundantly and certainly as a carefully tended fruit tree produces fruit.

But in actuality, Hills was an early Abramovich. At the same time, it is puzzling where the club might have gone other than the direction it took, if it was to flourish. For the committee the 'fruit' was the produce of its team. The club had to choose between being a recreational facility for the Ironworks or becoming a vibrant, professional football club for the East End and, despite these protestations, it was Hills' money that provided the committee with the necessary capital to invest in new players. Among the new signings was full-back E.S. (Syd) King, who, during his long tenure with Thames and West Ham, was perhaps the apotheosis of the transition from amateurism to full professional attitudes and organisation.

SYD KING – FULL-BACK AND APOTHEOSIS

King was born in August 1873 in Chatham, Kent. After his education in Watford he went to work in an ordnance depot in his home town. King started his football career as a full-back with Northfleet, where he claimed to have conceded a hat-trick of own goals in a match against Charlie Paynter's home town club, Swindon. Paynter was to have a long association with both West Ham and King himself.

Syd was transferred to New Brompton (the club that would become Gillingham FC) in 1897 and spent two seasons in Kent before joining Thames in the summer of 1899, along with team-mate Alec Gentle. At the time King was thought to be the best full-back in the Southern League and almost as soon as he signed, Derby made a bid for him.

A bad ankle injury sustained in the encounter with Spurs at the Memorial Ground on 10 March 1899 ruled him out for the rest of the season, but King did recover and went on to play for West Ham in 1901. Although he was still formidable as part of a full-back paring with Charlie Craig and played a total eighty-nine games for Thames and West Ham between 1899 and 1903, King was never quite the same player again.

Syd was appointed secretary of the club in 1902, while still playing. His final Southern League appearance was in a 1–1 draw with Kettering on 15 April 1903, although he did continue to play after this, on occasion in the London and Western Leagues.

It is fascinating to speculate on the possible future for football in East London had those overtures from Derby in the first days of King's career with Thames been successful. Anything that King achieved in his playing career was destined to be eclipsed by his success as the first manager of West Ham United. King oversaw the move to the Boleyn Ground in 1904, the transition to full professionalism and Football League membership in 1919. Through his understanding of the power of the press and skilful manipulation of the media over years, almost single-handedly, he introduced West Ham to League Football. With the assistance of Charlie Paynter, who would follow him as manager of West Ham, Syd improved the performance of his side throughout the Hammers first three League seasons and then in one eventful term, 1922/23, took West Ham to their first FA Cup Final (and also the first to be held at Wembley) and broke into the First Division of the Football League.

King kept West Ham in the top flight for nine seasons, finishing in sixth place in 1928/27. This feat was not to be equalled for twenty-two years and not bettered until John Lyall led the team that included Bonds, Brooking and Lampard to fifth place at the end of the 1978/79 season. As such, it is arguable if Syd King was not the greatest manager ever to reign at Upton Park. Whatever your opinion, Syd, to this day, casts a giant shadow over the Boleyn Ground.

King saw several of the players he worked with develop to international level, but West Ham were relegated at the end of the 1931/32 term. He had let his side grow old. This was evidenced by looking at the West Ham team beaten at Chelsea in the last First Division game of 1931/32 which included three members of the Wembley side. Although his position was not under threat, during a board meeting that took place on 7 November 1932, when team matters were being discussed, King, in a drunken rant insulted at least one director. At an emergency board meeting it was decided that, 'Mr King would be suspended for three calendar months from November 9 1932 without salary and further stipulate that he shall not visit the ground during this period.'

After this suspension, if the directors could be satisfied that his behaviour had improved, it was recorded that he might be reinstated as secretary only and that his salary would be reduced to £8 per week. Yet another meeting of the directors on the 3 January 1933 decided that King should not be employed in any capacity. The board had also expressed concern about King's honesty in the day-to-day business of running the club. This marked the end for King at West Ham. His ostracism and humiliation was complete.

The new secretary, Alan Searles (himself sacked for defalcation in 1940) advised King of the decision and informed him of the board's offer of an ex-gratia payment of £3 per week, 'as long as the company sees fit'. But less than a month later, the most successful manager in the history of West Ham United and Thames Ironworks to that point was dead. He imbibed an alcoholic drink laced with corrosive liquid. An inquest jury recorded a verdict that King had taken his own life whilst of unsound mind, after his son had told them that the Hammers' former manager-secretary had been suffering from paranoia. He was, however, quite satisfied with West Ham's offer of a £3 per week pension. A decade earlier, the East Ham Echo had stated in its FA Cup Final issue, 'West Ham is Syd King'. In many ways this is still true. Syd King laid the foundations of what we see now as West Ham United Football Club.

King was the antithesis of Hills. Syd was everything Arnold was not and vice versa. One can only conclude that the sanctimonious Old Etonian would have been horror-struck by the little braggart from Kent who swore like 'how's yer father', liked a drink or several, a bet and a big cigar. He was a sort of template professional in terms of future football. He persistently wore a straw boater and spats. In another time he would be unkindly called a 'spiv', who went out in a messy blaze of controversy. King's swagger was 'the finger' to the pious pomposity of Hills. One was 'Jerusalem' never ceasing from mental fight and the other was 'I've got a lovely bunch of coconuts' 'singing roll a bowl a ball a penny a pitch'.

'POACHING' CHARLIE BUNYAN

Francis Payne was still not satisfied with the Irons' playing strength. This was to prove to be his downfall. Payne procured the services of an agent, Charlie Bunyan, to seek out well-known players with a view of bringing them to the Memorial Ground.

Robinson's breakfast club included Robert Allan who made his debut in a 3–1 away defeat at Southampton on 16 December 1899. Allan was one of those who bridged the gap between the works team and the independent club, going on to appear for West Ham United up to the 1901/02 season. With his single goals for both the Irons and the Hammers, Allan became one of the relatively few players to score for both progenitor and successor clubs. In common with his teammate and fellow Scot, Charlie Craig, Bob hailed from Dundee.

Allan's wing-play was to be eulogised in a 1900/01 handbook:

Shows excellent judgement in everything he does, and can take hard knocks and play on as game as ever. Centres on the run, and occasionally contributes a long shot with plenty of steam behind it. Doesn't neglect his inside man and although weighty, can show a rare turn of speed when necessary.

Charlie Bunyan had been a professional footballer and kept goal for Hyde FC in an FA Cup tie against Preston North End. In that game he let twenty-six goals slip past him, making any subsequent accusations about the veracity of goalkeepers fade into insignificance (apocryphally he was to have it that there were several 'unlucky deflections' in this total). Whilst in pursuit of his duties for Thames, Bunyan had missed an appointment with a player in Birmingham. Not wanting to come away empty handed the nothing-if-not-time-efficient Bunyan approached another player unannounced and unsolicited. Charlie was subsequently deemed to have been indulging in the nefarious act of poaching. As such he was summoned to appear before an FA disciplinary panel. Following investigations it came to light that Payne had financed Bunyan's efforts to lure players to Canning Town and the club secretary was judged to have misused a large sum of money (rumoured to be as much as £1,000) given to the club by Arnold Hills.

The FA suspended Charlie Bunyan for two years. Payne failed to attend the FA hearing into the matter and was suspended until he did appear. In addition, the club was suspended for two weeks from 1 September and fined £25. Shortly after the FA ruling, Payne announced that he had resigned as secretary of Thames Ironworks Football Club at the close of the previous season. One can only speculate on the embarrassment and shame this affair brought to the door of the Corinthian-spirited president of Thames Ironworks Football Club, Arnold Hills. All his worse fears about the cancer of professionalism must have seemed to be encroaching on his vision of what his football club should be.

George Neill, who had played his last game for the club only six months earlier, became the club's third secretary. Neill was then aged 25 and during his term in office he continued the now traditional strengthening of the playing staff, particularly prior to the start of the 1899/1900 season.

BUILDING, BUILDING, BUILDING

As much heartache as the poaching scandal must have caused Arnold Hills, the committee of Thames Ironworks were not going to let this inhibit them. Before the start of the season the side was further bolstered by the arrival of Albert Carnelly, a much-travelled forward from Bristol City. At the same time three Tottenham Hotspurs players were brought to the Memorial Ground in something of a transfer coup masterminded by Irons secretary George Neill. The trio were Henry (Tom) Bradshaw, Bill Joyce and Kenny McKay.

Bradshaw, a winger from Liverpool, was to make play a dozen games for Thames and scored his two goals for the club in cup games. Born on 24 August 1873 he made his debut for Thames v. Reading on 16 September.

Tom started his footballing career with Northwich Victoria and was a regular member of Liverpool's Second Division championship-winning teams of 1894 and 1896. On two occasions he was selected to play for the Football League and won an England cap against Ireland in February 1897. Joining Spurs in May 1898, Tom coincidentally made his debut and scored against the Irons in a Thames and Medway League fixture.

Virtually ever-present in the Tottenham side during their 1898/99 campaign, Tom was chosen to represent the United League against the Thames and Medway League. He was also selected for the South v. the North in the annual international trial match and went on to play for an England XI against a Scotland XI in a match to benefit the players' union. After sixty-nine appearances in all competitions for Spurs that season, he transferred to Thames in the summer of 1899.

The highlight of Tom's all-too-short Irons' career was destined to be his four goals in an 11–1 Thames and Medway Combination thrashing of Grays United. Both Tom and the man who signed him, George Neill, were dead before they had reached the age of 30. Tom died on Christmas Day 1899 of consumption. Bradshaw was a key figure in terms of the future for Thames and his death, attributed to an injury received in a match against Bedminster the previous October, at the age of just 26, stunned the club. Neill was just four years older when he died.

Bradshaw was a courageous, fast and direct left-winger, he played and scored in the 1–2 FA Cup defeat at the hands of Millwall just sixteen days before his death in front of a record 13,000 crowd at the Memorial Ground. In his 1906 brief history of the club Syd King wrote of Bradshaw:

> The record of 1899/1900 however, would not be complete without some reference to poor Tom Bradshaw, who came from the Spurs with Joyce. How well I remember that match with Queens Park Rangers during the Christmas holidays, when Joyce brought over the sad message to the Memorial Grounds that our comrade had passed away. Poor Tom was one of the cleverest wing forwards I have ever known and he was immensely popular with everybody. He joined the club with me and with us in the team were MacEachrane, Craig – my partner full back – Carnelly and Joyce.

Spurs and Thames met on 2 April 1900 in a match to raise funds for Bradshaw's dependants.

The make-up of the Irons was to cause some disquiet amongst Thames' Southern League Division One opponents. For example, when the Irons travelled to Reading on 16 September for their first game in the upper heights of the Southern League, immediately after their FA suspension was lifted, Thames were greeted with some criticism.

The *Reading Standard* commented cynically that the Thames team lining up for the first game in the Southern League Division One, 'had a familiar look about them'.

The newspaper claimed that, 'anybody can get up a good team with plenty of "ready" behind them.'

They had a point of course, although Reading won 1–0, but two days later the Memorial saw McKay and inside forward Carnelly grab two goals each in a 4–0 win over Chatham. This was followed by a victory over Bedminster. Things started to look positive, and there was a feeling that the Irons were going on to repeat their feats of the previous season at the higher level. Four FA Cup games had produced twenty-one goals, including the seven that were smashed past the Dartford defence.

This was the start of Dundee man Charlie Craig's career with Thames. Craig, at 36, was one of the older members of the Thames squad. He was involved with both the last Thames side and the first West Ham team from 1899 to 1902. The tall Scottish full-back became one of East London's most popular players, making a combined total of 102 appearances for Thames and West Ham. He began his career in earnest with 'Our Boys' Dundee, played half-a-dozen matches and was promoted to the first team, which ultimately combined with the East End club to emerge as Dundee FC.

Charlie originally came south to work as a mechanic at Tate Sugar Refinery at Silvertown and then Thames Ironworks, but with the toleration of professionalism, football became Charlie's main occupation and he tried a number of positions before settling his 6ft 1in, 13st frame at left-back. One of the last links with the old Ironworks club was severed when he joined Nottingham Forest in the Football League.

Described by a writer of the time as being a 'genial, good natured giant', Craig was also a keen athlete and won a host of medals for his achievements on the track. He left Forest for Bradford Park Avenue, then moved on to Norwich City in 1908, only to return to Bradford PA at the end of the 1908/09 season.

Sadly yet poetically Charlie passed away on the same day in 1933 as his former full-back partner and Hammers Manager, Syd King. King more than once hinted at his friendship with Craig. However, Charlie Paynter saw them 'as different as chalk and cheese' and a pairing who could hardly understand what each other were saying. Indeed one can understand the mutual incomprehension between the man with an accent from the nineteenth-century banks of the Tay and King's antiquated Kentish brogue.

STRUGGLE AND VOLUME INVESTMENT

In their championship year Thames had played thirty individuals with eighteen (60 per cent) making less than ten appearances. The consistency of selection is one of the main differences between the modern game and its Victorian ancestor. For example, in West Ham's successful 1963/64 side twenty-one players were used in Division One games and only six (just over 28 per cent) of these appeared less than ten times that season. John Lyall's West Ham side that finished in the highest ever spot attained by a West Ham team used only sixteen players of which only three (under 19 per cent) failed to make double figures. Such is the impact of modern training methods and physiotherapy, but this also says something about how the economics of the game has changed.

Team squads in the early days of professional football were like regiments in number and organisation. The FA Cup and Southern League competitions were only the tip of the iceberg. Clubs like West Ham in the early part of the twentieth century would play in a range of leagues and cup competitions, fought out between national, regional and local opposition, using first and second teams, 'A', 'B' and sometimes 'C' squads. Later, youth and colt teams would also be involved. These competitions, that have been long forgotten and the details lost in the mists of time, drew big crowds, often on a par with the league and cup matches that we see as important from our modern vantage point, those that have counterparts in today's game. There was also a plethora of friendly encounters at all levels. Wages were relatively low, but employment was high. Again, it is useful to be reminded that a major pull of any game was an opportunity to bet on the outcome, goals scored etc.

There was a First World War mentality about the way players were used and a gladiatorial ethos within the game. The physical nature of the football in those days saw players cut down in their prime en masse. There were five players waiting to take the place of every man that limped from the field of play after, not during, the ninety minutes, as there were no substitutes and no quarter given then. One played on to exacerbate injury rather than stop to alleviate it.

With the coming of the modern era clubs began to invest in particular talent, nurturing individual players. Like the infantry soldier of today, the contemporary footballer is a highly trained professional, well equipped and supported by vast technical back-up, but in the early days skill and ability was exploited in a much more general way. Many went like lambs to the slaughter. Now investment in players is concentrated, it is rationalised in the same way as most modern capitalist production is. In the time of Thames and later the adolescent West Ham United, the investment was in volume – a high turn-out, high input strategy.

By mid-season it was clear that the Irons were finding life difficult in such exalted company as Millwall, Spurs and Southampton. With just three games left in the League they had won only three times in fifteen outings. When Thames met with Southampton at the Memorial Ground, a mere twelve days before the Saints were due to contest the FA Cup Final at Crystal Palace against Bury, it was clear that the Irons really needed to win all their remaining matches to avoid the threat of relegation. Perhaps Southampton were conserving their energies but Thames won 4–1. The hero of the match was Bill Joyce who scored a hat-trick and was carried from the field by Thames supporters, grateful for two badly needed points. Jubilation was cut short when, the very next day, Cowes and Brighton United announced their resignations from the Southern League and the East Londoners were left exposed at the foot of the table with Sheppey United. However, if Thames gained maximum points from their remaining games they could possibly overhaul both Chatham and Gravesend and claw their way to safety.

The Irons did indeed win both games, but so did Chatham and Gravesend. Thames finished bottom of the League, having won only eight of their twenty-eight games. This obliged the club to contest a Test Match for the second successive season. Unlike the previous season the Irons were looking to preserve rather than better their status. Fulham were the side looking to usurp Thames' place. The Cottagers were Southern League Second Division runners-up by the narrowest of margins from Chesham and Wolverton. The match took place at Tottenham's Northumberland Park ground. Former Thames forward David Lloyd was now a Fulham player, one of only six survivors from the previous meeting between the clubs, Thames had won that game1–0. A mighty charge in the first half saw the Irons go in at the break four up. This allowed Thames to play out a much more measured game in the second period. Just 600 people saw the 5–1 victory over the West Londoners. On his return to his old Spurs stamping ground Bill Joyce conjured up yet another crucial hat-trick.

Thames were safe for another season and by 1900 the club were pulling in new players from professional clubs from every part of Great Britain. However, the fact that the Memorial was unable to attract sufficient numbers to match rising expenses meant that the club had no option but to increase ticket prices. The committee swung its weight behind an aggressive ticket-selling campaign, using the *Gazette* and local newspapers. In the last two years of the nineteenth century, season ticket prices doubled from 5s to 10s. The committee did attempt to minimise any resentment about this inflation by introducing, for the first time, concessions at 5s 6d for ladies (tickets in the grandstand only) and 3s 6d for 'boys', but gate receipts were still insufficient.

It was clear that the club was still reliant upon the finances of Arnold Hills. However, the Thames president remained unhappy about the committee's increasingly professional outlook and behind this was the limit to his generosity and his lack of willingness to continue to invest in a project with no financial or productive return. A crisis was brewing, and something would soon have to give.

13

READYING FOR WAR

Many historians argue that the seeds of the First World War were being sown long before the sparks of Sarajevo a decade and a half into the twentieth century that ostensibly started the guns firing. An arms race had been going on for the best part of twenty years before that perhaps inevitable moment of violence, which historically causes Empires to dissipate, happened. Thames Ironworks had profited from this preparation, with protagonists from each side building their maritime means of defence and offence, just a couple of examples of this demonstrate the potted power of such vessels and their destructive potential. However, as you might have discerned from previous pages, the speed of nautical technological development and innovation meant that many of the great engineering constructions of attrition were out-of-date before they could be deployed in anger.

So what is the point of knowing this? It doesn't take an economics graduate to see the obvious waste of resources this represents, not that one can rely on economists for much that one might not get from a fortune teller. However, there is a lesson about upping the ante generally. The schema is as old as humanity itself – if you invest in research and development and create something on the basis of that, that thing you have created constitutes research in itself; it is a stage to be countered and bettered. This is pertinent to us today because it is the very same phenomenon that is manifested in cyber technology. Organisations and governments invest in tools, methods and means to disable each other's tools, methods and means. As such, any resultant process, arising as a consequence of the process it undermines, is the parent of its own demise – it inevitably gives rise to its counter (consequence) and the destroyer of itself. As you read this paragraph, billions of dollars were being pumped into projects and systems that are redundant at the very moment they bleeped, flashed and tapped into existence; ethereal they were, are and ethereal they remain as they are superseded as a consequence of their development.

This is why and how I own, or have at least bought, vinyl, tape and CD versions of the same albums, songs and tunes that for convenience sake I find myself downloading. I recently watched a film via Netflix. I first saw it in the cinema; I bought the video (which I never played). Over the following few years I acquired three DVD's of the same film (one is a 'directors cut' and one was bought because I forgot I had the other two). This is a web of mutual- and self-exploitation that is made up of producers, manufacturers, retailers, wholesalers and consumers. I know I am not alone is this cycle of wasted time and money. Are you reading the 'hard' or one of the range of potential 'e' versions of this book?

HMS *DUNCAN*

HMS *Duncan* was the leader of a class of six battleships, built with some haste for the Royal Navy in response to supposed threats. A risk of war between Great Britain, France and Russia was prevalent in the mid-1890s. In 1898, in response to what was understood as a renewed threat from both these nations, the Admiralty applied to the government for a supplement to the year's Naval Estimate. It immediately received the extra funding. This paid for four extra battleships, reduced versions of the *Formidable*-class battleships. Two more followed the following year.

The effort was ultimately unnecessary, as the French and Russian vessels posing the perceived threat proved to be substandard. HMS *Duncan* was the second ship of the class to be built. She was constructed, along with her sister ship *Cornwallis*, by Thames Ironworks; these were among the last major warships built by the yard.

Duncan was laid down on 10 July 1899 and the 14,900 ton ship was launched on 21 March 1901 and completed in October 1903. The ship was 432ft long with a beam of 75½ft. However, within three years, she was obsolete, having had an undistinguished career, although in June 1916, based at Salonika, she supported landings near Athens and operated against Greek Royalists from October to December.

Duncan was paid off at Sheerness and spent her final years in Reserve status, initially at Sheerness and then in April 1917 at Chatham. From April 1917 to January 1918 she had what was to be her final refit to make her suitable as an accommodation ship, which was her last mission. She served in this capacity as basically a floating hotel for naval personnel from January 1918 until March 1919. She was sold for breaking up in 1920.

The *Duncan*-class battleships were pretty much similar to their predecessors the *Formidable* and *London* classes, but with rather finer lines. They forfeited some protection in exchange for greater speed; the main armour belt was 7in instead of 9in thick. *Duncan*'s range at 10 knots was around 6,000 miles. Bulkheads and barbettes were also slimmed down, which reduced displacement by around 1,000 tons. This, together with an increase in power of 3,000hp, a consequence of the deployment of four, instead of three-cylinder triple-expansion engines, provided the Duncans with an extra knot flat out at about 19 knots. They carried four Mk VIII guns, 40 calibre long, mounted in pairs in turrets fore and aft. The secondary battery was twelve 6in quick-firing guns, located in casements on the main deck. This was the standard armament of the day, with her sixteen 12lb quick-fires on the upper deck, behind low breastwork.

One of the class, HMS *Albermarle*, had her secondary battery removed in 1917, and six of its guns relocated to the upper deck, correcting what had long been understood as a major design fault of the class.

BLACK PRINCE

As part of the 1902/03 Naval Estimates, two armoured cruisers of a new design, HMS *Duke of Edinburgh* and *Black Prince*, the latter named after Edward, the Black Prince, were ordered for the Royal Navy. These were the first ships designed for the Royal Navy under the supervision of Sir Philip Watts, the new Director of Naval Construction. The design was considerably larger than the preceding Monmouth and Devonshire class cruisers, mounting a heavier main armament of six 9.2in guns in single turrets.

Black Prince was laid down on 3 June 1903, launched on 8 November 1904 and completed on 17 March 1906. Initially, up to 1907, she served with the 2nd Squadron and from 1907 to 1908 she was with the 1st Cruiser Squadron. The ship joined the 5th Cruiser Squadron (as part of the Atlantic Fleet) from 1908 to 1912 and the 3rd Cruiser Squadron between 1912 and 1913.

Displacing 12,590 tons and 13,965 tons fully loaded, *Black Prince* had an overall length of 505ft 6in, her beam was 73ft 6in and she had a draught of 27ft.

Powered by four-cylinder triple-expansion steam engines, driving two shafts, producing 23,000hp *Black Prince* had a maximum speed of 23 knots. Her engines were powered by twenty Babcock & Wilcox water-tube boilers, together with six cylindrical boilers. She heaved a maximum of 2,150 tons of coal, along with 600 tons of fuel oil (this was sprayed on the coal to increase the rate of burn). At full capacity, *Black Prince* was capable of steaming for 8,130 nautical miles at 10 knots. Her complement was 789 officers and enlisted men.

The ship's main armament was six BL 9.2in Mk X guns in single turrets, two on the centreline and two on each beam, providing a broadside of four 9.2in guns. Secondary armament consisted of four BL 6in Mark XI guns, arranged in single casemates. The latter were mounted amidships on the main deck, their use restricted to calm weather. Twenty Vickers QF 3lb were fitted, six on turret roofs and fourteen in the superstructure. Three submerged 18in torpedo tubes completed *Black Prince*'s armament.

At the start of the First World War, *Black Prince* was one of the four armoured cruisers serving in the 1st Cruiser Squadron of the Mediterranean Fleet, which was under the commanded of Rear Admiral Ernest Charles Thomas Troubridge (a man with a biography that reflected world naval history during his time). She took part in the pursuit of German battlecruiser SMS *Goeben* and light cruiser SMS *Breslau*. Following the latter's arrival in Ottoman waters (hiding in the shadow of neutral Turkey) in the middle of August, *Black Prince* and *Duke of Edinburgh* were assigned to the Red Sea to defend troop convoys arriving from India and to seek out German merchant ships.

In August 1914 she captured the German ocean liners *Südmark* and *Istria*. On 6 November she was sent to Gibraltar to join a squadron of British and French ships to search for German warships still at sea off the African coast. However, on 19 November this duty was cancelled when the whereabouts of the German East Asia Squadron was discovered by survivors of the Battle of Coronel. Joining the Grand Fleet in December 1914 *Black Prince* was assigned to the 1st Cruiser Squadron under Rear Admiral Sir Robert Keith Arbuthnot.

As a consequence of experience at the Battle of Coronel, in March 1916 *Black Prince* was modified. Her 6in guns were removed from their casemates and replaced by six 6in guns mounted individually behind shields between the beam 9.2in turrets.

The Battle of Jutland saw the end of *Black Prince*. Having sustained some damage from a heavy shell during the day, she was later sunk under intense fire. How this happened was something of a mystery for a long time. It was uncertain if a submarine or surface ship had taken *Black Prince* down. The First Cruiser Squadron was positioned with a screening force during the battle, several miles beyond the main body of the Grand Fleet. Contact between *Black Prince* and the rest of the Squadron was lost as the latter made contact with the Germans, at around 5.42 p.m. Not long after this time HMS *Defence* and HMS *Warrior* (both members of the First Cruiser Squadron) were heavily engaged by German battlecruisers and battleships. *Defence* was blown up, while *Warrior* took heavy damage, subsequently causing her to sink.

After this the British fleet made no positive sightings of *Black Prince*, however at 8.45 p.m. a wireless signal, a report of a submarine sighting, was received from her. The British destroyer HMS *Spitfire*, having been severely damaged following a collision with the enemy battleship *Nassau*, sighted what seemed to be a German battlecruiser during the night of 31 May. It had two widely-spaced funnels and was described as, 'a mass of fire from foremast to mainmast, on deck and between decks. Flames were issuing out of her from every corner.' At around midnight the unidentified craft blew up. Subsequently it was thought that the ship sighted was in fact the *Black Prince*, her two midships funnels perhaps having collapsed or blow away.

Later the eyewitness account from a crewman on HMS *Spitfire* emerged:

We were just recovering from our ramming match with the German cruiser, and most of the ship's company were collected aft, when suddenly there was a cry from nearly a dozen people at once: 'Look out!'

I looked up, and saw a few 100yd away on our starboard quarter, what appeared to be a battle cruiser on fire, steering straight for our stern. To our intense relief, she missed our stern but just by a few feet; so close was she to us that we were actually under her guns, which were trained out on her starboard beam. She tore past us with a roar, rather like a motor roaring up a hill in low gear, and the very crackling and heat of the flames could be heard and felt. She was a mass of fire from fore-mast to main-mast, on deck and between decks. Flames were issuing out of her from every corner.

At first sight she appeared to be a battle cruiser, as her funnels were so far apart but afterwards it transpired that she was the unfortunate *Black Prince* with her two centre funnels gone. Soon afterwards, soon after midnight, there came an explosion from the direction in which she had disappeared.

However, the German account of the demise of *Black Prince* tells of a brief engagement, at approximately 11.35 p.m., with the German battleship *Rheinland*. Detached from the main body of the British fleet, close to midnight *Black Prince* sailed toward the German lines. She made an attempt to steer away from the German battleships, but *Thüringen* opened fire after catching *Black Prince* in her searchlights. As many as five other German ships, including battleships *Nassau*, *Ostfriesland* and *Friedrich der Grosse*, took up with the bombardment. Return fire from *Black Prince* proved ineffective. The majority of the German ships were between 750 and 1500yd of the British ship – for naval gunnery of the time, this was effectively point blank range. *Black Prince* took least a dozen heavy shells and several smaller ones. She was under the waves within a quarter of an hour. There were no survivors from *Black Prince*'s crew of 857 which included 37 officers.

Subsequently the *Daily Mirror* reported a statement by the Secretary of the Admiralty:

On the afternoon of Wednesday, May 31, a naval engagement took place off the coast of Jutland. The British ships on which the brunt of the fighting fell were the battlecruiser fleet and some cruisers and light cruisers, supported by four fast battleships. Among these the losses were heavy. The German battle fleet, aided by a low visibility, avoided prolonged action with our main forces, and soon after these appeared on the scene the enemy returned to port, though not before receiving severe damage from our battleships. The battlecruisers *Queen Mary*, *Indefatigable*, *Invincible* and the cruisers *Defence* and *Black Prince* were sunk.

Gunner Herbert Dash (service number: J/6403) from Malton, Meldreth, was among those lost on the *Black Prince*. News of his death on 31 May 1916 was conveyed in an article in the *Royston Crow* of the same date. Herbert was 24 years old. He had been in the Royal Navy for nine years at the time of his death, after which his commanding officer wrote that he was devoted to his work as a gunner and showed great promise.

Herbert's parents had one other son in the Navy and three in the Army. On 16 June 1916 an 'In Memoriam' notice appeared in the local newspaper:

Dash – On 31st May in the naval battle off Jutland, Herbert, the dearly loved son of Mr and Mrs Dash, Malton, Meldreth. To his memory 'Glory, honour and love'.

A tribute from one of his brothers followed:

In Memory of Brother Bert
He has gone on his last commission

In that beautiful ship called 'Rest'
And his brave head is pillowed
Safe on his Saviour's breast.

Sailor Brother Percy

Herbert is commemorated on the Portsmouth Naval Memorial, one of 9,666 Royal Navy seamen who died in the First World War and have no known grave but the sea.

Able seaman Frederick George Beames Hake of Oxford was another of those lost. Just three years older than Herbert he too is commemorated on the Portsmouth Naval Memorial.

Fred signed on for the Royal Navy on 25 August 1904 as a 16 year old. He left the Navy in 1913 after a well-travelled career, and joined the Oxfordshire Constabulary on 25 January that same year, but remained in the RN reserves, so was recalled to the service on 2 August 1914.

Transferred from shore-based HMS *Victory* on 23 August 1915, Fred joined the crew of the *Black Prince*. While home on leave in November 1915, he married Edith Stanley in Chipping Norton. Edith Hake re-married in Chipping Norton in 1922.

Several of *Black Prince*'s crew hailed from Malta which was not unusual given the close relationship between the Royal Navy and the island:

> G. Abela, a Canteen Server
> C. Baldacchino, a Canteen Server
> Edgar A. Borg, an Assistant Canteen Manager
> J. Cauchi, an Officer's Steward
> G. Cuomo, a Bandsman
> Angelo Formosa, a Bandsman
> L. Grasso, a Bandsman

Although Jutland was the only major naval battle of the First World War, in terms of the numbers of battleships and battlecruisers engaged, it was the largest sea battle in the history of naval warfare, with the two most powerful naval forces on the planet confronting each other.

Jutland involved 250 ships and approximately 100,000 men. While the Germans suffered fewer casualties than the British, the Royal Navy claimed victory given that the German fleet failed to set out on the high seas again for the rest of the war, relying instead on U-boats.

The wrecksite of the *Black Prince* is designated as a protected place under the Protection of Military Remains Act 1986.

14

LIFEBOATS

Thames Ironworks, as well as fabricating buoys for Trinity House, produced over 200 lifeboats ultimately deployed by the Royal National Lifeboat Institute (RNLI).

If ever you get the chance to visit any of the surviving brave, little life-saving craft Thames Ironworks built you might offer up the consideration of how the yard has directly contributed to the rescue of thousands of souls from fearful deaths and injury. However, the company was probably involved more in the prevention of nautical disasters than maritime rescue through its work for Trinity House, which was situated near East India Dock. This organisation was responsible for the stationing of lightships around the British coast and many of these vessels would come to Thames Ironworks for maintenance and repair.

Thames played an important part in the development of lifeboat design and early technology and were one of the shipyards on the River Thames that built Pulling and Sailing Lifeboats of the early twentieth century – other shipyards included Edwards & Symes (Millwall), Forrestt (Limehouse) and Wolffe & Son (Shadwell). The latter two also built boats for the HSB (French Volunteer Lifeboat Service). Pulling and sailing boats had oars, which were used to take the boat from the beach to carry out rescues, and sails to add to the speed of the craft.

Many lifeboats stations on the east coast would boast a Thames-made vessel including Aldeburgh, Casiter, Clacton, Cromer, Harwich and Sheringham, but craft built in Canning Town can be traced all over Britain.

Thames built four main types of lifeboat:

- ❖ Norfolk & Suffolk (N&S)
- ❖ Liverpool (Liv)
- ❖ Watson (Wat)
- ❖ Self Righter (S/R)

Some of these are listed below. Histories of most of them are traceable; all are in some way, distinguished:

Name	Date built	Length (feet)	No of Oars	Class
Covent Garden	1899	40	12	N&S
James Stevens No 10	1899	37	12	S/R
Licensed Victualler	1900	35	10	S/R
Forester (Reserve Boat)	1900	34	10	S/R
John Wesley	1901	43	10	Wat
Albert Edward	1901	43	12	Wat
54th West Norfolk Regiment	1901	37	12	S/R
City of Winchester	1902	46	12	N&S
Louisa Heartwell	1902	38	14	Liv
John Wesley	1902	38	10	Wat
Louisa Heartwell	1902	38	14	Liv
Nancy Lucy	1903	35	12	N&S
Alexandria	1903	35	14	Liv
Charles Decre James	1903	38	10	Liv
William and Emma	1903	35	-	Wat
Horatio Brand	1903	35	10	S/R
Charles Burton	1903	35	14	Liv
Ann Fawcett	1904	43	10	Wat
J C Madge	1904	41	16	Liv
James & Mary Walker	1904	38	12	Wat
James Finlayson	1905	35	10	Wat
Kentwell	1905	46	14	N&S
Edward Z Dresden	1905	38	14	Liv
Ann Miles	1905	43	10	Wat
Elizabeth Austin	1905	35	10	S/R
Hollan the Third	1907	43	10	S/R
Jacob & Rachel Valentine	1907	34	10	S/R
Charles Henry Ashley	1907	38	12	Wat
Ryder	1907	38	12	Wat
Susan Ashley	1907	35	-	S/R
Caroline	1908	38	14	Liv
John Ryburn	1908	43	8	Wat
Maria	1908	40	-	Wat
Lizzie Porter	1908	35	10	S/R
Eleanor Brown	1909	44	12	N&S
Janet Hoyle	1909	35	-	Liv
James Leach	1910	42	12	N&S
Jane Hannah MacDonald	1910	35½	10	S/R

Charles and Eliza Laura	1910	49	12	Wat
William and Laura	1910	43	10	Wat
Elliot Galer	1910	38	-	Wat
Helen Smitton	1910	40	-	Wat
William Henry Wilkinson	1911	35	-	S/R
Hugh Taylor	1912	34	12	N&S
Alexander Tulloch	1912	43	8	Wat
Frederick Kitchin	1913	43	-	Wat
James and John Young	1913	35	12	Liv

Just how prolific this production was, in terms of the overall number of lifeboats constructed during the period the Ironworks was making such craft, is demonstrated by the fact that around 70 per cent of operational RNLI boats during the First World War were made by Thames. Recent estimates have it that the total number of lives saved by Ironworks lifeboats was something in excess of 9,300 and that this is far more than the number of lives lost in conflicts, involving Thames-built warships, many of which saw action for both sides during the First World War, notably at Gallipoli and Jutland.

Wherever they were to be found, Thames lifeboats became part of the soul and history of their locality. For example the *Susan Ashley* needed six horses to launch her and ten to recover her when she was heavy with sea water. However, on her ceremonial last (literally) horse-powered launch on Whit Monday, in 1937, a huge crowd (for the time and place) saw her thirteen crew members, ten heavy horses and up to thirty helpers put her to sea. As the *Isle of Wight County Press* reported, 'Never before have the beach and cliffs at Brook presented such a scene of animation and interest as on Whit Monday afternoon, when a crowd, which must have numbered 2,000.'

The *Susan Ashley* served from 1907 to 1937 when the station closed. She was last known as a houseboat in 1980.

Most of the lifeboats built by Thames have heroic histories, far too many to relate in this chapter. However the tale of the tragic end of the *William and Emma* is worth relating. She was stationed at Salcombe, Devon and served for twelve years until the boat was wrecked in a tragic rescue attempt with the loss of thirteen crew members. A contemporary account can be found in the *Devonian Year Book* of 1917:

On Friday, October 27th 1916, an appalling calamity befell the South Devon port of Salcombe. The lifeboat (the *William and Emma*) had been called out about six o'clock in the morning to render assistance to the schooner Western Lass, which was reported to be wrecked on Meg Rock, near Prawle Point.

In spite of the furious gale that was raging and the tempestuous breakers on Salcombe Bar, the gallant crew of fifteen succeeded in getting out to sea, and in reaching the vessel that was in distress; then, finding that the schooner's crew had been rescued by the rocket apparatus (coastguard lifebelts) of Prawle, and that no further help was needed, they started on their return voyage, but in crossing the bar their little craft capsized, and all but two of their number were drowned. Most of them were married men, who leave not only their widows, but also twelve very young children to mourn their loss.

The victims were: Samuel Distin (coxswain)
Peter Heath Foale senior (second coxswain)
Peter Heath Foale junior (son of the second coxswain)
William James Foale (son of the second coxswain)
Francis (Frank) Cudd
John Ambrose Cudd (a volunteer)
Ashley Cook
Thomas Putt
Bert Wood
James Alfred Canham
Albert Distin
James Henry Cove
William Lamble

These names are included in the memorial at Poole, Dorset to all those lost on RNLI service.

Not much more than a handful of the lifeboats have survived (the exact number is not known) but a few have been, or are in the process of being, restored, for instance the *Helen Smitton*, the first lifeboat in St Abbs, Berwickshire. There are even fewer that remain seaworthy. The location of the wrecks of some others are known and it is a testament to the Ironworks that they have endured despite the ravages of nature. For instance the *Janet Hoyle*, a 35ft Liverpool-class lifeboat built by Thames in 1908, was found on a mudflat in Essex. Due to the quality of the materials used in her construction (principally Honduran mahogany) she has survived and significantly, is restorable.

The *Lizzie Porter*, which was based at Holy Island from 1909 to 1925, and then at North Sunderland from 1925 to 1936 has been on display at Chatham Historic Dockyard since April 1996. She was launched thirty-four times in total and saved seventy-seven lives. She was twice awarded the RNLI silver medal.

At the Wraysbury Dive Centre in West London, the *Elizabeth Austin* has been sunk to act as a visitor attraction. She saw service out of St Dogmael's in Cardigan Bay, Wales from 1905 to 1932. *John Ryburn* served at Stronsay in the Orkneys until 1915 and Peterhead, Scotland until 1921. She is now on the quayside in Caernarfon waiting to be brought back to East London into the care of the Thames Ironworks Heritage Trust.

Charles Henry Ashley was in service from 1907 to 1932 at Cemaes, Anglesey. She was sold and left in storage up to the 1960s. After becoming motorised she was used for fifteen years, but was abandoned until the 1980s when she was taken on by Amlwch Heritage Trust. She eventually returned to Cemaes where she has been totally refurbished and is now used for training.

Frederick Kitchin was one of only four 43ft Watson-class motor lifeboats built by the company. She had a fine record of service with the RNLI at Beaumaris from 1914 to 1948 – her thirty-eight launches saving forty-six lives. On the 6 August 1913, while on passage along the south coast, she stopped off at Cowes during the Regatta Week. King George V took the opportunity of hopping on board for short trip in the new lifeboat, getting an explanation of her workings from the Right Hon. Arnold Morley and Sir Godfrey Baring Bart, RNLI's Committee of Management members.

A cabin was added to her superstructure after she was sold in 1948, and she was converted to a yacht. Although the *Frederick Kitchin* sank in 2005, she was raised later in the same year and remains in a remarkably good condition, testifying to the skill of the Thames builders and the high quality materials used by the Ironworks. She is another craft currently in the hands of the Thames Ironworks Heritage Trust.

The first new lifeboat at RNLI Moelfre Lifeboat Station in 1910 was the *Charles and Eliza Laura*. In 1927 her crew was awarded two gold and thirteen bronze medals in recognition of the hazardous rescue of the ketch *Excel*. She had been obliged to sail right over the wreck to haul the three crew to safety. *Eliza Laura* was badly damaged and full of water but her air-cases kept her afloat. Two died, including one of the lifeboat crew. Second Coxswain William Roberts was completely blind for several hours after landing from the effects of wind and salt water.

In her nineteen-year career she was launched on thirty-six occasions, saving eighty-four lives. She was one of the 'little ships' that took part in the Dunkirk rescue of 1940. Today she awaits restoration in Scotland.

In fact, a number of Thames Ironworks lifeboats were part of the heroic rescue at Dunkirk, but just one helped with the evacuation of British troops from St Malo the same year.

The *William Henry Wilkinson* served at St Helier from 1912 to 1937, after which she was sold to the Yacht Club commodore, William Le Masurier. Following the evacuation of Allied troops from the Nord-Pas-de-Calais beaches at the end of May 1940 there were still large numbers of British and Allied troops stranded in the west of France.

On the 16 June 1940 the authorities in Jersey received a telegram from the Admiralty requesting that all available craft make for St Malo to help in the evacuation of the cornered Allied servicemen. The Commodore organised a little armada made up of craft of various sizes, including his former lifeboat, which had been motorised since her RNLI service; *William Henry Wilkinson*, once more went on her way to save lives.

By the evening of the 17 June, 21,474 men had been embarked without loss. The *William Henry Wilkinson* was destroyed only eleven days later, following the Nazi bombing of St Helier harbour.

The *James and John Young* survives to the present day and can be seen at the Eyemouth Maritime Centre in Berwickshire, in a partly restored state.

In April 1911 there was enormous enthusiasm in St Abbs on the arrival of the *Helen Smitton*, the village's first lifeboat. The *Berwickshire News* of April 25, 1911 reported:

The new St Abbs motor lifeboat is due to arrive today ... Lieut. Robes RN, district inspector of lifeboats is in charge; and the crew includes Mr John Wilson, coxswain; Mr Robt. Aitchison, motor mechanic, Mr Thomas Wilson (bowman); and Mr Hugh Rae, left Harwich with the boat on Tuesday, the stopping places being Girlestone, Scarbro, Tynemouth and Berwick.

On its arrival at St Abbs, it is expected that the boat will be taken out with its full crew for a trial trip.

The christening of the boat is not to be performed until August, and as is usually the case, the name is already settled in terms of a bequest (from Mr James Hodge in the name of his late wife, Helen Smitton).

At all the ports stretching from North Berwick to Berwick, new lifeboats have been provided during the last few years, all of which are of the most modern and up-to-date construction. Not only so, but the officials have recently acknowledged the necessity for the institution of additional new stations.

One of these was opened at Skateraw about three or four years ago, and is probably one of the most up-to-date and perfectly equipped in Scotland.

It is a far cry from Skateraw to Eyemouth, but up to the present time any service work along the coast had to be undertaken by either of those stations, particularly the former.

The need for an intermediate station was brought home to the parent institution by the shipping disaster of four year ago, when the 'Alfred Erlandsen' floundered on the reef of rocks close to St Abbs on a dark and stormy night.

The crew were left in the terrible position of facing death for some hours, and unfortunately all were lost.

Hence it was that after this shipping disaster a public meeting of the villagers was held, in conference with several officers of the Royal National Lifeboat Institution, and as the result of the appeal to the institution for a station and lifeboat for St Abbs, the committee of management in London at their next meeting assented to the application.

After testing various boats they approved of the Watson type and also to the boat being by motor power.

This is the first motor lifeboat that has been placed on the east coast and there is no question about it, no station more needs a vessel so propelled than St Abbs as its entrance-way is one of the worst on the whole of the coast, and it would have been quite impossible otherwise on many occasions to have 'pulled' the boat out to sea in the face of the kind of weather experienced there, when the wind sets up.

The new boat is propelled by motor power, but can also be managed by oar and sail. She is not a self-righter but belongs to the 'Watson' type.

Details of the boat: Official No. 603; built in 1910 by Thomas Ironworks, Rowedge [sic]; cost £3563; size 38ft in length by 10ft beam; engine one 4 cylinder, 24hp Wolseley; fuel 50 gallons capacity consumed at 4¼ gallons per hour; screw 21in Villinger reversible propellor; speed 7.5 knotts. Coxswains of 'Helen Smitton' - John Wilson, from 1911 to 1931 and James Nisbet, 1931 to 1936.

The customary carriage is dispensed with, and the boat remains when not in service at the top of the slip, on a tipping skid.

The boat will be stowed upon a raised platform at the head of the slipway, the deck of which is from 4 to 6ft above the pier surface. The storehouse where part of the equipment for the boat and crew will be housed has been erected on a site on the road to Northfield just above the harbour.

Thus readily adapted to work off Berwickshire, the new St Abbs lifeboat will certainly prove a most valuable addition to the life-saving equipment of the coast, and it may be taken for granted that nothing will be wanting on the part of management and crew to make her record worthy and honourable whenever danger calls.

In service of RNLI *Helen Smitton* was launched twenty-seven times and saved thirty-seven lives. She is now under the stewardship of the Thames Ironworks Heritage Trust.

The *Thomas Fielden* was a later example of this type of craft produced by Thames Ironworks. She was the Barrow lifeboat from 1901 to 1927, stationed at Roa Island. She was the second Barrow lifeboat to bear the name *Thomas Fielden,* her predecessor having had only a brief stay of three years at Barrow after her initial service in Holyhead. She was a 40ft by 11ft, Watson-class, non-self-righter. Built at a cost £1,327, she was delivered to Barrow in July 1901.

Thomas Fielden was launched on her first service on 26 August that year, going to the assistance of the Millom yacht, *Dorcas.* The following year the lifeboat assisted the Duddon schooner *T & EF,* which had grounded south of Walney Island.

In 1919 the *Thomas Fielden* saved ten men from the Faroese trawler, *Dorothea,* which was wrecked on Walney Island. In these years the lifeboat coxswain was Herbert Raby who was succeeded by Eb Charnley in 1917. In subsequent years other vessels assisted by the *Thomas Fielden* included the Barrow fishing boat *Daisy,* the Whitby trawler *Fairhaven* and the Fleetwood trawler *Davara.* On 23 June 1926 three people were rescued from a rowing boat that was drifting out to sea; this was the last time the *Thomas Fielden* was to come to the rescue. During her twenty-six distinguished years of service she was launched fourteen times and saved forty-five lives. She was replaced by a motor lifeboat, the *NT.*

In the Muckleburgh Collection Museum, at Weybourne, Norfolk, the *J C Madge,* can still be seen. RNLB *J C Madge* (ON 536) was a Liverpool-class, non-self righting lifeboat, stationed at Sheringham in Norfolk from December 1904 until June 1936. During this period she was launched on service thirty-four times, saving fifty-eight lives. She was built in 1903 (Yard number: TK68) at the cost of £1,436 16s 6d, the money coming from a legacy of £2,000 left to the RNLI by a chemist from Southampton, Mr James C. Madge. A pulling and sailing lifeboat, 41ft in length and a beam of 11ft, *J C Madge* was the largest lifeboat of that type made up to that point, and the only Liverpool-class lifeboat of this kind. She weighed 5 tons 7cwt and had a displacement of 12 tons 1cwt.

She left Canning Town on 30 November 1904, in the hands Coxswain William 'Click' Bishop and a crew of six. In fair weather she made her way around the east coast, stopping overnight at Harwich and Great Yarmouth, getting to Sheringham on 2 December 1904.

When *J C Madge* arrived at Sheringham she was located at Old Hythe (at the west end of Sheringham golf course) in a new purpose-built lifeboat house (situated about a mile west of Sheringham). She was inaugurated on 13 December 1904 at a ceremony at Old Hythe, at which she was given her name by the daughter of the president of the local RNLI branch, Mr H.R. Upcher JP.

She was clinker built and fitted with two sliding or drop-keels fitted out with two water-ballast tanks. *J C Madge* had two masts; the foremast carried a dipping lug sail, while the mizzen mast had a standing lug sail. Her crew of nineteen pulled sixteen oars that were double-banked for heavy weather. Her launching carriage, which was constructed by the Bristol Wagon & Carriage Works Company, arrived in Sheringham separately, carried by train. It was built with larger front wheels with a series of flat metal plates around the circumference of each wheel, which helped prevent the structure sinking in soft sand. Heavy ropes were tied to the carriage to allow thirty or more men to haul *J C Madge* into the sea, until the water was of sufficient depth for her to be rowed out on her mission. If, for some reason, the lifeboat could not be launched in this way, she would be pulled out into the waves using a haul-off warp (a windlass) and a thick rope anchored around 200yd into the surf, secured at the beach end to a post by the lifeboat house. There was a large manually operated winch to the rear of the lifeboat house to help to recover the craft on her return.

J C Madge was on station at Old Hythe over three decades. During this period she was launched thirty-four times, saving fifty-eight lives. Her first rescue took place on 6 January 1905, going to the aid of the London Barges *Gothic* and *Teutonic*. The crews were removed and landed in Sheringham. Later the *J C Madge*, along with the *Henry Ramey Upcher*, the fisherman's lifeboat, towed both barges to Great Yarmouth.

Early in the morning of 24 February 1916 the steamship SS *Uller* of Bergen was making her way from Sunderland to La Pallice. Carrying a cargo of coal, she foundered on Dudgeon Sands during a snow storm while gale force winds blew.

Uller was critically damaged as she floated off, and drifted for around eighteen hours, until she once more hit the bottom on the Blakeney Overfalls bank. In severe difficulty she drifted clear into deeper water, signalling for assistance. The maroons called out the Sheringham lifeboat.

But the only messages to be received by *Uller* gave the frightening news that neither the Cromer nor the Wells lifeboats were able to launch because of to the difficult conditions. However, the Sheringham crew made the long run, in the darkness, from the town to the lifeboat house, over the cliffs that had been trenched and barb wired.

The *J C Madge* was launched by means of the haul-off warp and the first wave she hit engulfed her, drenching her crew.

The courageous lifeboat found *Uller* just inside the Blakeney Overfalls at approximately 10 p.m. and put the second coxswain and a crewmember aboard the stranded ship. Following consultation with her skipper it was established that *Uller* still had steam and was able to accomplish half power. Thus, for what remained of the night, in the unforgiving conditions, the crew of the *J C Madge*, exposed to the elements, stood by.

As the morning broke, *Uller* made for Grimsby, towing the lifeboat on a 90ft line. *J C Madge*'s crew were obliged to do what they could to avoid being tossed onto the propeller of the *Uller*, which was, by that point, half out of the water as a consequence of her having taken on water in her damaged bow.

It took two days to cover the 53 miles to the Humber Estuary. The lifeboatmen spent the night in Grimsby, most had family and friends there. But back in Sheringham their family had received no report of the fate of their loved ones who had rowed into the black roaring sea days before.

A French steamer took the lifeboat in tow for a stretch of the voyage back to Sheringham and the *J C Madge* returned at last at 6 p.m. on the 28 February.

On 2 April 1936 *J C Madge* committed to her final service (poetically) to *Little Madge*, a Sheringham fishing boat. *Little Madge* had got into trouble and the lifeboat had taken off her two crewman and took her in tow. However both craft had to be hauled to safety by RNLB *H F Bailey III* (ON 777) – the Cromer Lifeboat.

J C Madge was replaced by the *Foresters Centenary* (ON 786) and sailed into retirement from service at Sheringham (she was decommissioned on 22 June 1936). She remained at Sheringham for more than a month prior to being sold out of service for £80 to W. Gillard of Wembley, Middlesex.

Converted into a private pleasure craft with an added cabin, *J C Madge* could be seen for many years trolling round the Norfolk and Lincolnshire coast. However, in 1988 she went on display at the Sheringham station's annual Lifeboat Day, raising £30,000, money that ultimately went toward saving even more lives. This motivated her purchase for restoration in 1989 by the Sheringham Museum Trust.

In the summer of that year the *J C Madge* sailed from Brancaster around the coast to the Lowestoft International Boatbuilding College at Oulton Broad. There she was renovated and returned to her service appearance. On 14 August 1999 the National Historic Ships Committee placed the *J C Madge* on the National Register of Historic Vessels (certificate no. 1763). From March 2010 she was placed on permanent display at the new Sheringham Museum.

While on station *J C Madge* had coxswains, William 'Click' Bishop (1904 to 1914), Obadiah Craske Cooper (1914 to 1924) and James Edward Dumble (1924 to 1936).

Service and rescues of *J C Madge* (ON 536):

Date	Casualty	Lives saved	Assistance
6 January 1906	Barge *Gothic*, of London	3	Gave help
7 January 1906	Barge *Gothic*, of London		Gave help to save barge
24/25 November 1909	Barge *Lord Morton*, of London	3	Save barge
8 April 1911	Whelk boats, of Sheringham	6	Saved two boats
8 April 1911	Whelk boats, of Sheringham (2nd launch of the day)	6	Saved two boats
24 February 1916	Steamship *Uller*, of Bergen		Stood by and escorted to safety
16 March 1916	Steamship *Rhenania*, of London (Prize vessel CT.5)		Assisted to save vessel
6 May 1916	Steamship *Theodor*, of London (Prize vessel CS.73)	7	Assisted to save vessel
18 April 1918	Steamship *Alice Taylor*, of Dundee	18	Saved
15 July 1919	Airship *NS11* crashed near Blakeney		Unsuccessful search

9 February 1924	Barge *Oceanic*, of London	3	Saved barge
15 November 1925	Four-mast schooner *Ingebord*, of Helsingborg	10	Assisted to save vessel
12 February 1927	Steamship *Helmsmen*, of Newcastle		Stood by
5 January 1930	Steamship *Lestris*, of Bruges		Gave help
31 May 1935	Three-mast schooner *Six Sisters*, of Hull		Gave help
2 April 1936	Fishing boat *Little Madge*, of Sheringham	2	Saved boat

James Stevens No 14 (ON 432) the second RNLI lifeboat to be stationed at Walton-on-the-Naze, was one of twenty craft financed from a £50,000 legacy by James Stevens, a businessman from Birmingham. The twenty vessels were all named after him. *No 14* was a 43ft Norfolk & Suffolk-class pulling and sailing type. TI 35 (her yard number at Thames Ironworks) cost £1,420 to build.

No 14's lifeboat house at East Terrace (now Walton Maritime Museum) needed to be enlarged to contain her. However, in 1900 she was put afloat on a mooring off the south side of Walton pier (the location where every Walton RNLI lifeboat has been stationed since that time) on a permanent basis.

In 1905 *No 14* returned to Thames Ironworks for the fitting of a 40hp Blake petrol engine, making her one of the first motor lifeboats to serve the RNLI cause. She was one of three N&S converted by the Ironworks. The others (which were not originally built by the Thames) were ON 350 *Bradford* (a 42ft S/R built in 1893) and ON 407 *Michael Henry* (a 37ft S/R built in 1897).

A mechanic, Frank Halls, was appointed to care for her engine. *No 14* was now able to reach speeds of 7 to 8 knots. However, the vessel retained its sails and oars, although one of the drop keels needed to be removed. On 26 October 1906, *No 14* returned to Walton-on-the-Naze, and on 26 January 1907 she made her initial service launch under motor power.

James Stevens No 14 was launched 126 times during her service career, rescuing 227 souls. On 29/30 December 1917 she gave her most celebrated service, rescuing ninety-two passengers and crew from SS *Peregrine* (London) which, in a force nine easterly gale, had run aground on the Long Sand Head. The coxswain of the time, William Hammond, was awarded a Silver Medal. John Byford, the second coxswain, received a Bronze Medal. A couple of cats were also saved from the waves.

It was on 29 March 1928 that *No 14* made her final service launch. She was sold out of RNLI service for £180 to a Maldon timber importing company (May & Butcher) to work on the Rivers Colne and Blackwater. At some point in the subsequent fourteen years *No 14* was purchased by J. Powles Ltd, and given the name *Mardee*. Under this moniker good evidence suggests that she played a role in the evacuation of Dunkirk in 1940. She returned to her birth place on the Thames with the Department of War Transport in May 1942 as a fire-boat – two big oval metal plates on her hull tell of the position of the water inlets for her fire hoses. She was still protecting and saving life.

Four years later she was decommissioned (at Ibbotson's yard at Beccles, Suffolk) and bought for £500 by Graham Starke. His son, Michael, recalled the removal of a plaque by the seller at the time *No 14* was sold, which made reference to the evacuation of Dunkirk. At this time she had a single Scripps V8 petrol engine fitted, an American Ford derivative used in Bren gun carriers during in the Second World War. At Lowestoft in 1951 a secondary Kelvin petrol engine was fitted on the starboard side. From 1952 *No 14* was moored at Brightlingsea, from where she was sailed regularly by the Starke family in the Blackwater and Colne estuaries.

During 1961 *No 14* was taken to Maylandsea for an extensive refit at Cardnell's Yard, which included a new stern post. She was kept in the Heybridge Basin from 1963. Four years on Mr Starke came across another Scripps V8 engine in a Ministry of Defence warehouse in Southampton. It was as good as new in its shipment crate, oiled and greased. This replaced the identical engine that had driven *No 14* for a couple of decades.

In August 1976, for the price of £1,200, *No 14* was bought by Mr R. Gale of Hornchurch. He had an ambition to sail her via the Bay of Biscay to the Mediterranean, but ultimately she was destined to sail on fresh water and the Heybridge Canal for a couple of years. Her next owner, Mr M. Burling, removed her engines and ancillary equipment and transformed the former lifeboat into a houseboat, to take up a mud berth at Maldon. In 1988 ownership passed to D.P. Orriss and three years later to J. Newton.

During the 1990s Tony Denton, a member of the Lifeboat Enthusiasts' Society, discovered and identified *No 14*. Notwithstanding a large ziggurat, she was recognisable for the craft she had once been. The stemhead fairleads and the wide fender so idiosyncratic to her class were discernable. Sadly alteration to her stem left only the '3' of her yard number (TI 35) visible. For all this, investigation and consultation revealed her to be *James Stevens No 14* and the world's oldest surviving motor lifeboat.

In 1996 Frinton & Walton Heritage Trust was told where *No 14* was located. The Newtons loaned the Thames Ironworks' builder's plate to Walton Maritime Museum for display and in 1998, they asked for the plate to be returned because they wanted to sell the vessel. This motivated the Trust to purchase her and restore her to her 1906 motorised state, so that she might be used by the public for short trips in the immediate vicinity of Walton-on-the-Naze.

Over a decade, with an investment of £250,000 along with thousands of hours of voluntary work, restoration was accomplished. September 2009 saw the relaunch of *James Stevens No 14* by Griff Rhys Jones at Titchmarsh Marina, Walton-on-the-Naze, her operational base and where she is usually on view. She was one of the historic craft that took part in Her Majesty the Queen's Diamond Jubilee Pageant on the River Thames on 3 June 2012.

Now *James Stevens No 14* is a working exhibit of Walton Maritime Museum (accredited by the Museums Libraries & Archives Council). Frinton & Walton Heritage Trust (registered charity no 289885) manages, operates and owns her. She works as a small commercial vessel in the Maritime & Coastguard Agency (MCA) Area Category 4 – in daylight and favourable weather, up to 20 miles from a safe haven. She can carry up to eleven passengers at any one time.

15

FRANK CLARKE·HILLS

THE GREENWICH CHEMICAL WORKS

In 1804, on the east side of an area then known as Greenwich Marsh on the Thames Peninsula, soap-maker George Russell built a large tide mill over the site of an artesian well. This area was later to become the Riverway area of Deptford and in 2000 was the site of the Millennium Festival,

The first organised Association football games played to common regulations were taking place within the sound of a blast of a big ship's hooter, not too long after George Russell built his mill to the east of Greenwich Marsh. It was designed on an industrial scale and used to grind corn. During its construction the boiler of a steam engine, designed by steam pioneer Richard Trevithick, exploded. This accident was to become famous in the history of steam engine development as it exposed innate deficiencies in the technology of the time, changing the way steam power was to develop.

In 1840, six years before Charles Mare watched his *Mosquito* glide into the waters of the Thames, Russell's mill, by then known as the East Greenwich Tidemill, came into the hands of Frank Clarke Hills as part of the settlement of his marriage to Ellen Rawlings. The large site had excellent wharfage facilities, ideal for a business that depended on water transport. Under the ownership of Hills it is probable that corn continued to be ground at East Greenwich. From 1845 it was described as a 'steam flour mill' and perhaps the tide mill itself was replaced by a 25hp steam engine.

On the riverbank to the north of the mill, Frank Hills erected a chemical works which was gradually extended. In the 1840s housing was built for the chemical works employees near the mill in Riverway. It was called River Terrace and added to the existing Ceylon Place, built at the same time as the mill. Parts of Russell's 'New East Greenwich' housing can still be seen and a public house, 'The Pilot Who Weathered the Storm' named in honour of William Pitt, is still open today as simply 'The Pilot'. There was a big house on the riverside, Frank Hills' riverside foreman's house. This is where the works manager Thomas Davies and his family lived. Today the Greenwich Yacht Club's clubhouse stands on the site.

The smell, of 'an acid and sickening character', caused widespread complaint in Greenwich and Charlton and annoyed the garrison at Woolwich, which was 3 miles away.

One of the firms operations might conjure up something of the impact of this stink. It manufactured manure from 'shoddy', which was a concoction made from waste leather, dry bones, bone ash and refuse from sugar bakers – whatever organic rubbish could be bought cheaply, piled up and mixed with sulphuric acid. The toxic fumes of manufacture took its toll on the workforce, not a few dying from their effects. In 1871, Mr Pink, the Medical Officer of Health for Greenwich gave advice designed for 'abatement of the nuisance which these works could scarcely have failed to occasion.'

VICTORIAN ENTREPRENEUR AND INDUSTRIAL INNOVATOR

Frank Hills, owner of the F.C. Hills & Co. Chemical Works, was an industrial chemist, who hitherto had been based in Deptford. He is an almost perfect example of the Victorian businessman. His chemical works at East Greenwich grew consistently over a fifty-year period and, with his brothers, he developed a model of early industrial capitalist development, controlling a range of linked commercial manufacturing and production concerns that amounted to an expansive empire stretching from East London to Spain, from Wales to South America.

Frank Hills has a rather opaque lineage. His father, Thomas, appears to have moved to Bromley-by-Bow just before 1810. At the start of the nineteenth century Bromley-by-Bow was a busy industrial area that boasted the largest alcohol industry in the country. It was a district of mills, mostly driven by the tides of the River Lea but not the Bromley Steam Mill, the mill that Thomas Hill had taken over from C. & J. Millward in 1811. Thomas used the mill for grinding corn and the manufacture of chemicals, converting the waste materials from the early gas industry. What he manufactured is unknown, but his accounts show that he used considerable quantities of this material between 1824 and 1827, indicating the Bromley Steam Mill was chiefly a chemical company during this period.

An account of Thomas' activity was written in 1827, about the time when he seems to have left Bromley-by-Bow, possibly because of bankruptcy. This account places his factory in Bromley, Kent. This inaccuracy has been replicated elsewhere, but as the St Leonards, Bromley Rate Books testify, Thomas Hills lived in Bromley-by-Bow. A letter also exists, written in large, careful letters on squared paper, which confirms this. It was addressed to Bromley Steam Mills and is from Thomas' son Frank who would have been about eight when he wrote it in 1815.

The Hills ancestry seems to have been Kentish. It was in this county, in Kemsing, in 1700 that a Richard Hills of Underriver rented a field to a William Wells. The families of Wells and Hills had a long history in Penshurst. The Wells family were shipbuilders, industrialists and politicians. However, it is uncertain what Thomas Hills had done or where he had resided before his arrival at Bromley-by-Bow, although there is considerable circumstantial evidence that places him in Somerset. Thomas married a Sara Clarke; her surname had been associated with the district of Lyme for hundreds of years. Thomas junior was born in Lyme Regis in 1804, having been named after his father and was probably their eldest son. Another, son, Henry, married Charlotte, who was from Lyme. In the eighteenth century Lyme was a holiday resort and a naval seaport, but it also had a relatively large chemical industry and was the source of the clay used for Coade stone, the terracotta used throughout London, the mixture of which was said to be a secret. Lyme may well have been where Thomas senior learnt the skills of industrial chemistry.

Thomas Hills and Uriah Haddock identified an innovative process for the manufacture of acid and took a patent out for this in 1818. It was revolutionary and chemists and industrialists came to Bromley to see how it was done. The discovery is described in almost every history of the chemical industry and this illustrates its importance in the development of the manufacturing and production in this area.

It was not long before Thomas was obliged to go to law following infringement of patent by Thompson and Hill of Liverpool. Defending his inventions and procedures related to the chemical and gas industries was a practice that one of his sons, Frank was to become adept at. In two or three cases Frank fought legal battles that dragged on for decades. A proportion of this legal action appeared to be less justified than it might have been, but he seemed to have made a good deal of money out of these proceedings through compensation and contract settlements. For example, an appeal from a consortium of gas companies that went to the Privy Council showed that Frank Hills had 'received £107,377 0s 9d in royalties. His expenses rated £16,942 … and … £6,450 for his own salary after paying the same sum to his brother, Thomas, and some large sums to other brothers'. This was a time when top gas executives and engineers could expect a salary of around £1,000 per annum. As such it can be seen that Frank Hills had an astute business instinct. He was involved in an almost endless process of developing and exploiting partnerships with other innovators.

Early in the 1830s Frank Hills began to contact the London gas companies from the Deptford Chemical Works that he rented from Frederick Beneke. Beneke, who came from a family with a strong background in chemistry and metallurgy, lived in Denmark Hill, Camberwell, not too far from Frank who resided in the same district, in North Terrace. In 1836 the London and Greenwich Railway was built across Deptford Creek, and included a gas works alongside the line on a site next to Deptford Chemical Works. It was said that when the gas works became independent of the railway, Frank provided a mortgage on it and experimented on gas industry waste. He carried out a great deal of research at Deptford, continuously experimenting in the laboratories and the engineering workshops chiefly focusing on gas works wastes. His collaborators at this time included the mysterious Reverend Dale and a German chemist by the name of Mr Baufe. Whilst testing the impurities of a batch of guano, he discovered a means of extracting iodine. This was an important breakthrough and the firm went on to undertake this industrially. Sulphur was also refined at Deptford and sold to Kentish hop growers.

By the mid-1830s several London gas companies were dealing with Frank Hills' methods and in the early 1840s the Hills' business expanded to include a short-lived chemical works at Battersea and could have been involved with the Hills Chemical Works in Wandsworth, which failed and was subsumed into Wandsworth Gas Works.

Frank Hills did not confine his business interests to the chemical industry. In the early 1840s he became known for the development of steam road vehicles. The best known promoter of steam road vehicles was Stratford based Walter Hancock. During 1839 Frank travelled on a Hancock vehicle on a trip to Cambridge, as a contemporary engineering journal was to relate, 'taking a lesson on steam carriage construction during the journey'. He later patented a gearing system that Fletcher in *Steam Locomotion on Common Roads* suggested had originally been developed by Roberts of Manchester. His work on steam cars appears to have been undertaken in collaboration with the General Steam Carriage Co. of East Greenwich. Some well-publicised trips were taken over particularly steep and difficult hills in the area but the venture seems to have been unsuccessful. Sixty years later his son, Arnold Hill, was to take up road vehicle manufacture in the 'Thames cars' line of coaches and cars.

The Hills brothers won prizes for their innovations in the chemical industry at the 1851 Great Exhibition, some of the products of which were recognised worldwide. This included material he exported to the West Indies to be used in the sugar cane industry.

The profits of the chemical industry appear to have been invested in heavy engineering. In 1871, at a time when he was at his peak of activity with the gas companies, Frank acquired a controlling interest in the Thames Ironworks and Shipbuilding Company.

Perhaps prophetically this was the same year the Football Association Cup competition was introduced. It was to help bring the game to a wider geographical constituency and promote an understanding of the rules throughout England and beyond. Former Upton Park player Alfred Stairs was at that meeting and was on the subcommittee that chose the trophy. His in-depth knowledge of the rules of the game was such that he was invited to referee the first three FA Cup finals.

Clubs were emerging with unprecedented speed in the Midlands and North. Whilst a number of these new clubs were the product of the activity of ex-public schoolboys, many of those who later joined their ranks were artisans, tradesmen and factory workers, and a substantial number of these men proved to have a talent for the game. The growing leisure industry that developed alongside the manufacturing industry, offered these individuals the chance of supplementing their earnings by playing in front of paying spectators, and not a few took up the opportunity. Some were sufficiently skilful to take up the game on a full-time basis. It is certainly true that well before professional football was legalised within the sport in 1885, many clubs had made payments to players to turn out for them.

Just as Frank Hills was pioneering within his industry, this was the beginning of what would become commercial football. It was the start of the laying of the necessary foundations for development. To understand football as an enterprise it has to be located in its beginnings in the industrial development of the first mature capitalist economy, Britain.

In the last third of the nineteenth century the Thames Ironworks and Shipbuilding Company were thought to be 'the greatest shipyard of all'. Frank Hills was to be chair of the board of this great enterprise until his death in 1895. However, Frank had been involved with the Thames Ironworks as a member of the board sometime before 1864, first appearing on the list of board members for a new shares issue. It is likely that he had an interest from the time that Thames Ironworks had been established following the bankruptcy of C.J. Mare in 1856, when the company had been launched with a capital of £100,000 in £5,000 shares, all sold on the first day of issue to local engineering companies.

Frank's involvement with Thames Ironworks paralleled the company's golden age. By the early 1870s the firm led in its field in every conceivable way. The peak of this period occurred in the 1890s when they specialised in quality work. The impetus from this era of excellence carried them, alone on the Thames, into the twentieth century.

Frank relished his role as chair of Thames Ironworks. Tales about his enthusiasm abounded. He explored each new battleship with all the excitement of a boy as, in the embrace of the Thames, it kissed the waves for the first time. He had no way of comprehending that he was living through the final phase of shipbuilding on London's river. He could not have guessed that it was his son's destiny to struggle in vain with the government and preside over the closure of his yards and the loss of the skills that had made his business renowned on the face of the planet.

THE FORGOTTEN GIANT

In the parish church of St Luke, in Chiddingstone Causeway, Kent, you will find a memorial to Frank Clarke Hills. Like a good number of London-based industrial entrepreneurs who scaled the heights of success on the banks of the Thames, Frank retired to the Kent countryside. He spent his final years at his home, Redleaf, on the hill above Penshurst Place with his zoophytes and a new gramophone. To his last days he could recite *Paradise Lost* in its entirety off by heart. In the first years of the twenty-first century only the gateposts and lodge endured of this once grand and beautiful structure. Designed by J.C. Loudon, a leading garden architect of the time, they had been commissioned by William Wells, the shipbuilder and owner of Redleaf before Frank acquired it, squaring a 300-year circle between the Hills and Wells families. When Frank Hills came to live at Redleaf in the 1880s, like Wells, he was also a father to battleships.

When Frank Hills died in May 1895, reports of his death were restricted to two or three lines in local newspapers. It took until 29 July for *The Times* to publish a report of his will, which had been lifted from the *Illustrated London News*. It had been discovered that this practically anonymous south-east London chemical manufacturer had left a personal fortune of £1,942,836 11s 1d. When W.D. Rubenstein analysed the wealth of the Victorian era in 1977 he showed that just forty individuals in the period between 1809 and 1914 left more than £2m. Frank Hills was very close to being included in this exulted company. Between 1880 and 1899, sixty-nine British millionaires had passed on – just three chemical manufacturers can be found amongst the names.

There is no evidence to suggest that Frank Hills inherited huge wealth. His brother Thomas, who died in comfortable circumstances, left just £3,657; another brother left £20,909. This being the case, Frank's final financial situation demonstrates that he was a remarkable businessman. Even from the grave he was still 'at it'. It took three years from the day he died to discover that the buildings and site of his main factory were not his and had to be removed from his estate. However, this only amounted to a value of £1,583.

Frank Hills was a great Victorian industrialist, probably a genius, but remains almost unknown. There is a document in the Kent County Archive that details Frank's agreement to hand power of attorney to his sons. It is signed in a feeble hand, his butler acting as a witness. His death at the close of the nineteenth century was closely followed by those of his two eldest sons. The Deptford Chemical Works was put into the hands of Thomas Herbert Hills, the son of his departed brother Thomas. The husbands of Frank's two daughters, Constance and Annie, administered the company from a distance. Within a few years the organisation that Frank Hills had founded and nurtured was bankrupt. The works at East Greenwich was taken over by the South Metropolitan Gas Company and George Russell's mill was converted to a power station. South Met had taken over most of the south London gas works during the 1870s and was one of the biggest concerns in the British gas industry by the last decade of the nineteenth century. During the First World War they were to use part of the site for research into chemical weapons.

Frank Hills filled a gap in the gas industry, doing the seemingly impossible, making a huge amount of money from its vile and noxious waste products. This was a man who followed the lineage of Merlin and the mystic path of the medieval apothecary. Guided by a sexton of the rough science that evoked the Victorian nightmares of Frankenstein, Jekyll and Hyde, he fulfilled the ancient dream of alchemy. In the bubbling, steaming, acidic atmosphere of the laboratory he turned base metal into gold. He exploited his own intelligence and the wisdom of others, being willing to learn from those around him and work hard on his enthusiasms. He rode roughshod over the patent system to mercilessly exploit the potential of his industry. His success blossomed out of his ingenuity and doggedness but more than anything else his energetic and seemingly boundless gusto. He left the gas company directors exhausted and exasperated. He left competitors gasping in his wake. However, he remains more or less unremembered by general history and uncelebrated by his own industry.

16

THE HILLS BOYS

Frank Hills was only one prominent member of an industrial and industrious family. There were several brothers, sons, daughters and nephews. Between them they achieved enormous success, stretching the bounds of their own family empire and pushing the parameters of their industrial context. As a phenomenon they represent a model of capitalist development in transition. The development of their informal consortium was very much based on a family nexus, but it was set in the secular and rational environment of commercial enterprise. It is unlikely that we will see their like again, but their example stands as an historical monument to them as a vibrant family and as creative individuals but also to their dynamic era.

FOUR BROTHERS, A SISTER, A NEPHEW AND AN UNCLE

In 1833 Thomas Hills, probably the eldest brother of Frank Hill, patented a boiler grate. However, by 1846 he was looking for a job. He applied for the post of Deputy Superintendent at the Phoenix Gas Works in Greenwich. He said that he was, 'a good practical chemist and accustomed to the control of workmen who would want a salary of £300 a year.' Phoenix turned him down because he was too experienced. After that he worked for his brother Frank, 'dealing with the commercial business at the works', both at Deptford and East Greenwich. In the early 1870s he joined Frank on the Board of Thames Ironworks.

As an old man Thomas lived at 8 The Grove, on Blackheath with his second wife and their young son, Thomas Herbert, who was described in 1891 as a 'student of chemistry'. It was he who inherited the Deptford Chemical Works. Thomas' four daughters, the eldest in her mid 30s, were still living with him in the 1880s. He died in 1885.

Another brother, George, seems to have worked for Frank at Deptford. He held joint patents with Frank, detailing his address as the 'Deptford Chemical Works'. George appears to have been active in dealing with these patents, because the record says that, 'he swore in Chancery'. This indicates that he was involved in the sugar industry. George was still alive when Frank made his will in 1890, and, although Frank left money to all his other brothers, he left nothing directly to George, choosing instead to bequest a sum to be used 'for his benefit'. That seems to imply that George was not able to make his own decisions and perhaps he needed to be cared for.

Arthur Hills gave his address as Norwood when he witnessed Frank's marriage agreement in 1847. It may be that he managed the chemical works, which the family owned at Nine Elms and, perhaps, another in Wandsworth. Arthur owned a chemical works in the 1850s on the Isle of Dogs at Millwall, immediately across the river from East Greenwich, called, significantly Anglesey Works. It was situated in an area known as Folly Wall where, in the 1990s, a housing complex was built. He also rented a plot of land at Deptford Creek next to the Deptford Chemical Works for nearly thirty years. He must have passed away in 1891 as he was alive when Frank made his will in 1890, but he was dead before Frank died.

Henry, who was younger than Thomas and Arthur, being born after the family moved to Bromley-by-Bow, spent much of his life commuting between Anglesey in North Wales and south London, where he lived in one of the high quality dwellings in Blackheath Paragon. His chemical works was situated in the industrial village of Amlwch, on the northern tip of Anglesey. It can be concluded that Henry probably lived part-time in Anglesey because he had a farm not far from his chemical works and several of his large family of children were born there.

Henry seems to have moved to Amlwch in 1840 and established a fertiliser factory at Llam Carw, the exposed headland overlooking the tiny harbour. It is now open cliff top where walkers enjoy sea views and the clinker of Henry's works remains underfoot. The Anglesey works closed in the 1890s.

There is some vague indication that Henry might have some connections with Birmingham since his eldest child, Alice, was born in Edgbaston in the late 1830s. *The Times* in 1859 recorded a partnership in a Bromsgrove salt works which involved a Henry Hills. Salt production is not so very far removed from some of the chemical manufacture that the Hills family was involved in. In 1863 there is evidence of a Hills sister, Jane, when Henry acted as executor to her will.

In 1860 Henry made an agreement with the Mona Mine Company. He became active in the small business community in Amlwch and was elected to the harbour board, perhaps reflecting his company's reliance on shipping. Harbour records relating to Henry's firm show shipments of raw materials from Spain and Antwerp. In 1889 the fiftieth anniversary of the chemical works in Amlwch was marked in these records together with details of its products.

At some time before 1897 Henry Hills had taken over a former smelting works complex on another harbour. This is now the site of a housing estate.

Henry and Frank probably co-operated with each other in business. Henry ended his days described as a 'chemist of Dartford' although clearly the Anglesey business was still thriving. Like Thomas he became a member of the Thames Ironworks Board in the 1870s. He died in 1897 at 6 Northbrook Road, Lee, a smaller and less fashionable address than the Paragon. He left a son, Charles Henry, who was to fulfil an important role in the family business. He seems to have had a home in Tynemouth, although he too appears to have spent much of his time in Blackheath and died in Bromley, Kent. In Newcastle he managed the Low Walker copper works. It was called the Anglesey Copper Company and sited on the Tyne with a smelter at Low Walker.

Edward Septimus Hills of Newcastle had some connection with the Anglesey works. He died in Hendon, north London in the 1880s. His brother, James, had a son, also by the name of James, who was a printer in Sunderland. The gas company minute books sometimes record a J. Hills. This could be another brother who kept the Newcastle end of the business going before Charles Henry went there. If there was also a James, then Edward Septimus could well have been Thomas senior's seventh child.

The Newcastle works is likely to have smelted copper extracted from the family mine in Spain. It would not have made sense to have brought copper from Anglesey which could have been dealt with by the existing smelter on site there. The common name given to the works in Newcastle and Millwall 'Anglesey' suggests that some of the by-products of copper smelting were used in London.

The Hills brothers' uncle Robert, who was probably a City of London-based merchant, had connections with South American metal mining, maybe having visited that part of the world himself, that, in the first part of the nineteenth century, was full of European fortune hunters. The Hills family had a continuing interest in metal mining and they also had enough capital to buy a substantial property in the 1820s. This may have been a family link with the Mexican copper mines. Many years later South American guano was used by Frank Hills at Deptford, and Thames Ironworks built vessels to aid in the exploitation of this material.

MAGNIFICENT DIVERSITY

During its history Thames Ironworks did not restrict itself to shipbuilding under any of its owners. Apart from leisure craft, lifeboats and warships, Thames Ironworks were involved in a range of other maritime, civil engineering and pioneering projects. A great many buildings continue to be kept upright by the iron structures supplied by the Hills foundry. In the latter part of its history the firm was feeling the need to diversify in response the competition from northern yards and perhaps reduce dependency on dwindling Admiralty orders. As such, the company at one point boasted several distinct departments:

- ❖ shipbuilding
- ❖ boatbuilding (encompassing production of lifeboats).
- ❖ civil engineering (which included projects like the Barry Docks Gates, Hammersmith Bridge, work on the Blackwall Tunnel and the roof of the Alexandra Palace).
- ❖ cranes
- ❖ switches, drills, marine and aeroplane engines
- ❖ motor vehicles

Its civil engineering projects included major roof building, for example at Fenchurch Street Station and, at one point, they put in a futuristic design for the Wembley Stadium. Under Peter Rolt, Thames Ironworks fabricated the iron for the International Exhibition

Building in South Kensington, the Royal Aquarium, Westminster and Alexandra Palace in the north of London. During Charles Mare's time, Thames Ironworks forged the ironwork for Blackfriars, Hammersmith and Westminster bridges, the North London Railway Bridge and sections of the rail bridge over the Menai Strait. Other bridge building included the Saltash and the Britannia Tubular bridges. Under the stewardship of Arnold Hills, Thames Ironworks built the 'New' Iron Bridge in 1896. Anyone who approached Newham from Tower Hamlets in the west up to the last years of the twentieth century will know this piece of engineering that effectively linked Canning Town and the Blackwall Tunnel, crossing the River Lea. It straddled the old boundary between Middlesex in the west and Essex to the east. The gradient of bridge it replaced always posed a problem to certain types of traffic, but the steep incline and awkward bends of the new structure was still an obstacle to horse-drawn vehicles in 1902. This was when a deputation of Silvertown traders pressurised West Ham Council to attend to the problem, and improvements were made, but not until 1929. The New Iron Bridge was replaced with a larger steel structure in 1932. Thames Ironworks produced all its own iron and steel for these projects.

The company took over Greenwich engine builders John Penn and Sons in 1902 and parts of Penn's works were given over to the production of a range of cars and lorries. It was this expansion which led to the manufacture of road vehicles at Greenwich and Vauxhall.

There were several models, one of which, a coach, can be seen today at Beaulieu Motor Museum. The prototype motor coach, which strongly resembled a stagecoach, was developed in 1902. Capable of 60hp, it had 5.0 litre, six-cylinder engine that was placed as far forward as possible to give the impression of a carriage, as do the small front and large rear wheels. The bodywork of this stagecoach was the work of Thrupp & Maberly, a company that would later provide the coachwork for deluxe manufactures such as Rolls-Royce and Mercedes-Benz.

Thames vehicles were to break all speed records from 50 to 300 miles, reaching over 75mph. A 12hp vehicle saw service as a London taxi. The firm had workshops at the famous motor racing track Brooklands, and used the circuit to test car components.

The only surviving example of a fleet of petrol-engine stagecoaches, commissioned by Motor Coaches Limited can be seen at the Louwman Museum in The Hague, Holland. The coaches were used to carry people to and from the races at Ascot and Epsom, within a 100-mile radius of London, seating passengers inside and sixteen on the roof.

This venture into motor vehicles might have hoped to have gone some way to addressing the drop in demand for marine engines. This part of the firm's operation as Thames Engineering Co. was based in Greenwich. In 1905 they exhibited at the Crystal Palace Motor Car Show and at Olympia, showing two steam carriages, a petrol delivery van and a bus chassis.

Though the core business of the Ironworks closed in 1912, the Thames Engineering subsidiary including vehicles continued, but lasted just two more years. The company's name was perpetuated in motoring history by the Thames range of trucks, vans and cars that endured well into the last quarter of the twentieth century.

Another interesting Thames innovation was the Hone's Patent Grab. The annual reports of Ironworks make regular reference to a steady income from the sale of this comparatively remarkable contraption. The U.S. Patent reads:

Be it known that I, GEORGE JAMES HONE, a subject of the King of Great Britain, residing at Clarence House, 176 Romford Road, Forest Gate, Essex, England, have invented new and useful Improvements in Grabs, of which the following is a specification … This invention relates to Grabs or excavators for coal, coke, clay, and other material …

The Hone's Patent Grab was used extensively in the gas industry, which of course the Hills family had an abiding interest in.

The Civil Engineering department of the Ironworks was responsible for a range of projects, part and whole constructions. One of these was the Admiralty Pier Lighthouse at Dover, completed in 1908, whose gun batteries protected the entrance to the Western Docks. The lighthouse continues in operation today as Grade II listed building which is open to the public.

But perhaps the most staggering (if not actualised) project was the Ironworks proposal for the Watkin competition to build a structure that might not only rival but dwarf the Eiffel Tower. It was proposed to erect this 2,007ft iron monolith at Wembley (double the height of the Parisian tower). If it had have been built it would now still be the fourth tallest structure in the world, bettered only by the Burj Khalifa skyscraper in Dubai at 2,722ft, the Skytree self-supporting tower in Tokyo at 2,080ft and the KVLY-TV guyed mast in Blanchard, North Dakota, USA at 2,063ft.

In 1911, almost as a final hooray, the company produced the dock gates for HM Dockyard at Devonport.

The Hills' also had interests in the field of mineral extraction. Above Amlwych stands Parys Mountain from which copper has been extracted for hundreds of years in a breathtaking landscape. About a mile to the west of the Parys Mine at Morfa Dhu, Messrs Hills and Sons of Amlwych worked a bluestone mine. This material was broken down into copper, lead, zinc, silver and other elements in smaller proportions. This is the only mine clearly identified as belonging to the Hills family, but they seem to have interest in other mines.

D.C. Davies managed a phosphate mine at Berwyn in North Wales on behalf of Frank Hills and its product may have been used at Amlwych. The mine was worked between 1872 and 1884 by Davies but it does not seem to have been successful. D.C. Davis could well have been related to Thomas Davies, the Greenwich Chemical Works manager. Both men were from Oswestry and were about the same age. Thomas Davies had a family of four daughters who produced a lively and interesting family magazine, much of it dealing with their holidays in Anglesey.

Frank Hills also owned the Ponderosa copper mine in Huelva, Spain from 1876. The district is now within the Rio Tinto area. In 1889 he acquired the Buitron Mines and, in 1891, the Buitron and Huelva Co.'s assets included a railway line. This meant that the family controlled the Buitron, Zalonea, Ponderosa and Conception copper mines. These Spanish mines were taken over in due course by United Alkali.

It is likely that the Hills family owned other foreign interests. Letters exist which indicate that Frank travelled extensively abroad on business. The company certainly imported South American guano into Deptford where it was refined.

Thames Ironworks (1900).

Launch of the HMS *Thunderer*.

Embarcation of artillery on board the *Argo* at Balaclava, bound for England (*London Illustrated News*, 12 July 1856).

Pervenetz.

Serapis.

Late eighteenth-century Russian sailors.

The twin-hulled paddle steamer *Castalia* (*The Graphic,* 19 September 1874) was nearly 300ft long with a beam of 60ft 6in. She had capacity to carry 700 passengers between England and France. Built in 1874 by the Thames Ironworks for the English Channel Steamship Company at a cost of about £70,000. The Prince of Wales travelled on board the relatively stable *Castalia* as part of his journey from London to India as he was prone to seasickness. In 1878, the English Channel Steamship Company was acquired by the London, Chatham and Dover Railway Company. In 1883, she was sold to the Metropolitan Asylums Board and converted to a hospital ship. She served until 1904 and was scrapped in 1905.

A view of the Ironworks in 1900.

The Turret of HMS *Victoria* (*The Engineer*, 30 June 1893). Nicknamed 'The Slipper' this 11,000-ton Victoria-class turret ship was the sister ship of HMS *Sans Pareil*. Built by Thames Ironworks at Elswick, she was launched in 1887 to become the flagship in the Mediterranean of Admiral Sir George Tryon. She collided with HMS *Camperdown* off the coast of Syria on 22 June 1893. *Victoria* gradually turned over then suddenly turned turtle and capsized. The disaster cost the lives of Admiral Sir George Tryon and 321 officers and men.

HMS *Benbow*.

SMS *König Wilhelm* (King William) was an armoured frigate of the Prussian and later the German Imperial Navy. The ship was laid down in 1865, originally under the name *Fatikh* for the Ottoman Empire. She was purchased by Prussia in February 1867, launched in April 1868 and commissioned into the Prussian Navy in February 1869. She was, up to 1891, the largest and most powerful warship in the German Navy serving as its flagship during the Franco-Prussian War in 1870–71. In 1878, the ship accidentally rammed and sank the ironclad *Grosser Kurfürst*, with great loss of life. By early 1904 she had been superseded by newer vessels. In May of that year, she was placed out of active service and used as a floating barracks and training ship, a role she held throughout the First World War. In 1921 the ship was ultimately broken up for scrap, after a career spanning fifty-two years and three German states.

Charlie Paynter and Syd King.

Fuji.

The launch of
HMS *Cornwallis*
– the latest
addition to the
King's Navy.
(*The Sphere*,
27 July 1901)

HMS *Albion* before her launch, 21 June 1898.

Motor bikes at the Memorial Ground.

The Duchess of York christening the *Albion*. (*Illustrated London News*, Saturday 25 June 1898)

Albion: The
aftermath.

The tragic launch
of HMS *Albion*,
21 June 1898.

Thames Ironworks FC.

HMS *Duncan*.

'The Iron Walls of the British Empire: The Building of HMS *Duncan*'. (*The Sphere*, 14 July 1900) The Duncan was a 14,000-ton, twin-screw battleship with 18,000hp. She was named after Admiral Duncan (1731–1804) who routed the Dutch fleet at Camperdown on 11 October 1797 and was created Viscount Camperdown ten days later.

Lifeboat *Nancy Lucy*. Designed by the Caister crew, the Caister No 2 lifeboat *Nancy Lucy* was built at a cost £1,603 9s 8d, donated by Sir Henry W. Lucy MP. She was built in 1903 and named by the Countess of Selbourne. The *Nancy Lucy* operated from 12 June 1903 to 1929, launching forty-two times saving 144 lives.

Lifeboat C. *Madge*.

Minotaur.

Vanbrugh steamer, built by the Thames Ironworks in 1905 for excursion services on the Thames for the London County Council. After withdrawal of the service in October 1907 she was sold in June 1909 for £990 to Boieldieu Cie Rouennaise de Navigation (Rouen) for services between Rouen and La Bouille, where she was renamed *Boieldieu*. She was named after architect Sir John Vanbrugh, who designed Blenheim Palace. Several buildings within the Royal Arsenal are also attributed to Sir John.

HMS *Thunderer*.

Petty Officer Gibbons pictured here with his wife during his service with HMS *Thunderer*.

Thunderer cartoon.

PUNCH, OR THE LONDON CHARIVARI.—FEBRUARY 1, 1911.

A PROUD PARENT.

NEPTUNE. "SHIP AHOY! WHAT SHIP'S THAT?"   FATHER THAMES. "*THUNDERER*. LITTLE THING OF MY OWN."

[*H.M.S. Thunderer*, the first *Dreadnought* built on the Thames, is to be launched from the Thames Ironworks on February 1.]

Theseus.

Grafton.

It is probable that Frank Hills and his family were involved with many more enterprises than are detailed here. It has recently come to light, for example, that Frank Hills had a large site in Stratford High Street. Stratford had a large concentration of chemical works. This interest was sold to a soap company.

It is perhaps too easy to forget that the innovatory nature of the products and projects developed by the Thames Ironworks were themselves at one time merely generated by a particular type of person. Nowadays we probably undervalue creativity, often regarding it with suspicion because, as the font of genius, it almost inevitably departs from the norm, which can look too much like rebellion or eccentricity. At the same time, as we mistake passion for anger, and invention as disruption, we celebrate the mundane and ordinary and, all too often, sacrifice the advantage of advancement.

However Thames indulged non-conformity to the company's and society's benefit. One such example was Barnes Wallis, who invented the 'bouncing bomb' that did much to shorten the Second World War. The Ironworks was his first employer in January 1905 after he left Christ's Hospital school, Horsham at the age of 17. His part in what was officially called 'Operation Chastise' was immortalised in Paul Brickhill's 1951 book *The Dam Busters* and the 1955 film of the same name (Barnes was played by the towering talent of Michael Redgrave).

Another Thames employee of a quite different stamp was Donald McGill, who would become the doyen of the 'cheeky' postcards. McGill started his working life at the Thames Ironworks as a naval draughtsman before falling into his lifetime's work. He was encouraged by his family after producing a get-well card for an ailing nephew. He fashioned more than 12,000 drawings in his lifetime, selling an estimated 200 million postcards, finding in almost equal portions fame and infamy. George Orwell penned an essay relating to McGill's work. However, approaching 80 years of age, Donald found himself prosecuted under the Obscene Publications Act. If there was ever an unsung hero of the battle against pompous and senseless prudishness McGill might take the plaudits. That said, it is doubtful how much the pious Arnold Hills might have appreciated the harmless if ribald character of Donald's humour.

This chapter gives a picture of the diversity and energy of the Hills family throughout the Victorian era. It also provides an idea of another part of the context out of which Thames Ironworks Football Club arose. The club that was to become West Ham United had, as its seed, the commercial and entrepreneurial forces of the most vibrant of times, its forefathers were energetic, industrious innovators, willing to take risks, looking to extend boundaries and fight in the face of all odds to achieve ambitions, part of which was to be the best. This was part of the institutional culture of Thames Ironworks. Like all the other influences that this book has analysed, the forces that shaped and moulded the football club, it could not be resisted or repressed. What the Hills family understood is that organisations must develop or die. Stasis is death. Maybe the reputation for limited ambitions that for many years West Ham United carried, to achieve 'their share' or mere 'respectability' needs to be understood in the light of the founding culture of the club. Raising its organisational gaze beyond confines of Green Street to the Olympic Stadium seems more congruent with the club's origins than the urge to seek out safety in the modest vacuum of relative obscurity.

IRONWORKS FADE, HAMMERS APPEAR

In the final months of the nineteenth century it seems that Arnold Hills realised that a club with a broad enthusiastic following might not be compatible with amateurism, and he began the slow process of drawing back from the rational consequences of the situation that he had created. This was evident in a piece he wrote for the *Thames Iron Works Gazette* during this period, which seemed at the same time to be proposing a kind of compromise:

> The clubs of ours have to grow, but let them always represent our own people. It may be necessary, at the beginning, to introduce a little ferment of professional experience to leaven the heavy lump; but even then let these professional experts come into the yards to work as well as play.

This idea, a mixture of naivety and 'shamateurism', was the concoction of a defeated and out-of-touch man whom time and events had passed by. Hills' problem, from his perspective, was that he had created a monster, but the logic of capitalist enterprise was at work and was about to offer him a way out.

Late in the nineteenth century the Ironworks bought out John Penn and Sons and, in order to raise new capital, Hills made his firm a public company. He had issued 4,000 10s shares, anticipating that they would be under-subscribed. He had offered to buy one share for every share purchased. Shares were offered first to staff at the Ironworks and then to the general public, but there was no rush to buy. At that time the typical working man in the East End would have been hard-pressed to find the money for even a single share.

However, Hills was to find himself, for the first time, accountable to shareholders. He was no longer an industrial potentate able to act in philanthropic ways as the whim took him. One of the first things that became clear was that the Ironworks could no longer retain their football club. From this new functional capitalist perspective of the public limited company, the Irons and the Memorial Ground represented a burdensome money-losing operation. It was only justifiable if it created better conditions in the Ironworks.

Hills no longer believed that its primary purpose was recreation for his workers. Neither did he feel that the club contributed to company morale or its bank balance.

Hills was still in a position to influence events, but what should he do? He could have done nothing and watch the company abolish the club. His other alternative was to transform Thames, create some initiative by which the continued existence of the club could benefit the Ironworks. He was undoubtedly emotionally involved. The club had not turned out as he had wanted, but it was his child and if it disappeared he ran the risk of this being seen as his failure. There was also the problem of the Memorial Ground. Like the club, its most salient characteristic was that it was there. If the Memorial Ground was not used it would stand as silent testimony to the demise of Hills' dreams to create a morally better society through sport and a football team with whom the local community could identify.

The next move that Hills made was a blend of capitalist inspiration, a last gasp philanthropy and good old British compromise. He kept the team in existence but severed its formal connections with the Ironworks. He proposed a limited company but did not use the situation to cut his personal losses and run. He became a major shareholder, urged fellow businessmen and workers to invest in the club and provided the Memorial Ground on very favourable terms (rent free for three years). It was, in fact, a brilliant solution but it made him a hypocrite. He had pulled in money from the sale of shares in his football club and made himself a sizable investor in an organisation devoted to making its financial supporters a profit from professional sport. The Hills family involvement with the club had endured. Patrick Hills (Arnold Hills' Grandson) served in the Navy as an officer in the Second World War. His cousin, Charles Warner was a West Ham United director up to the start of the twenty-first century.

At the end of June 1900, the Thames Ironworks Football Club resigned from the Southern League and was wound up. Within days, the club was reformed under the name of West Ham United and was elected to take the place of the Ironworks in the Southern League. A new secretary, Swansea-born Lew M. Bowen, a clerk at the Ironworks, and one-time match reporter for the *Gazette* was appointed. Lazzeleur Johnson, a clerk who lived in Forest Gate, was the first chair of the board. He worked for Thames Ironworks and had been connected with its Football Club. He purchased ten shares of West Ham United in July 1900 when they were first issued to the public.

There are a number of theories why the Hammers adopted their claret and blue strip, most claim some relationship with Arnold Hills, the azure element supposedly tying in with the cobalt of the Old Harrovians[13] and/or his representation of Oxford University. However, it is unlikely that Hills would have approved of the besmirching of his beloved amateur ties with the taint of professionalism.

My grandfather, Jim Belton, told me that Charlie Dove obtained West Ham's first claret and blue the kits 'cheap'. This was thanks to Jim's father William. The latter had been involved in the coaching of the Thames players, but he was also a professional sprinter,

---

13. For whom Hills had played club football.

who competed all over the country. In the summer of 1899 William had defeated four Aston Villa footballers in an impromptu race held at a fair in Birmingham. The Villa men had been so confident of victory over the scrawny cockney that they had gambled themselves with money they did not have. This being the case they were obliged to pay their debt by handing over a dozen or so Aston Villa kits (what at that time were called 'uniforms') to cover their loss – apparently one of the 'Villains' was responsible for the side's laundry and reported the kits missing on his return to the club. I took this to be just 'local colour' for many years until, when interviewing a former West Ham player from the 1930s, he told me a similar story, that the 'uniforms' had been won in a race held near to Villa Park and 'flogged' to a West Ham player for £3 10s. I first related this story in the West Ham United Miscellany in 2005. It has, over recent years, been confused, via a Wikipedia entry, and repeatedly stated in a number of publications that William (Bill) was the father of Charlie.

It seems likely that new colours were adopted partly to provide the new club with a new identity. That West Ham United might be associated with the success of Aston Villa, the club that had won the 1899/1900 Football League Division One Championship and three of the previous four League titles, could have been taken to be all to the good. Apart from the characteristic Hammers logo, West Ham's first strip was an exact replica of that worn by the 'Villains' of that period. Packaging and promotion were primary considerations from the very first moments of professionalism. Mercenary allegiances to Dagenham Motors, BAC Windows, Dr Martin's, JobServe, latterly Alpari FX but most shamefully SBOBET, have been mere contemporary expansions on a basic theme, to be consigned to the realm of 'the forgotten', melting into the thinnest of air, the ether of the insignificant – lost memories of superficial floss that signify nothing.

Events at Canning Town in the summer of 1900 could not be regarded entirely as a parting of the ways. The new club and the shipbuilders maintained a relationship, albeit an uneasy one, for some years afterwards. However, West Ham United Football Club was registered as a company on 5 July 1900 and Thames Ironworks Football Club passed into history.

CHAIRMAN GRISDALE

It is probable that Joseph Grisdale was too old to have turned out for the Ironworks side, but it seems he was involved with the team in some respect as, in 1901, when West Ham United was still based at the Memorial Ground, Joseph became a director of the club. When West Ham United moved to Upton Park in 1904, he became the Hammers' chairman, a position he would hold for the next five years.

In 1911 the former chairman and his family moved the family to the much leafier and generally more affluent west Essex district of Woodford Green. So it seems Grisdale had, as we used to say in East London, 'got the pig's head out of pawn'. He became a self-employed ship repairer and an employer himself. It seems likely that the disappearance of Thames Ironworks might have left enough residual work for a skilled and experienced man like him to make a good living and even start a more modest enterprise of his own, although the area clearly could not support a gargantuan enterprise like the one Hills had presided over. With war looming, and certainly during the First World War, there would have been a demand for his skills such as he possessed.

Grisdale had enough of a financial cushion to retire with his family to Holly Nook in Salisbury, an attractive rural location in Hampshire. He passed away in June 1921 leaving £7,490 in his will (in terms of purchasing power that would be worth about £300,000 today).

'OUR EXTREMITY IS GOD'S OPPORTUNITY ... '

Arnold Hills, Frank's third son, joined the Thames Ironworks and Shipping Company in 1880. When Frank Hills died Arnold oversaw the firm as it reached the very pinnacle of its development, between 1897 and 1902. However, at the same time when West Ham United came into being there were just 3,100 men working for the Ironworks and the losing battle against yards on the Clyde and in the north of England had begun. Twenty years after the completion of the *Warrior* the Ironworks were gradually starved of Ministry of Defence orders. Arnold Hills was obliged to make an ever-increasing effort to keep his business viable. The slow decline saw Orchard Place evacuated in 1903.

Through Parliamentary contacts he found out that northern syndicates on the Clyde and Tyne had been formed. This meant that they were able to keep production costs to a minimum and grab new orders from the Ministry. In response, Hills threatened to raise awkward questions in Parliament about the lack of orders his yard was receiving from the government, the works having only received £1 million out of an Admiralty budget of £67 million. It was at this point in 1910 that the Navy commissioned Thames Ironworks to build their biggest ever dreadnought, at 22,500 tons the largest and probably the most technically advanced battleship to sail the seas in the history of the world. The board were forced to pull the tender down to foolish levels, but HMS *Thunderer* was launched in February 1911. She was fitted out with her main armament, powerful 13in guns, at the company's works at Dagenham. She was the first ship to be fitted with directional gunfire equipment. However, the project incurred a tremendous financial loss and this, together with the First Lord of the Admiralty, Winston Churchill, refusing to give any further orders to Thames, led to the banks foreclosing on the Ironworks' debts.

Thunderer was to be the last major Thames Ironworks project. The super dreadnought was to be scrapped just sixteen years after her launch. Her career was a short one and without much in the way of incident (she fired just thirty-seven rounds at the Battle of Jutland). However, the technological innovation and advance she embodied in her design were to go on to become Royal Navy standard. These included Dreyer's fire control mechanism, which is considered by some to be the world's first modern computer, almost certainly as deployed for military purposes.

The Thames Ironworks decline was, to a significant extent, due to its heavy reliance on building warships for the Admiralty, which, despite the commission of the *Thunderer* in 1910, increasingly patronised the less expensive northern yards and Thames Ironworks came to an ignominious end.

However, this didn't happen without a fight and a degree of will to expose the character of the workings of state and capitalism in cahoots. A remarkable defence of the Thames Ironworks in 1910 by William Thorne,[14] MP for West Ham South (1857–1946) in a Commons debate, sheds some light on how the confederation of northern shipbuilders (the 'Shipping Federation') increasingly lobbied against the government awarding contracts to the London shipbuilder:

> I want to enter my emphatic protest against the way in which this firm's name has been brought before the House. I live in the division in which the Thames Ironworks is situated, and have taken a keen and lively interest in the work given to this yard. It is a well-known fact that all the Northern firms when building boats of this description have been absolutely opposed to the Thames Ironworks Company, chiefly because it is the only shipbuilding firm in the country which has given an eight-hour day. From that day to this the Northern 1129 firms have absolutely refused to allow this particular firm to become part and parcel of what is known as the Shipping Federation.

But overall it seems that, at least in part, the enlightened attitude toward working practice at the Thames Ironworks helped to lead to its downfall, as the other yards ganged up to lobby the Admiralty against awarding it contracts.

However, Winston Churchill, as First Lord of the Admiralty in 1911, held a crucial post at a critical time for Thames. Britain controlled an Empire that relied on the sea for its continued management, domination and exploitation. In 1912 the Admiralty tendered for two warships. The Thames Ironworks, out of twelve bidders, submitted the highest estimate. While it is true that London-based shipbuilders could not compete with the northern yards in terms of labour costs (the southern union movement at that time being much stronger than that in the north, where fourteen-hour days were still common), the lower costs of coal and iron ore transportation was another factor and one, even if all things had been equal in terms of employment costs, that would likely have been, in effect, a deal breaker.

For all this, probably the decisive consideration was the oligopoly[15] deal that a group of northern yards, led by Vickers, had with La Société le Nickel (a French mining company set up to exploit the nickel reserves in New Caledonia), which allowed them to access the crucial metal at a much lower price than competitors.

---

14. William Thorne, who was born in poverty in Birmingham, moved to London in 1882 where he found work at Beckton Gas Works. He got involved in the Union movement where he met amongst others Friedrich Engels, co-author of Das Kapital. Karl Marx's daughter Eleanor taught him how to read and write. Thorne was a leader of the Great Strike of 1889, which Thames Ironworks workers took part in. He went on to become a Labour MP in 1906 and retained his seat until his retirement in 1945 at the age of 87.
15. A situation in which a market or industry is dominated by a small number of sellers (oligopolists); oligopolies can result from various forms of collusion which reduce competition and lead to higher prices for consumers.

Arnold Hills petitioned Churchill about the number of disadvantages that the London-based shipbuilders faced, but his protests were, predictably, ignored and Thames Ironworks went into liquidation in November 1911. Workers at the Ironworks offered to work for reduced wages to secure Admiralty contracts for two more battleships, but the unions remained opposed. As a result, large-scale shipbuilding in London came to an end.

So, while some small fry businesses remained, the thousand years of vibrant shipbuilding on the Thames was brought to a conclusion. This was not exactly Churchill's finest hour but the list of his inequities is longer than history cares to remember. Just to name two, his bungling of the Namsos campaign at the start of the Second World War and his role in the slaughter that was Gallipoli from 1915 to 1916 caused untold, largely needless suffering and death. Many of the working people of East London, while appreciating his leadership qualities, saw Churchill as a warmonger. The failure of the pre-war and wartime governments to build adequate air-raid shelters for them didn't help of course. If the V3 supergun project had not been destroyed by 617 Squadron (the 'Dambusters') then the death toll this took on London would have been astronomically higher than it actually was.

As such it really was not 'Winnie' that saved even greater carnage than occurred in London during the blitz, but the pilots and machines of the RAF. For every statue of and eulogy to Churchill (no friend of the workers he) there needs to be homage paid to the men and women who designed, built and flew the Lancasters, Hurricanes and Spitfires that faced impossible odds.

Hills' physical health mirrored his company's degeneration. By 1910 he was arriving at the Ironworks, crippled by arthritis, but he fought to the bitter end, having to suffer humiliation and the constant threat of defeat. Supported in a specially made invalid basket, paralysed from the neck down, he addressed mass rallies in Trafalgar Square, arguing for the continuation of contracts for the building of warships in London shipyards. For all this, on 21 December 1912 a notice was pinned to Thames Ironworks' main gate. It read:

Our extremity is God's opportunity and I do not doubt there is still in store for us a Happy New Year.

On 7 March 1927, five days before his 70th birthday, Arnold Hills passed away. As a man tied to the fate of his company, perhaps he was always going to 'go down with his ship'. A plaque dedicated to the memory of Arnold Hills can be found on the stairway in Canning Town Station that was built in 2000.

A glowing tribute to Arnold Hills had appeared in the *Daily Mail* of June 1911. He was depicted as remorseless and a man who, despite not being in the best of health, persevered in his struggle to keep Thames Ironworks afloat. The article makes hints as to why Thames was failing to compete with its northern rivals who, because of the Fair Wages Clause in Admiralty contracts, could pay appreciably less to employees than was the case in respect of Arnold's operation. Hills' maintenance of an eight-hour working day at the Ironworks, while not a 'killer' in itself, would have been instrumental in its lack of a competitive edge.

It must be doubtful if the position Hills took on working conditions was totally motivated by human principles. He had always upheld the firm's right to employ non-union men, a principle that was deeply unpopular with his workforce. Under his watch industrial action was always a threat and Hills was at times 'hissed' by his own workmen as he entered the yard. Thus he was perhaps taking into account the limits his workforce might be realistically pushed to when he instigated practices such as the eight-hour day. The amicable relationship between Hills and his workforce is often over-egged. While everyone knew how their bread was buttered, the suspicion between the classes never came close to dissipating. As the Ironworks was on the ropes, a point at which few employees could have understood as being less than a critical time in the firm's history, Hills had been obliged to make an appeal to the trade associations to ensure their holiday matched the company's shutdown dates.

The Thames Ironworks and Shipbuilding Company, the premises of which had been described by the *Mechanics Magazine* in 1861 as 'Leviathan Workshops', closed just two years before the start of the First World War. The yard had built 144 warships and innumerable other vessels. If it had survived up to the outbreak of hostilities the firm might have ensured its future and perhaps also the survival of large-scale shipbuilding on the Thames. London's river lost its last major shipping concern at the height of the greatest naval shipbuilding boom Britain had ever had. The Great Eastern Railway later took over the Thames premises, but that too failed. Like the ill-fated *Albion*, that after serving in the Middle East during the First World War was sold for scrap in December 1919, Thames Ironworks had served its purpose and was consigned to local memory to become a fragment of Britain's industrial archaeology, an archetypical example of how capitalism, cannibal-like, consumes itself.

Ironically, on the other side of the river George Russell's tide mill lasted a bit longer. It had been converted to a power station and was replaced by a more modern structure in 1947 that was itself defunct by in the 1980s and demolished. This wiped out the last trace of the Hills family on the Thames.

One wonders what Frank Hills would have made of it all. Would he have kept shipbuilding going on the Thames? Would he have bothered with a football club? The answer to both questions is probably 'no'. One thing big Frank seemed to understand was when to move on – one of the secrets of business is knowing when to quit. He was an innovator, a man driven by instinct and energy for innovation. His third son Arnold was a public school boy through and through. He was motivated and in terms of his entrepreneurial activity, limited by ideals and beliefs. Perhaps nothing illustrates the difference between Frank and Arnold more than family stories of how, after Frank's death, Arnold poured a cellar of prize claret down the drain. Arnold, talented, honest, brave and idealistic, ultimately failed. Frank, a master of the cut and thrust, not averse to dancing on the cusp of scurrilousness, was the Victorian genius who made the money.

For so long Arnold Hills saw his workforce at Thames Ironworks as a threat, but they did not let him down. If Hills was betrayed at all it was by members of his own class: Churchill, the government who had asked him to overstretch his resources to the point of no return and the capitalists of the north who had undercut his production costs, not least by the maximum exploitation of workers. For all this, it is probably more accurate to say that Hills was overtaken by the direction of industrial development in shipbuilding.

In effect his East London yard had been used as a laboratory, to understand what was possible on the Thames, which ran through the centre of transport, government and commerce. In the end the contribution Hills and Thames Ironworks had made was to push ship production in this context to its limits, and may be represented in the *Albion* and the *Thunderer.* Thames Ironworks showed the world what was possible and shipbuilding went on from there. This was not without cost. Hills, his workforce and a significant proportion of the community that surrounded the Ironworks were chewed up by the grinding of the wheels of ship building capital.

PAST AND PRESENT

Thames Ironworks' place in history, especially of the 'murky' East End, occasionally flashes in and out of popular culture. One relatively recent example of this was a fight scene from the 2009 Sherlock Holmes film. This part of Guy Richie's gripping yarn is, in the original screenplay, set in the vicinity of the Thames Ironworks. However in the final production the name 'William Barnard' is depicted on the wall of the boatyard. Barnard was a wooden boat builder that went out of business about half a century before the time the film is set in.

The Ironworks was a sprawling industrial complex which covered up to 30 acres. In 1939, the better part of three decades after the demise of the Ironworks, its main building was still in relatively good repair. But it appears that by 1947, although the grand engineering department building was still recognisable, dilapidation had well and truly set in. Ultimately it disappeared and was replaced, covered by a humdrum warehouse. By the time Crossrail were developing the area at the start of the twenty-first century only the foundations of the Ironworks had endured.

In December 1990 West Ham Football Club was reunited with the Royal Navy after a gap of eighty-six years. A glass copper painting charting West Ham's football history and its connection with Thames Ironworks was commissioned by West Ham United and presented to Captain Allen of HMS *Warrior* at Portsmouth. Maybe if you ever look at this painting, perhaps as you watch the next match that West Ham play, whether it is by courtesy of the new tyrants of TV or the back-breaking investment in a season ticket, you might give a thought to who started it all, who made it all possible, the founding fathers of the Irons, C.J. Mare, Frank and Arnold Hills, Charles Dove, the hard working Ted Harsent and Dave Taylor, the unlucky Francis Payne. But most of all spare a memory for those whose final view of this world was the launch of a great ship, the *Albion* and the men who built her with the ceaseless 'clank' and 'thunk' of West Ham riveting hammers.

Build me ships, boats, cars and bridges too,
Build men, who can swerve, curl a ball and play me through.
And as the sun sets over the river,
Send me memories that will make me shiver.
For as the Thames rolls history's tale away,
The Hammers are on the field of play.
In a rainbow of claret and blue,
Please never forget me and
I'll always remember you.

Days and glory, winning, losing and goals,
Bubbles fly like silvery souls,
Of all the Hammers who have gone before,
Only see this, and the crowds will roar.

(Brian Belton)

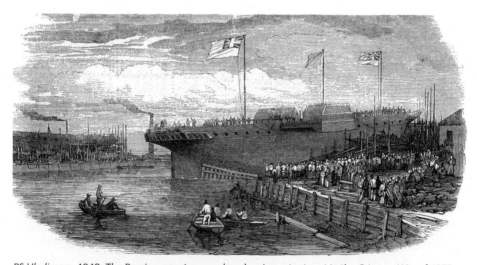

PS *Vladimere*, 1948: The Russian war steamer played an important part in the Crimean War of 1853.

WITH THE IRON WORKERS: A VISIT TO THE THAMES IRONWORKS AND SHIPBUILDING COMPANY

An article by F.M. Holmes, which appeared in 1885 in the *Church Monthly* – described as 'An Illustrated Magazine for Home Reading' (1885):

Nice catch-balls, are they not?

Yes, you answer, and not to be touched by hand; for, see, the boy to whom they are thrown picks them up with long pincers.

They are red-hot rivets, and the boy at the movable fire blows them to a glowing heat with his foot-worked bellows, and then tosses them to his colleague with the utmost unconcern.

Boy number two picks them up with his pair of long iron fingers, pops them through the holes of the iron plates prepared to receive them, and then, while the 'holder-up' workman keeps the head in its place with a massive iron instrument, the lower part is beaten flat to a head with hammers, and the rivet is fixed.

But why, you ask, is it necessary to fix rivets red-hot? One reason, of course, is that the end may be beaten down to form a head; but another is that the iron contracts as it cools, and thus draws more firmly together the plates of metal which it joins. But here are plates being bolted together by rivets without hammering. A hydraulic squeeze is used instead. The machine has two powerful jaws, one on either side of the two plates, and when the rivet is placed, a flame flashes out from the red-hot iron – as if in protest of the terrible squeeze – and the rivet is fixed with rounded flattened heads. It seems much easier than cracking a nut with your teeth.

Then as to the holes for the rivets – surely some time is occupied in cutting out these? No, for in another part of these extensive works they may seen stamped out quickly by powerful machines or drilled out almost as speedily by powerful drills, a stream of oil constantly trickling down on the work while it is in progress.

In yet another department you may see strong planes at work, driven by the all-powerful steam, and steadily whittling off shavings of metal from the plates or bars beneath; while in other divisions you may witness the moulders carefully building up the black sand into shapes they desire the molten iron to assume. Yet again, you may watch huge girders being built up and riveted for bridges, massive plates being bolted together and raised for dock-gates, or long, snake-like angle-irons being bent red-hot, and afterwards put up as the frames and ribs of a ship. It is the shipbuilding, indeed, which is the oldest and most important department of these works, and the directors claim that the commencement of English iron shipbuilding was made here by Messrs. Ditchburn & Mare. To them Mr. G.C. Mackrow – the present Company's naval architect – was articled; and in his time no fewer than 830 vessels have been built here – truly a notable record.

Where then, are these big works? Surely they must lie on Clydebank, or make busy the side of the Wear, the Tyne, or the Tees! Or nestle in the shipbuilding towns of Barrow or Belfast!

Nay, they rear their heads much farther south, even by despised Father Thames himself – despised, that is, for shipbuilding. Down by Bow Creek, which is the mouth of the River Lea, where it joins the Thames, these works have their dwelling-place; they occupy thirty acres on the Essex side and three on the Middlesex. They are known familiarly as the Thames Ironworks, and here are lengthy and capacious dry docks opening direct on the noble river, and capable of receiving with ease the huge *Dunottar Castle,* one of the crack, grey-coloured boats of the Castle Line trading to the Cape; and here also have been built some of the most noted war-vessels of Her Majesty's fleet. The *San Pareil,* the sister ships to the ill-fated *Victoria* the *Benbow*, the *Blenheim*, the *Grafton*, and the *Theseus* have all been born here. At these yards, too, was constructed from 1859 to 1861 HMS *Warrior*, the first seagoing ironclad of the British Navy in the world; and the details of that new movement in battleship building were worked out here.

But the Company is not proud. The managers build a humble barge as well as a huge battleship; and, indeed, here are two or three being constructed now. In these you can observe some of the chief principles of iron shipbuilding. Angle irons and plates – which may be of steel – are used. The angle-bars or irons resemble 'planks' of metal bent at right angles all along their length. These are also further bent by heating them to redness, and then quickly drawing them to the 'bending blocks,' which are heavy iron slabs placed on the ground, and filled with holes, into which are dropped stout iron pins. The pins are placed to form a rough outline of the shape to which the bar is to be bent.

See how speedily the men draw the red-hot iron from the furnace and force it to the required shape among the pins. It is bent round them in almost less time than it takes to tell the tale. Then, when fairly cold, it is hauled off to the 'screive board' close by. You would perhaps pass by this flat-looking floor quite unconcernedly, and give it no notice. Yet it is one of the most important pieces of apparatus in the whole thirty acres of works.

'What? That?' you exclaim in surprise; 'that flat-looking piece of floor with a few wavy lines on it, and pierced with a few holes? That?'

Ay, that, for on it is marked with accuracy the plans and outlines in full size of the frames and curves of the ship. The workmen therefore haul off their bent irons to this board and test them, in order that they may reach the exact shape with accuracy.

Chalk marks are mow made where the rivet holes are to be punched, and the frames and plates – the plates being rolled to the requisite shape or thickness – are taken outside to the spot where, amid high shores of timber to support its growing body, the ship is being put together. Everything, when it reaches this spot, has been formed to fit together with the accuracy of a watch. The bent angle-irons jut outward and upward from the keel to form the shape of the ship. One side of the angle is presented to the side, so as to give a surface upon which the plates forming the outside or skin of the vessel can be riveted. Where necessary a reversed angle-bar is riveted to the other side of the angle, forming a flat surface to which an inside 'skin,' or deck, or floor boards, or iron plates, can be riveted.

Riveting! riveting! riveting! It is nothing else but riveting where an iron or steel vessel is being put together; and gradually angle-bar after angle-bar – or bone after bone – is put in its place, and covered with plate after plate – or piece after piece of thick skin – until the shapely hull of a huge ocean-going liner or the squarer proportions of a knockabout barge have grown into sight.

Almost everything made of iron seems to be constructed here except guns. Here, is a huge 5ft casting of an iron cylinder for the immense engines of a mammoth steamship; there is the forging of the wrought-iron rivets for fastening ironwork together. Here are steam hammers which would forge a crank-shaft weighing forty tons, and there, are heavy rolling-mills which will turn out plates as thin as an eighth of an inch or as thick as 24in. Nothing comes amiss to these ready iron and steel workers by the Thames, whether it be a simple tank for oil or an armour-clad turret for Government – a wrought roof for a public building or a huge bridge. Indeed, it may be added that the iron superstructure for the famous Britannia Tubular Bridge was built at these works in 1846–7, as also was the ironwork for the new London, Chatham, and Dover Bridge at Blackfriars. But various as are the constructions, the principles pursued are much the same. Iron is melted and cast into moulds; or it is forged under hammers heavy or light; or it is twisted red-hot on the bending blocks; or rolled in ponderous mills to any thickness or shape required, so stupendous and so well directed are the powers employed.

And what of the workmen? Mr. A.F. Hills, the chairman of the directors, has said that a scheme is in operation by which the authority of the Company is determined and the legitimate function of the Trade Unions recognised. Every workman is paid a standard trade rate; but, in addition, a premium is also paid to specially skilled operators, thus obviating a general dead level of only average work.

Further, a system of profit-sharing has been adopted, by which all profits, after 10 per cent has been paid to shareholders, are divided equally between them and the workmen. As for the much-talked-of eight hours' movement, the Company have adopted it definitely, with a proviso, however, as to overtime when necessary. By such a scheme, which provides also for sickness and accidents, the proprietors and workmen are practically made to feel that their interests are identical.

RESULTS

1895/96

All home games played at Hermit Road

FRIENDLIES

Sep	7 (h)	Royal Ordnance	D	1–1
	14 (h)	Dartford	W	4–0
	28 (a)	Manor Park	W	8–0
Oct	5 (a)	Streatham	W	3–0
	16 (a)	Old St Stephens	W	4–0
	19 (h)	Erith United	L	1–2
Nov	2 (h)	Reading	L	2–3
	9 (h)	Grenadier Guards	W	4–0
	16 (h)	Charlton United	W	4–0
	23 (h)	West Croydon	W	2–0
	30 (h)	Coldstream Guards	W	3–1
Dec	7 (a)	Dartford	L	0–2
	14 (a)	Millwall	L	0–6
	16 (h)	Old St Stephens	W	3–1
	21 (h)	Grenadier Guards	L	1–4
	25 (h)	South West Ham	W	4–1
	26 (h)	Wandsworth	W	5–1
	28 (h)	Lewisham St Mary's	W	7–1
Jan	4 (h)	Novacastrians	W	6–1
	18 (h)	Upton Park	W	2–1
	20 (h)	Barking Woodville	W	6–2
	25 (h)	Civil Service	W	5–0
Feb	1 (h)	Manor Park	W	7–2

	6 (h)	Royal Ordnance	W	2–1
	8 (h)	Hornsey United	W	4–0
	17 (h)	Vampires	L	1–3
	22 (h)	St Lukes	W	1–0
	29 (a)	Reading	L	2–4
Mar	7 (h)	Fulham	W	5–1
	9 (h)	West Croydon	W	5–0
	14 (a)	St Lukes	W	1–3
	16 (h)	Woolwich Arsenal	L	3–5
	20 (h)	West Bromwich Albion	L	2–4
	28 (h)	Leyton	W	3–0
	30 (h)	Royal Ordnance	L	0–4
Apr	3 (h)	St Lukes	D	1–1
	4 (h)	Liverpool Casuals	W	3–1
	6 (h)	Vampires	W	6–2
	11 (h)	Commercial Athletic	W	3–1
	18 (h)	South West Ham	W	3–0
	25 (h)	Millwall Athletic	D	1–1

FA CUP

Oct	12 (a)	Chatham	L	0–5

1st Qualifying round

WEST HAM CHARITY CUP

Feb	15 (a)	Park Grove	W	1–0

Park Grove protested and forced a replay

Mar	7 (a)	Park Grove	W	3–0
	21 (a)	Barking	D	2–2
	28 (a)	Barking	D	0–0
Apr	20 (a)	Barking	W	1–0

Club secretary: A.T. (Ted) Harsent
Captain: Robert Stevenson
Biggest win: 28 Sept 1895, 0–8 v. Manor Park (a)
Highest attendance: 12 Oct 1895, 3,000 v. Chatham (a) FA Cup 1st qualifying round
Biggest defeat: 14 Dec 1895, 6–0 v. Millwall (a) Friendly
Major transfers in: J. Lindsay from Old Castle Swifts
                     Sam Hay from Victoria
                     G. Sage from Old Castle Swifts
                     Robert Stevenson from Old Castle Swifts

1896/97

All home games played at Hermit Road

LONDON LEAGUE

Sep	19 (h)	Vampires	W	3–0
Oct	8 (h)	1st Scots Guards*	W	2–0
	22 (h)	3rd Grenadier Guards	L	1–4
	24 (a)	Crouch End	W	1–0
Nov	28 (a)	Ilford	D	2–2
Feb	27 (a)	Vampires	W	2–1
Mar	6 (h)	Ilford	W	3–2
	13 (a)	Barking Woodville	L	0–1
Apr	1 (h)	3rd Grenadier Guards	L	0–5
	3 (h)	Crouch End	W	4–1
	8 (h)	Barking Woodville	D	1–1

London League	P	W	D	L	F	A	Pts
3rd Grenadier Guards	12	9	1	2	32	13	19
Thames Ironworks	**12**	**7**	**2**	**3**	**17**	**17**	**16**
Barking Woodville	12	6	3	3	20	11	15
Ilford	12	7	1	4	26	14	15
Crouch End	12	4	2	6	14	19	10
Vampires	12	3	1	8	10	28	7
London Welsh	12	0	2	10	9	26	2

* The Scots Guards withdrew during the season and their record was deleted. London Welsh were suspended near the end of the season and as a result Thames Ironworks were awarded two wins.

FA CUP

Oct	10 (a)	Sheppy United	L	0–8

1st Qualifying round

WEST HAM CHARITY CUP

Mar	11 (h)	Manor Park	W	2–0
	20 (n)	West Ham Garfield	L	0–1

LONDON SENIOR CUP

Oct	17 (a)	West Norwood	W	2–1
Nov	7 (a)	Marcians	W	4–0
Jan	9 (h)	Wandsworth	W	3–1
	16 (h)	Barking Woodville	W	2–0
	30 (h)	Bromley	D	3–3
Feb	6 (a)	Bromley	D	2–2
	13 (a)	Bromley	L	0–2

ESSEX SENIOR CUP

Dec	5 (a)	Leyton	L	2–3

Club secretary: Francis Payne
Captain: Robert Stevenson
Biggest win: 7 Nov 1896, 0–4 v. Marcians (a) London Senior Cup
Biggest defeat: 10 Oct 1896, 8–0 v. Sheppey United (a) FA Cup 1st qualifying round
Major transfers in: Davey from Reading
                     E.G. Hatton from Reading
                     Robert Heath from West Ham Garfield
                     Holmes from Reading
                     Rossitter from Reading

1897/98

All home games played at the Memorial Grounds

LONDON LEAGUE

Sep	11 (h)	Brentford	W	1–0
Oct	2 (h)	Leyton	W	4–0

	23 (a)	3rd Grenadier Guards	W	1–0
	30 (a)	Leyton	W	3–1
Nov	13 (h)	Barking Woodville	W	3–0
Dec	2 (h)	2nd Grenadier Guards	W	5–1
	11 (a)	Ilford	D	3–3
Jan	1 (h)	Ilford	W	4–0
	8 (h)	Stanley	W	4–2
	15 (h)	Bromley	W	7–3
Feb	26 (a)	Stanley	D	1–1
Mar	12 (a)	Barking Woodville	D	0–0
	19 (a)	Bromley	W	5–1
Apr	2 (h)	3rd Grenadier Guards	W	3–1
	23 (a)	Brentford	L	0–1
	30 (a)	2nd Grenadier Guards	W	3–1

London League	P	W	D	L	F	A	Pts
Thames Ironworks	**16**	**12**	**3**	**1**	**47**	**15**	**27**
Brentford	16	12	2	2	43	17	26
Leyton	16	8	4	4	41	33	20
3rd Grenadier Guards	16	7	3	6	34	33	17
Ilford	16	5	7	4	33	25	17
Stanley	16	5	4	7	22	22	14
Barking Woodville	16	2	6	8	16	37	10
Bromley	16	4	2	10	20	49	10
2nd Grenadier Guards	16	0	3	13	17	42	3

FA CUP

Sep	18 (h)	Redhill	W	3–0
	25 (h)	Royal Engineers Training Battalion	W	2–1
Oct	16 (a)	St Albans	L	0–2

LONDON SENIOR CUP

Nov	27 (a)	Novacastrians	W	1–0
Jan	15 (h)	2nd Grenadier Guards	W*	
*Walk-over after the Guards withdrew				
	22 (h)	Ilford	L	1–3

Club secretary:	Francis Payne
Captain:	Walter Tranter
Biggest win:	15 Jan 1898, 7–3 v. Bromley (h) London League
Biggest defeat:	22 Jan 1898, 1–3 v. Ilford (h) London Senior Cup
Major transfers in:	Simon (Peter) Chisholm from Inverness
	George Furnell from Old Castle Swifts
	Henry Hird from Stockton
	George Neill from West Norwood
	James Reid from Reading

THAMES IRONWORKS IN THE FA CUP 1895/96 TO 1897/98

1895/96

1ST QUALIFYING ROUND

12 Oct v. Chatham (a) 0–5
Watson; Tull, Williams, Stewart, French, Parks, Woods, Sage, Lindsay, Freeman, Darby. *Att: 3,000*

1896/97

1ST QUALIFYING ROUND

10 Oct v. Sheppey United (a) 0–8
Southwood; Stevenson, Holstock, Bird, Bandridge, Davie, Nicholls, H.Rossiter, Hatton, Gresham, Morrison. *Att: 800*

1897/98

18 SEP v. REDHILL (H) 3–0

Chisholm 2, Opp own-goal
Furnell; Chalkley, Tranter, Dove, Dandridge, Chisholm, Older, Hatton, J.Reid, Gresham, Edwards. *Att: 1,000*

25 SEP v. ROYAL ENGINEERS TRAINING BATTALION (H) 2–1

Hatton, Reid
Furnel; Chalkley, Tranter, Dove, Dandridge, Chisholm, Older, Hatton, J.Reid, Gresham, Edwards. *Att: 1,000*

16 OCT v. ST ALBANS (A) 0–2

Furnel; Chalkley, Taylor, Dove, Dandridge, Gillies, Hird, Gresham, Hatton, J.Reid, Edwards. *Att: 1,000*

1898/99

Game	Date	Opponents Home/Away	Result/Score	Thames Ironworks Scorers	Attendance
1	Sep 10	(a) Shepherds' Bush	W 3–0	Atkinson 2, Adams	1,500
2	24	(h) Brentford	W 3–1	Hay 2, Dove	1,200
3	Oct 8	(a) Uxbridge	L 1–2	Gresham	2,000
4	29	(a) Wycombe	L 1–4	Reid	1,000
5	Nov 5	(h) Shepherd's Bush	W 1–0	Wenham	1,000
6	12	(a) St Albans	W 4–1	Lloyd 3, Reid	800
7	26	(a) Watford	D 0–0		1,000
8	Dec 3	(h) Fulham	W 2–1	Reynolds, Gresham	2,000
9	17	(h) Watford	W 2–1	Lloyd 2	1,500
10	24	(a) Chesham	W 3–0	Hird 2, Hounsell	1,000
11	31	(a) Maidenhead	W 4–0	McEwan, Hird, Reynolds, Reid	2,000
12	Jan 14	(h) Wycombe	W 4–1	McEwan, Lloyd, Opp own-goal	1,000
13	21	(a) Wolverton	W 4–3	Dove, Chisholm, Leonard 2	200
14	28	(h) Chesham	W 8–1	Lloyd, Reid, Reynolds 2, Dove, MacEachrane, Gresham 2	2,000
15	Feb 11	(a) Brentford	W 2–0	Reynolds, Leonard	2,000
16	18	(h) Uxbridge	W 4–0	Henderson 4	1,500
17	Mar 4	(a) Southall	W 2–0	Henderson 2	4,000
18	11	(h) St Albans	W 1–0	J.Reid	2,000
19	18	(h) Wolverton	W 2–1	J.Reid 2	1,000
20	25	(h) Southall	W 2–0	G.Reid, Gilmore	3,000
21	Apr 8	(a) Fulham	W 1–0	Lloyd	3,000
22	15	(h) Maidenhead	W 10–0	Lloyd 3, Leonard 4, J.Reid 2, Henderson	3,000

FINAL TABLE SOUTHERN LEAGUE DIVISION TWO

		P	W	D	L	F	A	Pts
1	Thames Ironworks	22	19	1	2	64	16	39
2	Wolverton Railway	22	13	4	5	88	43	30
3	Watford	22	14	2	6	62	35	30
4	Brentford	22	11	3	8	59	39	25
5	Wycombe Wanderers	22	10	2	10	55	57	22
6	Southall	22	11	0	11	44	55	22
7	Chesham	22	9	2	11	45	62	20
8	St Albans	22	8	3	11	45	59	19
9	Shepherds Bush	22	7	3	12	37	53	17
10	Fulham	22	6	4	12	36	44	16
11	Uxbridge	22	7	2	13	29	48	16
12	Maidenhead	22	3	2	17	33	86	8

THAMES IRONWORKS HOME/AWAY RECORD

Played	W (h)	D (h)	L (h)	F (h)	A (h)	W (a)	D (a)	L (a)	F (a)	A (a)	Pts	Pos	Div
22	11	0	0	39	6	8	1	2	25	10	39	1st	SL

FA CUP

1Q	Oct 1	(h) RE Training Battn	W 2–0	MacEachrane, Gresham	1,000
2Q	15	(a) Brighton United.	D 0–0	2,000	
R	19	(h) Brighton United.	L 1–4	Hird	2,000

CHAMPIONSHIP DECIDER (PLAYED AT MILLWALL)

Apr 22	(n) Cowes	W 3–1	Lloyd, Henderson, Gresham	1,000

TEST MATCH (PLAYED AT CHATHAM)

Apr 29	(n) Sheppey United	D 1–1	Lloyd	2,000

PLAYERS/TEAMS

Southern League Division Two

Player/Game	1	2	3	4	5	6	7	8	9	10	11	12	13	14	15	16	17	18	19	20	21	22	A*	G*
Moore	1	1	1	1	1	1	1	1	1	1		1	1	1	1	1	1	1	1	1	1	1	21	0
Trarter	2	2		2	2	2	2	2	2	2		2	2	2	3	2	2	2	2	2	2	2	20	0
Marjeram	3				3	3	3	3	3	3	2												8	
Chisholm	4	4	4	4		6		6					5	4	5	4	4	4	4		4	4	15	1
Dove	5	11	3	3	4			4	4	4	1		4	4	4	5				4			14	3
MacEachrane	6	6	6	6	6	11	6	11	11	6	6	6	6	5	6	6	6	6	6	6	6	6	22	1
Hird	7	7	7	7	7		7	7	8	7	5	4	8	6	6	4	7	7	7	7			19	3
Brett	8																						1	
Atkinson	9	9																					2	2
Adams	10		9																				2	1
Foss	11																						1	
Lloyd		3	2			9			9	9	9	9	9	9							8	8	11	12
Hitch		5	5	5																			3	
Hay		8	8	9			9	9	6														6	2
Gresham		10	10	10	10	10	10	10	10	11	11	10	10	10							10		14	4
Hounsell										10	8												2	1
Cobb			11		11																		2	

Player/Game	1	2	3	4	5	6	7	8	9	10	11	12	13	14	15	16	17	18	19	20	21	22	A*	G*
Reid, J.				8	8	8	8				10	8		10	8	8	8	8	8			10	13	9
Buller			11																				1	
McEwan					5	5	5	5	5	5	4	5											8	2
Reynolds					7		11	8	7	8	7	7	7	11	7	7	7						12	5
Wenham					9																		1	1
Niel						4					3												2	
Dunn												3	3	2	3	3	3	3	3	3	3	3	11	
Leonard												11	11	7	11	11	11	11	11		11	11	10	7
Henderson															9	10	9	9	9	9	9	9	8	7
Reid, G.															10	9	10	10	10	10			6	1
McManus																		5	5	5	5	5	5	
Bird																				8			1	
Gilmore																				11			1	1
1 own-goal																								

FA CUP

Player/Game	1Q	2Q	R	A*	G*
Moore	1	1	1	3	
Tranter	2	3	3	3	
Chisholm	4	6	4	3	
Dove		2	2	2	
MacEachrane	6	4	6	3	1
Hird	7	8	7	3	1
Adams	10	9	9	3	
Lloyd	3	7	8	3	
Hitch		5	5	2	
Hay	8			1	
Gresham	9	11	10	3	1
Cobb	11	10	11	3	
Niel	5			1	

A* = Appearances
G* = Goals scored

CHAMPIONSHIP DECIDER V COWES (PLAYED AT MILLWALL)

22 Apr (n) 3–1
Lloyd, Henderson, Leonard.
Moore; Tranter, Dunn, Chisholm, Dove, MacEachrane, Rynolds, Hitch, Henderson, Adams, Leonard.

TEST MATCH V SHEPPEY UNITED (PLAYED AT CHATHAM)

29 Apr (n) 1–1
Lloyd
Moore; Tranter, Dunn, Chisholm, McManus, MacEachrane, Reynolds, Hitch, Henderson, Gresham, Leonard.

Club secretary:	George Neill
Captain:	Walter Tranter
Top scorer:	David Lloyd – 14
Biggest win:	15 Apr 1899, 10–1 v. Maidenhead (h), Southern League Div. 2
Highest attendance:	4 Mar 1899, 4,000 v. Southall (a), won 0–2 Southern League Div. 2
Biggest defeat:	29 Oct 1899, 4–1 v. Wycombe Wanderers (a) Southern League Div. 2
	19 Oct 1899, 4–1 v. Brighton United (a) FA Cup second qualifying round, replay
Major transfers in:	Thomas Dunn from Chatham
	Henderson from Warmley
	David Lloyd from 3rd Battalion Grenadier Guards
	Patrick Leonard from Manchester City
	Peter McManus from Warmley
	Roderick MacEachreane from Inverness Thistle
	Arthur Marjeran from Swanscombe
	Tommy Moore from Millwall
	George Reid from Warmley
	J. Reynolds from Gravesend
Major transfers out:	George Furnell to Hammersmith Athletic

1899/1900

Game	Date	Opponents Home/ Away	Result/ Score	Thames Ironworks Scorers	Attendance
1	Sep 16	(a) Reading	L 0–1		3,000
2	18	(h) Chatham	W 4–0	McKay 2, Carnelly 2	1,000
3	Oct 7	(h) Bedminster	W 1–0	Joyce	3,000
4	Nov 4	(a) Tottenham Hotspur	L 0–7		7,000
5	11	(h) New Brompton	D 0–0		2,000
6	25	(h) Swindon Town	W 1–0	Adams	2,000
7	Dec 2	(a) Bristol City	L 0–2		3,000
8	16	(a) Southampton	L 1–3		4,000
9	23	(h) Millwall	L 0–2		12,000
10	25	(a) Queens Park R.	L 0–2		4,000
11	30	(h) Queens Park R.	L 1–2	McKay	4,000
12	Jan 6	(a) Chatham	L 1–3	Carnelly	5,000
13	13	(h) Reading	L 0–1		4,000
14	15	(a) Bristol Rovers	D 1–1	McKay	6,000
15	20	(a) Sheppey United	W 3–0	McKay, Carnelly, Joyce	4,000
16	24	(a) Gravesend	L 1–2	Carnelly	1,200
17	Feb 10	(a) Bedminster	L 1–3	Carnelly	2,000
18	17	(h) Bristol Rovers	D 0–0		4,000
19	24	(a) Portsmouth	L 0–2		2,000
20	Mar 10	(h) Tottenham Hotspur	D 0–0		9,000
21	17	(a) New Brompton	L 1–3	Opp own-goal	2,000
22	24	(h) Gravesend	W 2–1	Carnelly 2	3,500
23	31	(a) Swindon Town	L 1–3	Opp own-goal	3,000
24	Apr 5	(h) Portsmouth	L 2–4	Joyce 2	5,000
25	7	(h) Bristol City	D 0–0		5,000
26	9	(h) Southampton	W 4–1	Joyce 3, Allan	4,000
27	17	(h) Sheppey United	W 4–2	McKay, Joyce, Taylor, Opp own-goal	3,000
28	28	(a) Millwall	W 1–0	McKay	8,000

FINAL TABLE SOUTHERN LEAGUE DIVISION ONE

		P	W	D	L	F	A	Pts
1	Tottenham Hotspur	28	20	4	4	67	26	44
2	Portsmouth	28	20	1	7	58	27	41
3	Southampton	28	17	1	10	70	33	35
4	Reading	28	15	2	11	41	28	32
5	Swindon Town	28	15	2	11	50	42	32
6	Bedminster	28	13	2	13	44	45	28
7	Millwall Athletic	28	12	3	13	36	37	27
8	Queens Park Rangers	28	12	2	14	49	57	26
9	Bristol City	28	9	7	12	43	47	25
10	Bristol Rovers	28	11	3	14	46	55	25
11	New Brompton	28	9	6	13	39	49	24
12	Gravesend United	28	10	4	14	38	58	24
13	Chatham	28	10	3	15	38	58	23
14	Thames Ironworks	28	8	5	15	30	45	21
15	Sheppey United	28	3	7	18	24	66	13

Played	W (h)	D (h)	L (h)	F (h)	A (h)	W (a)	D (a)	L (a)	F (a)	A (a)	Pts	Pos	Div
28	6	4	4	19	13	2	1	11	11	32	21	14th	SL

RESERVE TEAM RECORD (LONDON LEAGUE DIVISION ONE)

Played	W	D	L	F	A	Pts	Pos
18	10	2	6	42	23	22	4/10

FA CUP

	Date	Opponent	Result	Scorers	Att.
P	Sep 23	(h) Royal Engineers	W 6–0	Joyce 3, McKay, MacEachrane, Reid	1,000
1Q	30	(a) Grays United	W 4–0	Joyce, McKay, Carnelly, McManus	750
2Q	Oct 14	(h) Sheppey United	W 4–2	Carnelly 2, Joyce 2	2,000
3Q	28	(a) Dartford	W 7–0	Carnelly 2, Mckay 2, Joyce, MacEachrane, Bradshaw	1,200
4Q	Nov 18	(a) New Brompton	D 0–0		3,000
R	23	(h) New Brompton	W 2–0	Carnelly, McKay	3,000
5Q	Dec 9	(h) Millwall	L 1–2	Bradshaw	13,000

TEST MATCH (PLAYED AT TOTTENHAM)

Apr 30	(n) Fulham	W 5–1	Joyce 3, Stewart, Opp own-goal	600
Moore; Craig, Dunn, MacEachrane, Stewart, Dove, Taylor, Carnelly, Joyce, McKay, Allan.				

Club secretary: George Neil
Captain: Tom Bradshaw
Top scorer: Bill Joyce – 15
Biggest win: 28 Oct. 1899, 0–7 v. Dartford (a), FA Cup Third qualifying round
Highest attendance: 9 Dec. 1899, 13,000 (h) v. Millwall Athletic
Biggest defeat: 4 Nov. 1899, 7–0 v. Tottenham Hotspur (a)
Major transfers in: Henry (Tom) Bradshaw from Tottenham Hotspur
                        Albert Carnelly from Bristol City
                        Alec Gentle from New Brompton
                        William Joyce from Tottenham Hotspur
                        Syd King from New Brompton
                        Ken McKay from Tottenham Hotspur
Major transfers out: Tom Bradshaw (deceased)
                        William Joyce to Portsmouth
                        Patrick Leonard to Manchester City
                        Walter Tranter to Chatham

FA CUP

Player/Game	P	1Q	2Q	3Q	4Q	R	5Q	A*	G*
Moore	1	1	1	1	1	1	1	7	
Dunn	2	2	2	2	2	2	2	7	
King	3	3	3	3	3	3	3	7	
Dove	4	4	4	4			5	5	
McManus	5	5	5	5				4	1
MacEachrane	6	6	6	6	6	6	6	7	2
McKay	8	8	8	8	8	8	8	7	5
Joyce	9	9	9	9	9	9	9	7	7
Carnelly		10	10	10	10	10	10	6	6
Bradshaw	11	11	11	11	11	11	11	7	2
Hird	7	7	7					3	
Craig				7	4	4	4	4	
Gentle					7			1	
Reid	10							1	1
Bigden					5	5		2	
Adams						7	7	2	

A* = Appearances
G* = Goals scored

PLAYERS/TEAMS

Southern League Division One

Player/Game	1	2	3	4	5	6	7	8	9	10	11	12	13	14	15	16	17	18	19	20	21	22	23	24	25	26	27	28	A*	G*
Moore	1	1	1	1	1	1		1	1	1	1	1	1	1	1	1	1	1	1	1	1	1	1	1	1	1	1	1	27	
Dunn	2	2	2	2		2							2	2	2	2	2	2	2	2	2	2	2	2	2	2	2	2	21	
King	3	3	3	3	3	3	3					2	3	3	3	3	3	3	3	3									16	
Dove	4	4	4	4	5			4	4									4		4			4	4	4	4	4	4	15	
McManus	5	5	5	5				5																					5	
MacEachrane	6	6	6	6	6	6	6	6	6	6	6	6	6	6	11	11	6	6	6	6	6	6	6	6	6	6	6	6	28	8
Corbett	7	7					7																						3	
McKay	8	8	8	8	8	8	8	8	8	8	8	8	8	8	9	8	8	8	8	8	8	8	8	8	8	8	8	8	28	8
Joyce	9	9	9	9		9	10	9	10	9	10	9	9	9	8	9	9	9	9	9	9	9	9	9	9	9	9	9	27	8
Carnelly	10	10	10	10	9	10	9	10	9	10	9	10	10		7	10	10	10	10	10	10	10	10	10	10	10	10	10	27	8
Bradshaw	11	11	11	11	11																								5	
Hird			7																										1	
Craig				7	2	4	2	2	2	2	2				6	6	4						3	3	3	3	3	3	17	
Gentle					4																								1	
James					7																	7							2	
Reid					10																								1	

Player/Game	1	2	3	4	5	6	7	8	9	10	11	12	13	14	15	16	17	18	19	20	21	22	23	24	25	26	27	28	A*	G*
Bigden						5	4	5	5	5			4	4	4	4			4		4								11	
Adams						7	11	3	3	3	3	3																	6	1
Walker						11	11	11	11	11	11	11																	7	
Sunderland							1																						1	
Allan								7	7	7	7	7	7	7	10	7	7	7	7	7	7	4	7	7	7	7	7	7	21	1
Gilmore										4	4	4									3								4	
Turner										5	5	5		10								3							4	
Stewart													5	5	5	5	5	5	5	5	5	5	5	5	5	5	5	5	16	
Taylor													11	11	11	11	11	11	11	11	11	11	11	11	11	11	11	11	14	1

BIBLIOGRAPHY

Barnett, Henrietta and Barnett, Samuel: *Practicable Socialism* (1915).

Belton, B.: *Founded on Iron* (2003).

Belton, B.: *Johnnie the One* (2003).

Belton, B.: *The West Ham Miscellany* (2005/2006).

Gibson, A., Pickford, W. *Association Football and the Men Who Made it* (1906).

King,S. *Book of Football* (1905).

Lambert, Andrew: *Warrior: Restoring the World's First Ironclad* (1987).

Mason, Tony: *Association Football and English Society 1863–1915* (1980).

Mills, M.: *The Early East London Gas Industry and its Waste Products* (1999).

Morgan, T. Fraser: *Notes on Warrior Rigging 1860–1997*.

Morris, J.: *The Story of the Barrow Lifeboats, Lifeboat Enthusiasts Society* (1988).

Powles, J. *Iron in the Blood* (2005).

'Third International Conference on the Technical Aspects of the Preservation of Historic Vessels', San Francisco, CA (1997).

If you enjoyed this book, you may also be interested in…

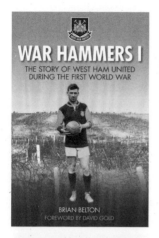

WAR HAMMERS I
BRIAN BELTON

This book tells the fascinating story of West Ham United Football Club during the First World War, charting the relationship between war and football by following the pursuits of West Ham from 1913/14 to 1918/19. It documents the social implications of war on Londoners and the social and political influence of football, the armed forces and civilians alike. Looking closely at the 13th Service Battalion, also known as the 'West Ham Pals', the book includes such players as George Kay, Ted Hufton, and their manager and coach, Syd King and Charlie Paynter.

9780750956017

BRUNEL: pocket GIANTS
EUGENE BYRNE

Through his ships, bridges, tunnels and railways Brunel helped create the modern world. In the soaring ambitions of the Victorian age, nobody thought bigger than Brunel. Never tied to a dusty office, he crammed enough work, adventure and danger into a single year to last a lesser person a lifetime. He was also a brilliant showman, a flamboyant personality and charmer who time and again succeeded in convincing investors to finance schemes which seemed impossible. Brunel made plenty of mistakes, some of them ruinously expensive. But he also designed and built several structures which are still with us to this day.

9780752497662

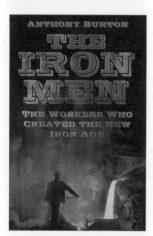

THE IRON MEN
ANTHONY BURTON

The eighteenth century saw the second Iron Age. Practically everything was made of iron: the machines of the Industrial Revolution; bridges and the ships that went under them; the trains running on their rails; and the frames of the first skyscrapers. But progress was bought at a price and the working classes paid it. Tracking both the brilliant innovation of the period and the hardship and struggle that powered it, this is the story of how iron changed the world. Anthony Burton is the author of more than seventy books many dealing with different aspects of industrial and transport history.

9780750959551

Visit our website and discover thousands of other History Press books.

www.thehistorypress.co.uk